It is fashionable to speak of trade unions in the UK as organisations in decline. They have lost membership, power, and influence over the last decade. However, those who have commented on the possible long-term decline, or even disappearance, of unions have not generally examined their organisation or, in particular, their financial status, and these are the factors which ultimately dictate unions' ability to survive, recruit, and influence employees.

This book provides the first systematic picture of union financial status for thirty years, and reveals a dramatic picture. Though, overall, unions have become financially less healthy in the post-war period, many unions experienced an improved financial position during the membership contraction of the Thatcher years. The authors analyse the reasons for this, and also reveal the extent to which unions are highly dependent on overt or covert financial support from employers. They show that the long-term financial decline of unions has been more affected by the competition between unions for membership than by the effects of traumatic industrial disputes.

Union business: trade union organisation and
financial reform in the Thatcher years

Union business
Trade union organisation and financial reform
in the Thatcher years

Paul Willman
Timothy Morris
and Beverly Aston

London Business School

CAMBRIDGE
UNIVERSITY PRESS

Published by the Press Syndicate of the University of Cambridge
The Pitt Building, Trumpington Street, Cambridge CB2 1RP
40 West 20th Street, New York, NY 10011–4211, USA
10 Stamford Road, Oakleigh, Victoria 3166, Australia

First published 1993

Printed in Great Britain at the University Press, Cambridge

A catalogue record for this book is available from the British Library

Library of Congress cataloguing in publication data
Willman, Paul.
   Union business: trade union organisation and financial reform in the
Thatcher years / Paul Willman, Timothy Morris, Beverly Aston.
      p.   cm.
   Includes bibliographical references and index.
   ISBN 0 521 41725–2 (hardback)
   1. Trade-unions–Great Britain. 2. Trade-unions–Great Britain–Finance. I.
Morris, Timothy, 1953–. II. Aston, Beverley. III. Title.
HD6664.W563 1992
3187′0941′09048–dc20   91–47165   CIP

ISBN 0 521 41725 2

AS

Contents

Acknowledgements

The authors are grateful for the financial assistance of the Department of Employment, which funded the research through two grants between 1987 and 1989. We are particularly indebted to Dr Mark Stevens. None of the views expressed or conclusions drawn herein reflect those of the Department. We are also grateful to the Warden and Fellows of Nuffield College, Oxford for the award of the Norman Chester Senior Research Fellowship to the first named author in 1989 in order to pursue this research.

Many people helped with the research, not least the many respondents in our case-study unions who gave generously of their time. The staff of the Certification Office were unfailingly helpful and patient in the face of our sustained demand for access to the returns. We would also like to thank Phillipa Buckland for statistical assistance on the first project.

Earlier drafts of this volume benefited from the comments of academic colleagues, most notably those attending the British Universities' Industrial Relations Association Conferences of 1989 and 1991. The authors are grateful to George Bain, William Brown, John Kelly, David Metcalf, Ben Roberts and Roger Undy for comments on all or part of the work. Material in Chapters 2, 4 and 8 has appeared elsewhere in different form. We are grateful to the editors of the *British Journal of Industrial Relations* for permission to reproduce material in Chapter 2 and of the *Industrial Relations Journal* for similar permission for Chapters 4 and 8.

The usual disclaimer applies. The errors we have retained we covet as our own.

1   Introduction: unions in the 1980s

It would be hard to argue that the 1980s was a successful decade for British trade unions. Whether one turns one's attention to membership levels, to union density, or to the outcome of several of the larger disputes of the decade, the picture is one of retreat or defeat. Union influence over various aspects of government policy directly or indirectly affecting industrial relations was minimal. Successive pieces of legislation dealing with the rights of trade unions and of their members were criticised and rejected by unions themselves yet enacted, apparently with a level of popular support which must have included that of many union members. In 1983 and 1987, many of those members reaffirmed their rejection of the policies of the Labour Party, the preferred political party of many union leaders, voting instead for the confirmation of policies which, not just pragmatically or occasionally but ideologically and systematically, rejected values and beliefs close to the core of British trade unionism. The latter half of the decade saw a distancing between the previously closely linked institutions of the labour movement. Not only was the Labour Party in opposition seeking to reduce a perceived source of electoral disadvantage by stressing the independence of its policy making from the views of trade union leaders but also, within the TUC, there were splits over both organisational and political matters, resulting in the expulsion of EETPU in 1988, the most serious split within the movement since 1945.

If all was not gloom, the bright spots were scarce, and did not illuminate any clear path to recovery. As strike rates fell, and public perception of mighty union bosses attenuated, the overall popularity of unions appears to have risen (Edwards and Bain, 1988): popularity did not, however, translate into a willingness to join. If the decline of union membership at the outset of the decade abated, it was not reversed. When employment began to expand again in late 1982, it was not reflected in a rise in union membership. Real earnings rose substantially across the decade but union membership and, in the opinion of many observers, union power, declined. It was not a good advertisement.

1

The response of trade union leaders varied, both over time and between unions. There emerged in the early part of the decade a fundamentalist reaffirmation of the socialist principles of trade unionism manifest in a total rejection of 'Thatcherism' and a faith in the good offices of a returning Labour administration to restore the rights and privileges accorded to trade unions in the Social Contract period, for which a certain nostalgia emerged. It had not seemed such a golden age when they were in the midst of it. Over time, in the face of attempts to assert a 'new realism' by the TUC leadership, fundamentalism died but its demise was a lingering one in NUM and several other public-sector unions. By contrast, in EETPU and several other private-sector unions – particularly those made into private-sector unions – fundamentalism was stillborn. For several, the events of the 1980s which caused trade unions organisational and financial problems were seen to be the result primarily of irreversible economic changes rather than ephemeral political ones and the appropriate response was both adaptive and strategic, involving changes to organisational structure and union policy, rather than simply reactive, involving rejection of government policy.

In the 1980s, therefore, analysts were presented with the spectacle of a union movement unevenly committed to and unevenly capable of change. Trade unions are ostensibly democratic, poorly resourced organisations whose rejection of commercial values and practices has in the past often left them devoid of the services of those with business expertise. Many are specifically designed *not* to be led from the top and several have constitutions involving a mixture of checks and balances which imply that they are not to be led at all. If one combines this appreciation of the structural difficulties with the observation that many of those then in charge of trade union affairs had, in their careers, seen only expansion, then the public image of a union movement appearing simultaneously to be in crisis but unable to respond becomes more understandable.

In such circumstances, many analysts questioned whether trade unions had a future. The reemergence of a crude form of convergence theory encouraged comparisons with the long-term decline of union membership in the USA. Financial matters were often to the fore. Both the TUC and the Labour Party suffered retrenchment after well-publicised financial difficulties. In both 1990 and 1991, Congress was told about the TUC's financial problems and about proposals for settling them. Unions themselves suffered unevenly and in different ways, but NUPE, MSF, and AEU all experienced financial difficulties covered in the press. The financial problems of NUM were recurrent news items from the time of the strike itself to the publication of the Lightman Report in 1990. Several mergers, such as that leading to the absorption of the Boilermakers' union by NUGMW at the start of the decade and the merger of NUR with NUS at the end, were induced by financial crisis.

Others, notably Bain (1986) took a more relaxed view, arguing that the events of the 1980s, though traumatic, could not be understood in isolation. From this viewpoint, the unusual *rise* in membership from 1974 to 1979 was at least as exceptional as its subsequent sharp fall, notably to 1982. It remains the case that levels of union membership and union density are not unusually low for the post-war period. The events at the start of the decade were, in the more extreme view, simply a one-off adjustment of union membership following a rapid, perhaps overdue, structural adjustment in sectoral employment shares in the UK in which highly unionised manufacturing industries suffered rapid contraction while private services, in which union density has been low, expanded.

Neither view captures the nature of change in British trade unions in the 1980s. It does not sit well with the former, 'structural decline' view that the rate of decline in union density in the UK has been slow in the latter half of the decade nor that many of the large, TUC-affiliated trade unions are reporting membership expansion at the turn of the decade; none has 'gone broke'. The 'structural adjustment' view may well be closer to the truth but it fails to spell out the extent of change in British trade unions across both the 1970s and 1980s.

Across the two decades, there has been a substantial shift in membership composition: male manual workers now comprise a smaller proportion of total union members than in the past and female, white-collar workers, particularly in the public sector, a higher. Union membership has, through mergers, become more highly concentrated in the larger unions. Particularly in the 1980s and partially under the pressure of statutory requirements, both the policies and internal procedures of trade unions have altered. In many unions, an older generation of leaders has retired and a younger set, often of different social and educational backgrounds, has taken their place. There has been a considerable amount of organisational change, often exogenously induced.

Rapid and severe membership loss in the early 1980s also induced in many unions an organisational response, which focused on a concern with financial matters. Such loss was, with its attendant income loss, literally unprecedented for incumbent union managers charged by the membership with stewardship of the union in general and its funds in particular. In many unions, financial information was scarce and systems of financial control non-existent. Moreover, rule-book provisions, often of considerable antiquity, made such systems difficult to implement. Even where union concerns were not primarily financial, or financial crisis was not imminent, policies adopted in the face of membership difficulties often had financial implications. There emerged concern with the effective management of union resources which required both policies and personnel which trade unions, emerging from the relatively benign membership environment of the 1970s, did not possess.

The main purpose of this book will be to document these changes in the management of trade unions in the 1980s. The central argument is that, although unions are not primarily concerned with the maximisation of any measures of financial return, the availability and management of financial resources becomes particularly important in periods of crisis or change. We shall seek to substantiate the proposition that the last decade has seen considerable, perhaps unprecedented, change in the management of trade union resources. Although such change has in many cases been induced by external events, we shall argue that it has subsequently offered opportunities for trade union leaders to develop policies and services which are to the unions' advantage. We shall thus, through documentation of financial changes, seek to understand changes in the overall pattern of union government.

The perspective adopted throughout is thus that of the union manager whether termed General Secretary, President, or Secretary/Treasurer, and the problems discussed are the problems they have faced. This is very much a study of what has been termed 'formal' union organisation, but the importance of lay organisation and participation is not ignored. Throughout, we shall consider the impact of lay, 'free' participation on union resources and policy. In different unions, the proportion of total resources provided by subscriptions, levies, 'free' membership activity, and by employers through provision of facilities varies substantially.

Our perspective thus differs from many recently adopted, both in its focus on the formal rather than informal union and in its concern with financial matters. The justification for this is partly pragmatic. On the basis of arguments we hope to justify in the body of the text, we feel that, compared to the 1970s, formal union activity was becoming more important as, in many unions, lay activists' influence declined. Similarly, financial crisis induced unprecedented financial concern which seemed worthy of investigation.

However, there are other reasons. It seemed appropriate to look at the unions' formal structure in the 1980s as no serious study had focused on the period from 1975 onwards (Undy et al., 1981). There was thus a gap in our knowledge of the evolution of union structure and management of over a decade. It seemed appropriate to begin with financial matters not only because they were of concern to union leaders but also because no serious analysis of union finances had occurred for over 20 years. The financial resources and rules of trade unions were important factors in explaining the rise of trade unions in the nineteenth century (Webb and Webb, 1907) and in the 1950s, Roberts' analysis of union government contained the famous dictum: 'Those who control the purse strings control the union' (1956: 343). However, we know little about the financial structure and performance of the UK trade unions since the 1960s (Latta, 1972).

The structure of the book is as follows. Chapters 2 and 3 present aggregate and disaggregated data on union financial performance. Chapter 2 looks in the aggregate at the period since 1950. Chapter 3 looks in more detail at the fortunes of different unions in the 1980s. Both chapters provide a picture of recurrent financial difficulties, which raises the question of how unions seek to manage their financial affairs. Chapter 4, a theoretical chapter, therefore describes the role of financial matters in union behaviour. It attempts to derive testable propositions about union behaviour emerging from analysis of their financial structure and objectives. The implications of this are explored in Chapter 5 which looks at the politics of union finances, focusing in particular on the ways in which financial arguments are brought to bear on policy formulation and their influence on union behaviour.

Chapter 6 looks specifically at the importance of union size and union growth: the influences of financial matters on membership decisions, including arguments about economics of scale, are assessed as is the role of financial matters in the encouragement or impedence of union mergers. Chapter 7 focuses on strikes and assesses the impact both of strike activity on union finances and of union financial status on the decision to strike.

Chapters 8 to 12 present five short case studies of trade unions. Chapter 8, on NUM, indicates the impact of a major dispute on the union's financial position, and also discusses the extremely unusual financial structure of NUM. Chapters 9 and 10 focus on and contrast the very different financial structures and fortunes of GMB and AEU. Chapter 11, on BIFU, describes the move from impecunity to solvency through membership growth of a private-sector, white-collar union. Chapter 12, on EETPU, looks at a system of tight sophisticated financial controls. The purpose of these cases is not simply descriptive. We hope to show the close relationship between financial changes and changes in union government and policy: the argument will be offered for all unions that financial reform has been a prerequisite for the achievement of the union's objectives.

Chapter 13, in conclusion, draws out some of the implications for trade union structure and policy in the 1990s of the data presented. The argument is that unions are employer-dependent organisations with reasonably flimsy resources which exacerbate the difficulties of their financial position by inter-union competition. Expansion of trade unionism into poorly unionised areas implies the need for greater employer dependence, for the preservation of managerial discretion by union leaders, and, above all, for the avoidance of competition.

Throughout, we base our analysis both on the statutory returns made by trade unions and on our independent research conducted between 1987 and 1989. A full description of the research methods appears at Appendix 1. We have covered events up to the end of 1989, though on occasion we have included consideration of subsequent events where this seemed appropriate. Unless stated to the contrary, all figures are expressed in 1989 prices and the present tense is used to refer to the state of events at the end of that year.

2   The financial status of British trade unions, 1950–1989[1]

1   Introduction

There have been three systematic studies of the financial status of British trade unions in the post-war period. All relied on the statutory returns described in Appendix 1. Roberts (1956: 343–95) analysed change across the period 1936–50, Latta (1972) looked at the decade 1960–70 and Willman and Morris (1988) looked at the period 1975–85. All three studies described the financial performance of particular unions as well as the financial status of unions as a whole. Their findings indicate that the financial fortunes of British trade unions have been highly variable over the last 40 years. In this chapter, we shall seek to present an up-to-date picture of the aggregate financial status for the post-war years and in the next a more detailed, disaggregated picture of events in the largest unions in the 1980s. We shall try to provide an explanation of aggregate changes and an account of the sources of variation in financial performance between unions.

The structure of the chapter is as follows. Section 2 discusses the findings of previous studies, and outlines the ratios used here. Section 3 presents the overall picture of union finances from 1950 to 1989. Section 4 discusses the implications of these trends. Section 5 concludes.

2   Previous studies of trade union finances

Although analysis of the financial status and arrangements of trade unions was central to the Webbs' classic study, particularly of the 'new model' unions (1907: 162–283), many more recent studies have not considered financial matters. The major exception is Roberts' (1956) study of trade union government and administration which systematically considered subscriptions, the management of union funds, expenditure, assets, and political funds. Roberts was concerned to document changes between 1936 and 1950 both in the aggregate and on a disaggregated basis. Across the period, he found that union subscriptions increased less than wages

7

and prices; union administrative costs per capita also rose by more than per capita subscriptions. Subscription income thus came to account for a smaller proportion of total income and unions were required to 'fill the gap' with other forms of income, notably from assets, including income from investments. In addition, between 1936 and 1950, union expenditure rose, but working expenses increased far more rapidly than expenditure on friendly society benefits in part, Roberts argues, because of the post-war expansion of state benefits.

Roberts also found substantial differences in subscription levels, often related to the level of benefits paid, in expenditure, and in assets. In 1950 assets were held in British government securities (50%), in municipal securities (10.5%), and as cash deposits (23.9%) (Roberts, 1956: 387). Compared with 1936, this represented a shift away from municipal securities. He noted that, because of the risks of high levels of unemployment and large-scale strikes, unions required substantial liquid funds. He also speculated, in advance of more recent developments, on the likely beneficial impact on the necessary level of liquidity and on rates of return on assets of a centralised, rather than piecemeal, investment policy.[2] Overall, the picture he presented for 1950 was one of a solvent union movement, but one which was inhibited by a lack of finance. The trends for income and expenditure did not, at the time, give him cause for optimism.

Latta focused on the decade 1960 to 1970 but, referring to Roberts' work, he prefaced his analysis with a brief resume of changes since 1950. He noted that, despite the optimistic views of several commentators in the early 1960s, the financial position of many unions remained poor (1972: 393). In that decade, the TUC itself, in its evidence to the Donovan Commission, had remarked that trade unionism was provided to members 'on the cheap' (TUC, 1966: 137).

Latta's own analysis of the decade looked at data for the set of unions with more than 30,000 members in 1970. His conclusions focused on differences between unions, such as that between manual industrial unions with a secure financial base and relatively stable or declining membership on the one hand and, on the other, poorer white-collar unions which needed to expand to remain solvent. However, he did note widespread loss of assets and, for several unions, periods when expenditure exceeded income. Overall he observed 'a marked decline from the period surveyed by Roberts' (1972: 409). He suggested that a change in financial policies on the part of many unions was a prerequisite for financial security in the 1970s.

The third study, by Willman and Morris (1988), looked both at the aggregate picture and at the financial affairs of the set of 56 unions with more than 20,000 members in 1984. They found that, between 1975 and

1985, real income both from subscriptions and investment grew. Real worth was static, despite substantial membership loss from 1979. However, real expenditure also increased substantially. In the aggregate, unions were solvent across the period; short periods of insolvency for several unions were associated with national strike action or very rapid membership loss in the period 1979–81. Subscription income fell as a proportion of total income, while investment income increased, particularly after 1981. Expenditure on benefits fell as a proportion of total expenditure, continuing the trends noted by Roberts. Overall, they concluded that, given the loss of members, 'the data convey a picture of remarkable financial health' (1988: 96), even though, historically, the union movement as a whole was relatively impoverished.

Willman and Morris also found substantial differences between unions. White-collar unions in particular experienced massive percentage increases in real subcriptions and assets from 1975 to 1985. Older, manual unions remained rich but accounted for a much smaller proportion of total union wealth. The richest unions tended to be the largest; both per capita subscription income and per capita administrative costs, which were highly correlated, were lower in the largest unions. This may be evidence of economies of scale in administration in the larger unions, or it may simply indicate that levels of membership service are lower in the larger general unions than in the smaller craft or industry unions.[3]

Taken together, these studies provide a set of snapshots of union finances at particular points in time; the entire picture is not visible. Some findings are difficult to reconcile. Given the general picture of financial difficulty and decline in 1950 and again in 1970, how have unions continued to survive? Is there any simple relationship in the aggregate between union membership and union solvency or wealth; in particular, how have union finances weathered the substantial membership losses since 1979? Why were unions able to raise real per capita subscriptions in the period 1975–85 but not in previous decades? Why did real wealth apparently decline overall between 1950 and 1985?

In order to answer these questions, we shall focus on the returns from 1950 (i.e., the end of Roberts' period of study) to 1989, the latest year for which a full return is currently available, and specifically on income, broken down between income from members and other income, expenditure, divided between administrative expenditure and benefits, and net worth, that is the value of year-end union funds. This measure is preferred to the gross assets figure, which takes no account of liabilities.[4] In all cases, figures are calendar year-end totals. Several per capita measures of income, expenditure, and assets are also used and in all cases the membership series used is that of the Certification Officer's returns.

Our measures and several ratios derived from these basic data are defined as follows.

(a) *Source*: Certification Office Returns

Solvency = $\dfrac{\text{Total income}}{\text{Total expenditure}}$

Subscription dependency = $\dfrac{\text{Subscription income}}{\text{Total income}}$

Acid test = $\dfrac{\text{Total net worth}}{\text{Total expenditure}}$

shortfall = $\dfrac{\text{Subscription income}}{\text{Total income}}$

Subscription ratio = $\dfrac{\text{Real per capita subscription income}}{\text{Real weekly pay}}$

Return = $\dfrac{\text{Total other income}}{\text{Total net worth}}$

(b) *Source*:   Department of Employment

Inflation	Average annual inflation rate
Unemployment	Average annual percentage rate
Strikes	Working days lost, in thousands, per annum
Real weekly pay	Weekly gross earnings of full-time male manual workers over 21 (on adult rates) whose pay was unaffected by absence. This is a proxy for average earnings, a full series of which from 1950 was unavailable.

3   Union finances: the aggregate picture

Figure 2.1 shows an index of aggregate union net worth, total income, and total expenditure, all in real terms at 1989 prices; it also shows an index of union membership. Across the post-war period, real income and expenditure have risen steadily and broadly in line. As a result, the union movement has remained solvent, although the short-term stagnation of real income in the late 1960s and late 1970s caused solvency to decline; in the early 1970s, the series is interrupted. During the sustained membership loss of the 1980s the union movement has, in the aggregate, remained solvent. Real net worth has, however, fallen since 1950. Rising at broadly the same rate as income and expenditure in the 1950s and 1960s, it began a steady decline in 1967 which lasted until 1981. The union movement as a whole is poorer in real terms in 1989 than it was in 1950 and its reserves

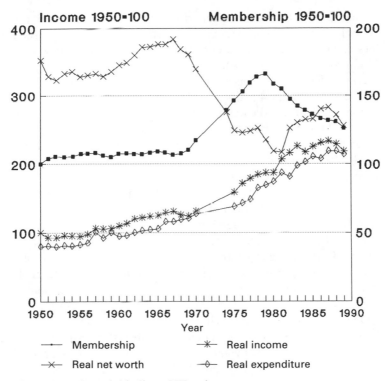

Figure 2.1. Financial indices, UK unions
Source: Certification Office

have fallen sharply as a multiple of annual expenditure. This is a point
of some importance and we shall return to it below.

Overall, Figure 2.1 indicates financial health and stability from 1950 to
1966, a period of financial decline during membership growth from 1967
to 1981 and some financial recovery during membership decline in the
1980s. However, the figure conceals important changes in the composition
of income and expenditure over the period.

There has been a long-term decline in subscription dependency. In 1950,
89% of union income came from subscriptions, falling slowly to 85% by
the interruption of the series in 1971 and to 82% by 1989. Income from
investments has filled the gap.[5] There has been a more radical shift in the
composition of union expenditure. While there has been a steady rise in
real total expenditure and real administrative costs, real benefit expenditure has been roughly static; indeed, there has been a fall since 1970. In
1950, for example, administrative costs accounted for 58.7% of the total
and benefits for 32.3%. As late as 1970, these figures were 60% and 29.6%
respectively. By 1986, a steady and steep rise in administrative costs led

to their share in total expenditure rising to 75.6%, while benefits accounted for only 11.9%. 'Friendly society' benefits and strike pay account for a very small proportion of union expenditure, the bulk of which goes on administration.[6] In fact, *real* expenditure on benefits in 1989 is lower than that in 1950; the fall has been particularly rapid across the 1980s. We shall discuss the implications of this below.

Figure 2.1 also indicates a complex relationship between membership levels and the financial measures. As the figure implies, per capita income, expenditure and net worth moved broadly in line up to 1968. Thereafter, to 1979, real income and expenditure per capita continue to rise as membership rises, but real net worth per capita falls very steeply. The financial and membership conditions of the 1980s differ again. This is a period of rapidly rising per capita income, expenditure, and net worth, but of sharply contracting membership.

What, then, do these trends imply for the financial health of trade unions? In the absence of any clear view of what union finances *ought* to look like, one cannot be definite in answering this question. However, there are several indicators one might use to assist in some form of assessment.

One concerns the net worth of trade unions. This is important in at least two respects. The first, noted by Roberts, is that the accumulated wealth of unions is a safeguard against the sudden experience of a strike or high levels of unemployment. In the 1980s, the evidence is that some unions can generate large increases in revenue through levy to protect reserves during strikes (Willman and Morris, 1988: 62–8) and that, with the decline in the provision of benefits and the relative unimportance of observed membership fluctuations in determining union wealth, loss of members does not *in itself* raise expenditure. Nevertheless, one crude test of union financial health might be the level of reserves expressed as a multiple of average annual expenditure. This would, at least, indicate the ability of unions to survive interruptions to revenue. Although liquidity is not considered here, it approximates the 'acid test' ratio one might use in assessing the financial status of a firm.

Wealth is important in another respect. Since the early 1960s, and prior to that in the period studied by Roberts, subscription income has not covered expenditure. The gap has had to be made up from other sources, and return on assets has been the major source. A second financial measure is thus the shortfall of subscription income over total expenditure, which is an indication of the return from assets the union must secure to balance the books.

A third measure is solvency. The balance of income over expenditure in a given year may be modified by various accounting devices, but it

Table 2.1. *Financial indicators, British trade unions, 1950–1985*

Date	'Acid test' Net worth / Total expend.	'Shortfall' Sub. income / Total expend.	'Solvency' Total income / Total expend.	Subscription proportion ratio
1951–5	4.13	1.04	1.18	0.42
1956–60	3.54	0.97	1.11	0.40
1961–5	3.60	1.03	1.19	0.40
1966–70	2.92	0.87	1.08	0.37
1971–5	N/A	N/A	N/A	N/A
1976–80	1.47	0.96	1.14	0.31
1981–5	1.29	0.90	1.12	0.37
1989	1.20	0.84	1.03	0.39

remains the case that insolvency, defined in these terms, cannot be sustained indefinitely. The average solvency sustained over a five-year period may give some insight into the financial performance of unions at that time.

A fourth measure is the proportion of earnings taken as subscription income. Again, this is a rough measure, but it indicates the extent to which unions can maintain their income as earnings increase.[7] The percentage is very small but, equally, small changes in the subscription share can have a large impact on union financial performance.

Table 2.1 lists averages of these four indicators for five-yearly periods from 1950 to 1985, and for 1989. Although some of the measures are crude, the table indicates a poorer financial picture overall in the period 1980–5 than at the outset. Both solvency and the shortfall of subscription income over expenditure were worse in the 1960s, but union financial reserves, measured against expenditure, hit a post-war low in 1989. The proportion of earnings taken as subscriptions has increased since the late 1970s, but remains lower than that of 1950. Figures for 1989 do not give grounds for any greater optimism.

One may raise objections to this on the grounds that, on several measures, the period since 1980 has seen improved wealth and markedly improved real income. Assessed against the ability to generate revenue from a declining membership base, unions have become quite successful. From this point of view, unions have become much more effective managers of assets and collectors of subscriptions and are back on the road to health. These considerations indicate the difficulties of any simple assessment, particularly from aggregate data.

Nevertheless, it emerges that Roberts' fears about the financial health of the union movement were well founded, if a little premature. The period to 1967 was one of steadily rising real income, expenditure, and net worth. Commentators in the early 1960s could be optimistic, based on available trends, about the future of union finances. Latta, writing in 1970, could not. By 1975, the decline was pronounced and Willman and Morris, looking at the decade to 1985, came to the apparently counter-intuitive conclusion that the 'Thatcher years', involving rapid membership loss, saw an improvement in financial performance over that achieved during membership expansion under the previous Labour government.

This discussion raises the question of the importance of membership levels for financial health. Empirically, union growth in Britain, particularly in the 1970s was associated with a loss of real wealth. Since new members bring in no accumulated wealth, the per capita fall was more marked; at 1989 prices, unions were 'worth' approximately £111.6 per member in 1967 – the post-war peak – and approximately £43.80 per member in 1979. There is an extremely strong negative correlation between union membership and union real net worth.[8] On the other hand, there is also a strong positive correlation, as one might expect, between membership levels and the aggregate measures of real income from and expenditure on members.[9] While in the first case it is difficult to attribute any causal relationship, there does appear to be a logical relationship between size and income and expenditure.

4   Implications

The fall in real net worth is, at first sight, surprising. Between 1967 and 1981, while net worth fell, the union movement was solvent, membership was growing, and real income was rising. There are several possibilities. One is that unions sold assets to remain solvent. Another is that the return on assets and investments failed to keep pace with higher inflation in the late 1960s and 1970s; if the pattern of union investments in 1950 noted by Roberts were maintained – with a bias towards fixed-interest securities – this would be likely to happen. A third possibility is that unions continued to declare merely the book value of intrinsically healthy asset portfolios so that decline is apparent rather than real.

Union net worth is held in the form of tangible assets such as property, a portfolio of investments including gilts, municipal securities, and equity and as liquid funds. Over time, the real net worth of unions will be influenced by: (a) the surplus or shortfall of subscription income over total expenditure, generating flows into and out of funds, and (b) the real rate of return on assets.

Figure 2.2. Return and real worth, 1950–89

The returns allow calculation of a crude measure of the rate of return on investments across the period, compared to the rate of inflation, illustrating in more detail the mechanics of the decline in real net worth. Again the contrast is broadly between the periods before and after 1968. From 1950 to 1968, the percentage return supported maintenance of real net worth. However, from 1968 to 1980, the rate of return was normally at or below the rate of inflation; this is consistent with the hypothesis that union investments were not inflation-proof. In the 1980s, however, return on assets and the real value of total assets both increased[10] (Figure 2.2). There is thus some evidence here of a change in the policies of asset management, which can be corroborated from other data.[11]

Low subscriptions, a shortfall of subscription income, and a poor rate of return would therefore generate the observed long-term decline in union real net worth. We may term this a structural model of financial decline, the key feature of which is the inability to raise real subscription income to cover expenditure.

However, there is a second model, which explains decline in terms of expenditure crisis. Roberts (1956) noted that unions retained funds against the risk of high unemployment or prolonged strikes. It might be supposed that high incidences of both would deplete union net worth, by reducing income from members and increasing expenditure. Empirically, therefore, one might expect a negative relationship between real net worth on the one hand and the measures of unemployment and strike activity on the other.

The results of a stepwise regression model using both *structural* and *crisis* variables (detailed in Appendix 2) indicate that the *structural* explanation is more likely. Observed levels of unemployment and strike activity have financially debilitated the trade union movement less than have low subscription income and the inability to generate sufficient other income from investments without disposing of assets. The determinants of union income, particularly the 82% of total income which comes from subscriptions, are thus of interest.

Real income from members is some function of the number of members, their real income and the proportion of it they are prepared to give as subscriptions (or the proportion of it unions are able, at reasonable cost, to collect). As the trend on union income in the 1980s indicates, a combination of rising real earnings and improved collection methods through more extensive use of devices such as employer check-off (Millward and Stevens, 1986) may have offset membership loss even where the subscription proportion was static. In addition, the increased use of indexation methods may make it easier to raise nominal subscriptions by avoiding conference debates on the matter.[12] Roberts' observation, that executives are more likely to be defeated on this rather than any other issue, may still be true (Roberts, 1956: 343).

If unions could increase the subscription proportion to 1950 levels, their financial position would be transformed. They have, in the aggregate, increased it since 1975, but still fall short of the figure of 0.5% of average earnings achieved in 1950. On 1989 figures, a 0.5% collection rate would have given a surplus of membership income over total expenditure of approximately 8.2%, and an overall surplus of income over expenditure of approximately 26.6%.

The pressure on income is maintained by the tendency for real expenditure levels to rise. This is not due to benefit expenditure – as we have seen real benefit levels have fallen – but to a steady rise in administrative costs. Administrative expenditure in trade unions, as defined in the Certification Officer's returns up to 1986, consist, on the one hand, of a number of relatively fixed items such as premises, cars, permanent staff, the union journal, and the hire of rooms for recurrent meetings, as well as, on the other, variable items such as postage, stationary, transportation, and extraordinary costs.

Salary costs are a substantial proportion of total costs for most unions. As real earnings rise, therefore, the increased real income from subscriptions is absorbed by the labour-intensive process of membership servicing and recruitment and the shortfall of membership income on total expenditure is maintained. This occurs despite the fact that there is a persistent surplus of subscription income over administrative expenditure; unions make a 'profit' from membership servicing, but it is absorbed by other costs and makes little contribution to assets.[13]

The final point to make about the expenditure trend is that it reflects a shift in the nature of service provision by trade unions. In Pencavel's (1971) terms, they have shifted from provision of individual goods to reliance on collective and semi-collective ones. Since many of the collective goods are appropriable by free-riders, this shift has done nothing in itself to provide incentives for union membership, and it may be that the trend towards membership-dependent benefit provision emerging in the 1980s is an attempt to redress the balance (TUC, 1988). We shall return to this point below.

5   Conclusions

Overall, the data imply that unions have experienced considerable financial difficulties, particularly since the mid 1960s. From a relatively weak financial base in the early 1960s, assets were shed rapidly to fill the shortfall of membership income over total expenditure. Real income actually fell in the late 1960s, while real expenditure continued to rise.

This problem arose against a backdrop of increasing membership, and remained unresolved during the more rapid membership expansion of the 1970s. Indeed, one of the more interesting contrasts to draw is that between the poor financial performance during expansion and the improved performance during rapid contraction in the 1980s. The increase in union real income and worth between 1980 and 1988 has not been matched before in the post-war period, nor has the rate of membership loss; the membership and real worth curves for the post-war period are almost mirror images. This contrast thus serves to emphasise that financial improvements do not depend solely on membership performance.

The trends, and the noted difficulty in making prescriptions for union financial health, set some problems in assessing the position in 1989. The financial position remains relatively weak. Reserves are historically low as a multiple of expenditure. There remains, in addition, the structural problem of the shortfall of membership income. It is difficult to resist the conclusion that the low post-war level of subscription income is at the core of the financial problems faced by unions. Crises may be induced by high strike rates or rapid job loss, but the endemic financial weakness of trade unions lies in the income shortfall.

Increases in real subscription income appear to be easier to generate when real earnings are rising rapidly. This, in part, explains the maintained solvency at a lower membership level in recent years. However, the proportion of income taken as subscriptions must rise to generate an excess of income over expenditure which would allow replenishment of the asset base in real terms. This does not require anything unprecedented, merely a return to the proportion of members' income secured as subscriptions by unions in the early 1950s, without a commensurate rise in expenditure.

Across the period covered by this chapter, the structure of the union movement as a whole changed markedly; in particular, the number of unions declined and the proportion of white-collar and public-sector unions increased. The internal structures of many union organisations underwent substantial change, for example in the growth of shop steward networks since the 1960s. These changes may have affected financial performance but, since unions do not exist primarily to optimise such performance, these financial consequences may not have been seen as important. For example, it may be that many unions were prepared to acquiesce in the loss of wealth in the 1960s and 1970s because the resources available on the balance sheet were less important than previously, compared to those supporting workplace activity supplied by employers and lay activists. The view taken here is, firstly, that the financial problems of the late 1970s were so severe that unions were required to pay more attention to financial matters – hence the partial recovery in the 1980s – and, secondly, that this higher priority for financial matters will have considerable repercussions for the process and outcomes of policy formation within particular trade unions in future.

The partial recovery of trade union finances in the 'Thatcher years' is not without its ironies. It perhaps indicates some of the difficult organisational problems facing unions in the modern era. In order to remain solvent, unions must manage their assets effectively and they must avoid inordinate expenditure on strikes and fights against redundancy. They are to some extent the beneficiaries of the recent rapid increases in real income and recent improved rates of return on equity. Since real incomes affect both income and expenditure, real income increases do not of themselves guarantee solvency, but it is plausible to suggest that, at higher real income levels, it is easier to raise the subscription proportion; in practice, most unions have done so. A corollary of this is that financial performance will benefit from the direction of organising activity away from low paid groups, which cannot afford higher subscriptions, or from groups whose subscriptions cannot be cost-effectively collected: in practice, groups of workers without bank accounts and with hostile employers who resist check-off. Going further, one might suggest that a policy of transferring costs to the employer and work to lay activists would also help to improve financial status. However, the pursuit of such policies might make trade unions as a whole more dependent on employers (Willman, 1989).

These considerations are explored more fully in Chapter 4. However, it becomes clear at this point that the improvement in union financial status might require policies which some or all union members might object to. At the extreme, polices which optimise financial performance would almost certainly cut across some of the principles which trade unions have espoused for some time. The politics of trade union finances may be complex and it is not always clear that union leaders seeking to put their organisations on a financially more sound footing will always receive support. We return to this issue in Chapter 5. However, the ability of trade unions to pursue their chosen policies depends on the availability of financial resources and the ways in which such resources are managed. Financially, the British trade union movement cannot afford another decade like the 1970s.

The final set of observations concern the relationship between membership and financial health. The membership data used here are imperfect, but the analysis does imply that there is no straightforward positive relationship between union membership and financial performance, particularly net worth. However, one might expect some relationship between the two, particularly if one allows the possibility that trade unions may achieve rather than merely receive membership growth (Undy et al., 1981). A wealthier trade union movement might sustain a better membership performance than a poor one ceteris paribus through the devotion of more resources to membership retention and acquisition. Such resources might also be better targeted. The experience of cost-ineffective growth in the 1970s may cause trade unions to discriminate in their choice of new members and thus to affect the aggregate membership level. In short, the financial status of trade unions may be an important intervening variable between the conventionally identified macroeconomic determinants of union growth and the actual rate of membership change.

However, these questions are difficult to examine in the aggregate. The data presented here mask significant differences in financial fortunes between unions. We turn to a disaggregated analysis in the next chapter.

3 Financial differences between unions

1 Introduction

Differences in financial performance between trade unions have been discussed in previous studies (Roberts, 1956; Latta, 1972; Willman and Morris, 1988). It emerges from all studies that there are both rich and poor, that some unions rely heavily on subscriptions while others live at least in part on investment income and that there is variance both in the subscriptions charged and the services rendered. However, although substantial variance persists, the pattern has altered over time. For example, Latta's dichotomy between poor white-collar and rich manual – industry unions had become blurred by 1985 (Willman and Morris, 1988). The progressive reduction in the number of unions and the concentration of membership in the largest unions (Buchanan, 1981) has influenced the disaggregated pattern of union financial performance.

The objective of this chapter is, firstly, to present the pattern of financial differences between unions in 1989, the last year for which full financial information is currently available and, secondly, to document changes since 1980; we are concerned to understand what lies behind the aggregate picture of recovery in union finances outlined above. There have, within the aggregate picture, been both winners and losers.

The structure of the chapter is as follows. Section 2 looks at the pattern in 1989. Section 3 analyses the pattern of change since 1980. Both sections use data from the set of 56 unions with over 20,000 members in 1984 which was the basis for Willman and Morris (1988). These sections thus update that publication in some respects. Section 4 focuses more closely on the largest unions which account for the bulk both of membership and resources. Section 5 concludes.

2 The disaggregated pattern in 1989

While unions overall were solvent in 1989, almost a third of this set had a shortfall of income over expenditure. The worst cases were NUR and

NUS, which covered less than three-quarters of their expenditure; we discuss the latter in more detail in Chapter 7. Most shortfalls were marginal, but MSF, NUT, and NATFHE all had shortfalls of over 10%. The greatest surpluses were in ISTC and NUTGW with surpluses of over 50%. Solvency can be affected by unusual events in a given year, and recovery from deficit can be quite rapid. Despite major financial problems left over from the strike, for example, NUM was solvent in 1988 but again experienced a shortfall of income over expenditure in 1989 (Aston, Morris, and Willman, 1990). However, some shortfalls, such as that at NATFHE and NUT, are more enduring and may indicate deeper-seated problems. For the majority of solvent unions, income exceeded expenditure by between 5% and 20%.

Dependency on subscription income has been falling for this sample, with 82% of total income from that source. It remains the case that several unions gain less than 50% of their total income from subscriptions; in 1989, these were ISTC, BGSU, and MU. At the other extreme, RCN declares no income other than subscriptions. There are, in fact, very strong correlations between solvency, subscription dependency, and net worth per capita. Highly solvent unions are rich and not heavily dependent on subscriptions. Insolvent unions are subscription-dependent and poor.[1]

By definition, unions with low subscription dependency cover a substantial proportion of expenditure through investment income. This investment income is fairly concentrated. In 1989, six unions, TGWU, GMB, NALGO, NUM, NGA, and ISTC, accounted for 35% of all union investment income. Many of the rich, manual-industry unions observed in previous studies have high per capita investment income, but, because they are by now relatively small, they account for a relatively small proportion of the aggregate figure. They do, however, contribute more than several of the very large unions with low net worth and low investment income; together, the investment income of AEU, MSF, NUPE, and UCATT was less than that of ISTC in 1989.[2]

Subscriptions per capita are highly variable, but the distribution, plotted against size in Figure 3.1, is skewed. Most unions, including many of the largest, cluster to the left. Of the top 12, only TGWU, NALGO, NUM, and NUT collect more than £35 per head per year. Several, including USDAW, MSF, UCATT, and RCN collect less than £30. The lowest per capita yield is BGSU, with £21.77. The highest, and the only unions to collect more than £100 per capita are STE (£104.87) and NGA (£101.48).

The pattern is not easy to explain. There is a very strong correlation between subscriptions per capita and administrative expenditure per capita; either unions collect what they need from members or, alternatively, spend all they get. There is also a negative correlation with size, but

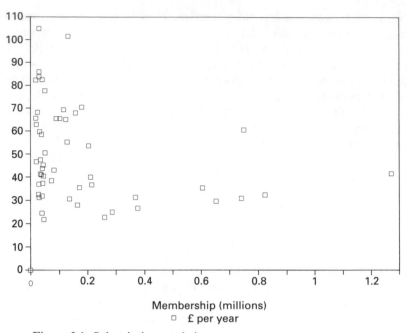

Figure 3.1. Subscriptions and size

weaker than in some previous years. The largest unions may be providers of a lower quality service, they may benefit from economies of scale, or they may simply not be very good at collecting subscriptions. The richest unions in per capita terms tend to charge the highest subscriptions, although the correlation is relatively weak.[3]

Table 3.1 shows the relationship between net worth per capita and subscription income per capita by dichotomising each variable around the mean. The position of each union is shown and the emerging pattern is rather striking. Both distributions, particularly that of net worth per capita, are highly skewed, hence the concentration of unions in the lower left quadrant. The character of the unions therein is not. With the exception of NALGO, all of the large unions are in this quadrant as are the majority of unions in the banking and teaching sectors where competition for members is fierce. Old, manual-industry unions cluster to the right of the figure, with the majority in the lower right quadrant. Many of these unions are sufficiently rich to have low subscriptions; few experience membership competition. The unions in the top right-hand quadrant, with high net worth and high subscriptions, are a mixture of managerial, craft, and industry unions. Those in the top left are mainly public sector

Table 3.1. *Per capita net worth and subscriptions: all unions, 1989*

Av. net worth (£84.90)			
NUCPS	AUT	NUM	NALGO
UCW	NUS	SOGAT	TSSA
CPSA	ACTT	NUR	EMA
NCU	POA	NGA	STE
NUJ	FBU	IPMS	NUMAST
		ASLEF	

Av. subscription Income (£50.90)			
TGWU	NAS/UWT	NUHKW	MU
AEU	BIFU	NUTGW	CATU
GMB	RCN	ISTC	URTU
NUPE	AMMA	IRSF	NUFLAT
EETPU	NATFHE	FTAT	
USDAW	BGSU	EIS	
MSF	BFAWU		
NUT	EQUITY		
UCATT	NAHT		
COHSE	LBGSU		
NWGSU			

unions but there are also two unions whose funds have been eroded by strikes, NCU and NUS, and two media unions, NUJ and ACTT.

The key point to make about the figure is that unions which compete for members cluster to the lower left. Competition appears to be associated with low net worth and low subscriptions per capita. High per capita net worth and subscription income accrue to those unions which avoid membership competition. Some of the latter find it hard to charge high subscriptions, presumably because in the presence of large assets the argument is difficult to sustain. Others, mainly those with a high-income job territory or with a strong benefit orientation, charge more.

However, there are complications to the simple competition argument. We are dealing with a highly skewed size distribution and larger unions cluster to the lower left. They may be cheaper (i.e., charge lower subscriptions) because they benefit from scale economies in the provision of union services. Those in the top right, charging high subscriptions, are relatively small. We shall assess the merits of the 'competition' and 'scale' arguments in Chapter 6 below.

It is important here to distinguish the richest unions from those which are the richest per capita. The richest unions, i.e., those with the highest end of year funds, tend to be the largest. In 1989, the three largest unions, TGWU, GMB, and NALGO, accounted for approximately 27% of union funds and 28% of union members. The richest per capita unions among this sample are, as Table 3.1 implies, in the medium size range. ISTC remains the richest, with NUR, NGA, TSSA, and MU all having funds in excess of £200 per capita (see Willman and Morris, 1988: 39). The RCN declares a net worth of £0. The list of other unions with funds of less than £20 per capita is lengthy; it consists of AEU, UCATT, AMMA, NATFHE, BFAWU, EQUITY, ACTT, NUS, and LBGSU.

Of course, some unions, such as AEU, have low subscriptions, low costs, and low net worth; they may operate so successfully through employer and member subsidy that the balance sheet of the union gives little information on its viability or its strength. We therefore constructed 'acid test' ratios, as defined in the previous chapter, for this sample. It will be recalled that the average for all unions was 1.2 in 1989. Sixty-five per cent of this sample have more than one year's expenditure in reserves, but only 20% have more than two years'. ISTC has more than five years' expenditure in funds; TSSA and CATU have more than four. At the other end of the scale, several large unions performed badly on this measure in 1989; NUPE had less than six months' expenditure in reserve, AEU, NUT, UCATT, UCW, and BIFU less than nine months' and smaller unions including AMMA, NATFHE, BFAWU, EQUITY, NUJ, NUS, ACTT, NAHT, and LBGSU less than six months' – in some cases much less.

Since the acid test ratio deals in total and not liquid funds, the position of these unions, particularly some of the teaching unions, may seem very serious indeed. Three points may be made, by way of explaining why, at the time of writing in mid 1991, only NUS and NUTGW have disappeared. The first, noted above, is that there may be wealth which does not appear on the balance sheet. The second is that some assets, such as property, may be substantially undervalued; this is certainly true of AEU, discussed in detail in Chapter 10. The third is that unions do not necessarily need to plan for income interruptions; LBGSU is a good example of one which is unlikely to strike and unlikely to experience withdrawal of employer support. Nevertheless, it remains the case that the financial positions of some large TUC affiliates such as NUPE and UCATT remained serious in 1989.

Only 54% of this sample made a profit out of the provision of membership services in 1989.[4] This is down on previous years, when most unions in this sample showed a surplus (Willman, 1989), but the reason for this has principally to do with a move to a more comprehensive definition of administrative expenditure by the Certification Officer from 1986 onwards.[5] The differences between unions are again of interest. Those with the greatest per capita margins of subscriptions over administrative expenditure were all single industry unions; in order, they were CATU, FBU, POA, and NCU. All service only one major set of negotiations. However, several of those with the biggest per capita deficits were also single industry unions. They were, in order, BGSU, MU, NUT, ISTC, NUFLAT, and NUM.

For the large unions, however, these relatively small margins can translate into large sums overall. TGWU generated over £5 million and AEU over £4 million from membership servicing in 1988. If this money is invested and benefit expenditure controlled, then the medium-term financial position is not merely healthy but very good. However, these returns are variable; TGWU made only £0.5 million in 1989, whereas AEU made £3.4 million. Unions which cover shortfalls of subscription income over administrative expenditure through investment income can also prosper. The untenable position is one where a union of low net worth with little investment income cannot make a profit from the servicing of its job territory. This was the position of MSF which lost nearly £4 million, half its net worth, in 1988 and a further £2 million in 1989 on membership servicing. We shall look more closely at this position below.

The major remaining expenditure item, benefits, was highly variable across the sample, despite the overall trend towards declining share. Expressed as a percentage of total annual expenditure, the highest benefit spenders in 1989 were CATU (36%), POA (33%), and FBU (31%). At the other extreme, AMMA and LBGSU spent nothing. There is no longer a simple craft/non-craft division in benefit expenditure; SOGAT and ASLEF spent less than 10% of expenditure on benefits whereas GMB and TGWU spent 20% and 14% respectively.

In summary, then, the variance in financial structure and performance between unions in 1989 remains considerable, but is rather harder to summarise than the position reviewed by Latta in 1972. There are no longer simple relationships between finances and union type. There are rich white-collar unions such as NALGO and IRSF and poor craft or manual-industry unions such as ACTT and NUS. Both proportionately and absolutely, general unions spend more on benefits than do many craft societies. There remains a substantial concentration of union resources in the largest unions but such unions tend to have lower than average subscriptions and net worth per capita. In order to understand how this position emerged, we need to look at change across the 1980s.

3.   Changes since 1980

It will be recalled from Chapter 2 that the main changes in the aggregate were membership loss, recovery of net worth, particularly net worth per capita, and the rise in real subscription income, both overall and per capita. Since large unions account for most of the aggregate change, one might expect similar patterns in this set. This is the case overall, but several unions did experience adverse changes in financial performance across the period. Moreover, in this set, 40% experienced an *increase* in membership across the period.

The total union membership loss from 1980–9 was approximately 2.6 million. TGWU, AEU, and NUM account for over half of this net loss. NUM, together with ISTC and NUS lost over 50% of their members during the period. Large percentage gains were, however, reported by the financial services unions such as BIFU and the staff associations, by RCN and by some teaching unions.[6] However, as in the aggregate, there was no correlation between changes in membership and changes in subscription income or net worth on a disaggregated basis. The argument of the previous chapter is further reinforced by the strong correlation between changes in real subscription income and real net worth. Unions which generated the greatest absolute increases in subscriptions gained wealth most rapidly.[7]

In Table 3.2 we have once more classifed the sample in terms of per capita net worth and subscriptions but in this instance we focus on average *changes* across the period. Once more the characteristics of the unions to the right of the table, those with large increases in real net worth, include the absence of membership competition and, for many, negotiations with few employers or via an industry association. Again, most of the large, competing unions cluster to the bottom left. The characteristics of those with high increases in subscriptions but below average growth in net worth per capita are more mixed. NCU, NUT, NUS, and NAHT have all, to a greater or lesser degree, been affected by disputes in the period.[8] NUCPS is the result of merger between the financially healthy SCPS and the poorer CSU, which effectively diluted the assets of the smaller union. In short, then, the winners across the period avoided membership competition and large strikes; they maintained strong positions in the membership and employer markets.

The table deals with absolute values and in per capita terms. If we simply calculate changes to unions' total real net worth, the picture is slightly different. Figure 3.2 plots percentage changes in real net worth against membership over the period 1980–9. This shows that some small, often poorer unions expanded net worth rapidly across the period. For example, the largest increases in real net worth were by BGSU (815%), STE (467%) and NWGSU (395%). Among the larger, richer unions the largest percentage increase was that of NALGO (190%). Among other

Table 3.2. *Changes in real per capita net worth and subscriptions: all unions, 1980–9*

Av. change in real net worth (£36.13)			
TGWU	NUS	NALGO	SOGAT
NUT	NAHT	EMA	NGA
NCU	POA	IPMS	AUT
NUCPS	LBGSU	ISTC	IRSF
FBU	NUR	TSSA	STE
COHSE	NUJ	NUMAST	

Av. Change in real subscriptions per capita (£14.30)		
AEU	BIFU	BGSU
GMB	AMMA	NUHKW
NUPE	NATFHE	NUFLAT
EETPU	FTAT	EIS
USDAW	URTU	NUM
MSF	BFAWU	MU
UCATT	NWGSU	NUMAST
RCN	EQUITY	URTU
CPSA	ACTT	
NAS/UWT	UCW	

Note: Changes for GMB are based on NUGMWU figures for 1980. Changes for MSF are based on the average of TASS and ASTMS figures for 1980.

unions with over 100,000 members in 1989 SOGAT, COHSE, BIFU, and NAS/UWT had real increases of over 100%.

If these were the winners in the period, there were also losers. Large losses in real net worth were experienced by AEU (60%), NUPE (44%), NUM (55%), NUS (92%), and ASLEF (46%). There were different reasons for this. In NUM and NUS, strikes were largely to blame. The case of AEU is rather more remarkable; all three cases are examined below. If we seek to account for the *overall* increase in union real net worth over the period, then events in TGWU and NALGO are the most important. The increase in real net worth in NALGO was 42% of that observed in the aggregate and that of TGWU 6.5%. On the other side of the coin, there was a *loss* equal to almost 50% of the observed aggregate real increase in wealth by AEU and NUM together. These figures indicate the importance of financial success, and perhaps effective financial management in the largest unions for the health of the union movement overall.

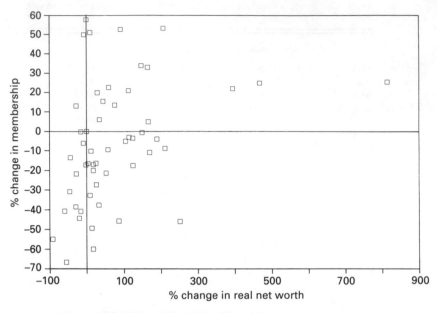

Figure 3.2. Change in membership and net worth

This is particularly the case since the unions whose wealth grew most rapidly were also those whose subscription income showed the largest absolute increases. The largest absolute rises in real subscription income per capita are in STE (£57), NGA (£44), POA (£38), and SOGAT (£36). There are also large rises in NALGO (£28) and NUR (£21). Only three unions in the set could *not* raise real subscriptions per capita, namely UCATT, EQUITY, and EIS.[9] However, some unions had low increases, for example GMB, USDAW, MSF, and RCN had real increases in subscriptions per capita of less than £5 overall. Given, as we have noted, that unions are labour-intensive organizations and that this was a period of rising real earnings, it is unlikely that such a low rate of increase would cover rising administrative costs. Once more, the picture looks rather different in percentage terms. Five unions managed an increase of over 100%; they were LBGSU (181%), POA (126%), BGSU (136%), and SOGAT (104%).

Given the more inclusive definition used by the Certification Officer from 1986 onwards, one would expect an increase in reported real administrative costs. In per capita terms, all unions except EQUITY experienced an increase. This increase was over 200% at NALGO, and over 100% at NUT, SOGAT, NUR, NGA, BGSU, STE, and LBGSU. In some cases, the long-term effects of disputes may be to blame. We discuss this in Chapter 7. Nevertheless, some of these large increases are difficult to explain, particularly when contrasted with the increases of less than 20% in per capita costs in UCATT, NUTGW, FTAT, EMA, and ACTT. Industry unions fall into both sets.

4   Success and failure in the top ten unions

Given their dominance in financial terms, it is appropriate to look more closely at the ten largest unions. Table 3.3 gives key indicators on membership, subscription income, and net worth for this set, as well as some measures of change over the period. The table emphasises not only the variance in capital structure among large unions, but also that there are both winners and losers financially across the period.

We can illustrate the variance by comparing the four largest unions. AEU is financially by far the most flimsy. As we shall show in Chapter 10 below, which focuses on the union, this is primarily because most of the union's collective bargaining and governance functions are kept off the balance sheet through heavy reliance on lay participation. However, the massive decline in real net worth does indicate some problems. NALGO, by contrast, is a high income, high expenditure union with massive growth in real net worth. Of the four, NALGO, GMB, and TGWU have acid test ratios substantially greater than unity. It is unlikely that multi-employer, multi-sector unions such as GMB or AEU would ever experience complete interruptions to income in circumstances other than sequestration of assets, but both had financial worries in both 1988 and 1989.

Apart from NALGO, other winners across the period were EETPU and RCN. The former has a relatively light capital base compared with certain other craft or manual-industry unions but it has grown substantially in financial terms despite membership loss to a position in 1989 where it had the highest acid test ratio of the top ten unions. Subscriptions per capita have been held down and are lower than those of the general unions.

RCN is extremely difficult to evaluate, since its accounting policies for the union side of its overall activities show it exactly balancing income and expenditure – with no accumulated funds – in any given year. The assets and funds actually deployed in support of union activity are accounted for elsewhere. Nevertheless, on the basis of a 58% increase in membership and a 23% increase in per capita subscriptions, it has had a much more successful period than either NUPE or COHSE, its main TUC-affiliated competitors.

Table 3.3. *Key indicators: Largest UK unions: 1980–9*

| Union | Membership (000) | | Per capita measures | | | | Change measures | | |
	1989	1980–9 change	subs £ per yr	admin cost £ per yr	net worth £ per yr	Net worth (£ million)	real net wealth per cap.	real subs %	Acid test ratio 1989
TGWU	1270.3	−616.2	41.5	41.1	56.5	71.8	9.2	73	1.18
AEU	741.6	−509.4	30.8	26.22	19.95	14.8	−60.1	26.4	0.61
GMB	823.1	−92.9	32.3	34.2	50.7	41.7	12.1	10.0	1.29
NALGO	750.5	−31.5	60.4	65.7	79.4	59.6	190.1	86.4	1.20
MSF*	653	−30	29.6	33.2	27.9	18.2	42.9	−1.3	0.79
NUPE	604.9	−94.1	35.3	34.3	22.4	13.5	−44.2	46.9	0.57
USDAW	375.9	−74.1	26.6	31.4	30	11.3	8.8	10.7	0.90
EETPU	367.4	−72.1	31.3	31	49.3	18.1	25.4	23.7	1.41
RCN	285.5	97.3	24.9	23.9	0	0	0	22.7	0
UCATT	258.3	−53.7	22.7	23.6	16.8	4.3	−1.5	−5.97	0.65

Note: *MSF change data based on TASS and ASTMS in 1980.

Four large unions have had an unhappy time in the 1980s. NUPE has suffered a large fall in its net worth, despite a large rise in per capita subscriptions and a relatively small percentage fall in members. USDAW and UCATT both make a loss on membership servicing. USDAW only raised real per capita subscriptions marginally and UCATT actually suffered a decline and its net worth per capita is the lowest of the top ten. Both unions suffered not only membership loss but also very high membership turnover. They service job territories characterised by temporary or casual work, large numbers of small establishments, and, frequently, employer hostility. Their finances indicate the difficulties of intractable employer and membership markets.

The position of MSF is in some ways as severe. We have already noted the substantial losses the union incurred on membership servicing. In addition, very low per capita net worth and a poor acid test ratio characterised the union in 1989. Evaluation of changes over time must rely on the slightly dubious retrospective comparison with TASS and ASTMS in 1980, but on this basis there has been a decline in subscription income per capita. One popular view is that this was a merger between a financially stable union, TASS, and an overstretched one, ASTMS. However, the picture in 1987 immediately before merger is more complex. TASS had higher nominal net worth per capita than ASTMS, £35.72 compared to £10.78. It also had a better acid test ratio, although at 0.94 and 0.36 respectively both were poor. Both unions were insolvent in that year, but in this respect TASS, covering only 89% of expenditure, was in a worse position. Moreover, ASTMS made a profit from membership servicing but TASS did not. Both unions were thus in some respects financially weak prior to the merger and, by 1989, the merger had done little to solve these problems. We discuss this, and the financial aspects of merger activity, Chapter 6.

Because of the skewed size and net worth distributions, these changes in the top ten affect the aggregate figure markedly. We can illustrate this by considering the contribution of these unions to the two most marked trends in the aggregate picture in the 1980s, namely the recovery in real net worth and subscription income. We have already indicated the importance of financial recovery in NALGO and TGWU for the aggregate figure on net worth and the negative effect of events within AEU and NUM.

However, there are difficulties here. If we widen the scope of consideration a little, it emerges that SOGAT and NGA contribute 14% and 16% respectively to the rise in real net worth and 11% and 13% to the rise in real subscription income. CPSA shows a negative share of the subscription income increase of approximately 7%. Many of these changes, then, are simply the result of mergers or membership transfers between unions, rather than changes which might directly affect the overall figures. The success of TGWU, SOGAT, and NGA in this respect is, in fact, the result of redistributive market share unionism which may have a neutral or even negative influence on the aggregate figures (Willman, 1989). By contrast, losses in wealth, income, and membership in AEU and NUM were real in the sense that the monies and employees went out of the unionised sector.

The financial success of NALGO is thus the more remarkable since it occurred without the inflow of funds from other unions. For Latta (1972), NALGO was an example of a relatively poor white-collar union but its financial transformation since then has resulted in a rise from the tenth ranking to the second most wealthy trade union. It has lost a low percentage of its members in the 1980s and its subscription income is supported by the inclusion in membership of relatively highly paid employees who pay a percentage of income rather than a flat rate. The union has become a substantial property owner and holds a diversified investment portfolio.

However, as we noted in Chapter 2, financial success for a trade union is a contestable idea. NALGO shows all the signs of having grown financially through a troubled period for trade unions, but it does not follow that the leaders of the union have pursued a policy of net revenue maximisation or even that the union leadership has accumulated wealth at its disposal. In NALGO, branches and districts retain 27.5% of contribution income. Of the remainder, only 57% goes into the general fund; the rest is specifically earmarked as a result of conference decisions about premises and strike reserves. Despite the healthy overall financial position, therefore, the union leadership experiences recurrent cash-flow problems (Willman, Morris, and Aston, 1989: 226–66). An increase in disposable wealth for a trade union implies nothing about disposal rights.

5   Conclusion

In this chapter, we have sought simply to present the pattern of variance in union finances in 1989 and to show the differing fortunes of unions across the 1980s. This pattern of variance is difficult to summarise. The union movement remains financially dominated by the top four unions, but there is no sign that financial concentration is increasing. There remain vast differences in income and wealth per capita. Some small managerial unions have become extremely wealthy. Many of the richest unions are still medium-sized manual-industry unions, but others have been absorbed through merger and several have been impoverished by large national disputes. Several white-collar unions, by contrast, have prospered, particularly in the public sector and despite involvement in disputes. It appears that the effects of strike involvement on financial status are variable.

Apart from large strikes, two related factors appear to be associated with the experience of financial difficulty in the 1980s. They are the inability to raise real subscription income per capita and the inability to make a profit on membership servicing. Unions have incurred massive membership losses but avoided financial difficulties through subscription increases. However, few unions – and none in the top ten – have been able to hold down the rise in real administrative costs per capita below 30%. In some cases, the rise has been much higher and the variance in administrative costs per capita implies either a variance in quality of service or that some job territories are more expensive to service than others. Revenue increases and cost controls have both been necessary.

These considerations also indicate the conditions for financial success. Financially successful unions, namely those which both raised subscription income and made a 'profit', tend to be those which avoided competition. An additional consideration is merger, but its effects cannot be generalised. TGWU, together with some smaller unions such as SOGAT, NGA, and BIFU, has absorbed smaller unions, apparently producing some financial benefits. Other mergers, such as that producing MSF, have not. Some mergers appear to be part of a policy of membership expansion through increase in market share, others purely defensive with one or both partners already in financial difficulty. Some of the manual-industry unions with declining membership are attractive merger partners but it is difficult to see what their own motives for merger might be.

By 1989, the problem observed by Roberts (1956), that the funds of trade unions were concentrated in non-recruiting unions while those seeking to expand trade union membership were poor, has been alleviated. The largest, richest unions are open recruiters. However, they compete, and there is some indication that competition affects both income and wealth. It may be, as the aggregate analysis implied, that a concentration of wealth in competitive recruiters and the effects on wealth of competitive recruitment will impoverish the union movement as a whole. Certainly, unions such as UCATT and USDAW which compete both with non-unionism and the general unions are impoverished.

As the brief discussion of NALGO indicated, the financial data do not, in the absence of information on financial management, give an idea of the real funds available to union leaders under any given set of circumstances. An analysis of such systems of management will be the focus of much of the remainder of the book.

4   The role of financial matters in union organisation

1   Introduction: why should trade unions care about money?

Those who have concerned themselves with the economics of trade unions have often not been concerned with their internal structure. Most economists are concerned with the economic *impact* of trade unions, particularly on absolute and relative wages, on profitability or on labour productivity (see Hirsch and Addison, 1986). When economists ask the question, 'what do unions do?' they are less concerned with union activity itself than with such consequences (Freeman and Medoff, 1984) and a concern with the effects of trade unions does not require an economic model of trade union organisation.

By contrast, those who have concerned themselves with the internal structure of unions have not generally been concerned with economics. The attention paid to trade unions by sociologists and by those in the more descriptive British industrial relations tradition has encompassed union government and democracy, the relationship between 'formal' trade unions and lay representation, the factors which encourage or discourage merger and the relations between unions and government, but not the economics of union organisation. For example, Undy *et al.*'s (1981) discussion of change in British trade unions focuses on the degree of centralisation of decision making and on the role of union general secretaries. It has little to say on the role of resource constraints in enforcing change in British trade unions between 1960 and 1975, other than to remark upon certain circumstances, notably merger negotiations, where resource considerations are important.

It has not always been so. The Webbs (1907) suggested that sound financial management had played a key role in the development of the 'new model' unionism and that financial concerns subsequently influenced both the structure and policy of unions. More recently, Roberts (1956) as noted above, accorded a central role to financial matters both in the determination of union policy and in limiting the ability of union leaders to deliver services to members. Latterly, however, concern with such matters has abated. There has been very little concern with the economics of

34

union organisation and few attempts to link such concern to an explanation of union policy and behaviour.

This absence of concern is perhaps understandable. The Webbs were concerned with the establishment of permanent trade unions in a hostile environment. Financial probity was a necessary condition for 'new model' unionism but, once established, a concern with economic matters could recede. Unions were, after all, concerned with other objectives and, although a minimum level of resources was necessary, union policies were based essentially on non-economic considerations, at least as far as the internal management of the organisation itself was concerned. Subsequently, on this argument, a solvent union movement has pursued its objectives untrammelled by such mundane considerations. However, as we have shown, unions in general have experienced financial decline across the post-war period and some unions have suffered financial embarrassment during the 1980s.

In such circumstances, might it not be the case that financial matters are now more important for both trade unionists and their leaders? In trying to answer this question, we are hampered by the absence of any model of the role of finances in voluntary, ostensibly democratic organisations like trade unions. Between the statements, first, that unions need a minimum level of funds to survive and, second, that they are not in the business of maximising profits there lies a large grey area in which to flounder.

2   The economist's approach: revenue maximising models

Several economists interested in the explanation of union bargaining behaviour have attacked this problem, occasionally indirectly. They have done so primarily by addressing the issues posed by the existence of divergent interests *within* the union, notably between union leaders and the rank and file. Paradoxically, perhaps, they have tended to lean heavily on a non-economic, essentially political model of the trade union developed by Ross (1948).[1]

Ross saw the union as: '... not only a group, but an institution as well: it leads a life of its own, separate and different from its members' (1948:7).

Union behaviour involved the reconciliation of three sets of objectives. These were defined as:
(1) the provision of an acceptable level of wage and non-wage benefits to members, the level being determined by rank-and-file comparisons with benefits elsewhere;

(2) the institutional aim of the survival and growth of the union organisation;
(3) the personal objectives of union leaders. Ross noted that attainment of the third objective is often satisfied by the second and his work essentially focuses on differences between member and leader interests.

He did not, however, concern himself with financial matters. As Burton (1984: 139) has noted, there is no subsystem of the model concerned with financial variables. Beyond a certain pessimism Ross has little to say. He notes:

corporate managers must operate under the surveillance of cost accountants and financial officers who have the function of steering leadership activities towards the formal purpose of the enterprise. Corresponding agencies of a rudimentary form are sometimes found in a union organisation, but they are probably less of a drag on the leadership ... because the formal purpose of the union is less capable of measurement. (1948: 27)

In general, economists have subsequently resolved this problem in the conventional way, namely by assuming that union leaders have a maximim-and. For example, Berkowitz (1954) assumes that trade union officers run their unions for their own interests, seeking to maximise net revenues. Net revenue is that surplus available after administrative costs incurred have been deducted from the income generated from the membership. Unions may, for certain purposes, be considered as if they were business enterprises, particularly in considering their organising activities. The implications are clear:

there is no necessity that it (i.e., the union) conducts its operations so that each and every bargaining unit shows a positive profit. The only survival requirement is that the total revenues from all units be at least equal to the total cost of running the union. (1954: 587)

In essence, then, Berkowitz, is acknowledging the likelihood of non-economic motives; but his argument is essentially for the need to look upon the economics of union activity as an 'aspect of their role which we need to be reminded of periodically' (1954: 589).

Membership preferences appear in the Berkowitz analysis as a constraint on union leaders. They are more central to Atherton's (1973) far more systematic discussion of union bargaining goals. Atherton identifies the *formal* purpose of the union as the maximisation of membership utility, defined in terms primarily of wages, employment, and the avoidance of strikes. The *institutional* objectives are similar to those of Ross, namely institutional survival and the political survival of the union's leaders, but in practice Atherton focuses on net revenues defined in Berkowitz's terms. Union activity consists in the balancing of these objectives but, for leaders at least, utility maximisation is proxied by net revenue maximisation, that is the maximisation of residual receipts available for the private use of the leadership.

One problem with the net revenue-maximisation approach is that union leaders typically have no enforceable property rights over residual income. As Martin (1980) has noted, very few US unions are 'proprietary', i.e., offer members available property rights over the present value of their union card. Most are 'non-proprietary', in which the ownership of residual assets is unclear, and it is precisely in such common structures that leaders' considerable managerial discretion in the use of funds is constrained by elaborate formal rules (1980: 90–106). It is thus difficult to see why union leaders would seek to maximise revenues which they cannot subsequently appropriate.

In the UK, the status of the accrued contributions which form trade union reserves at any point in time is in some ways unclear. It is certainly the case that the majority of unions in the UK are, in Martin's terms, 'non-proprietary'. New union members seldom overtly 'buy in' to unions although in many there is a qualifying period of membership prior to access to the full range of benefits. Departing members are *decreasingly* likely to take accrued contributions with them in the form of benefits. However, accrued funds are the nearest thing to equity possessed by UK unions in that they are held in trust and deployed by the leadership on behalf of existing or prospective members.

Martin goes on to reject all 'wealth maximising' models of trade unions on the basis that this proprietary right is absent. This is surely too fundamental a rejection. As Burton has pointed out, union officers, like managers in other not-for-profit organisations, may gain in power and status, as well as in terms of indirect income from larger rather than smaller treasuries. Asset growth may support higher salaries or more secure tenure, and its pursuit may encourage membership growth beyond the level which maximises per capita rent (1984: 144).

The emphasis on proprietary rights does, however, help to explain certain aspects of the *management* of union funds. Without full proprietary rights on membership, members may be expected to experience lower opportunity costs in non-rent maximising behaviour (Martin, 1980: 88). In particular: 'the absence of a proprietary interest in the present value of union monopoly rents lowers the cost to members of ignoring sound financial management practices' (1980: 15). This effect is likely, for Martin, to be manifest in more conservative investment policies than would be expected in the presence of full proprietary rights.

The economic approach, then, is to develop simple models of the institutional arrangements within unions to develop predictions concerning their bargaining behaviour. The contest for control of the union between leaders and members is the central issue in revenue or wealth maximising approaches. At one extreme lies the *member dominated* union, collective voice pure and simple, with the objective of maximising members' per capita rent. Union wealth or assets can be seen merely as the resources necessary to achieve this objective. An undifferentiated membership seeks simply to maximise:

$$\frac{\text{Total monetary and non-monetary returns following from union activity}}{\text{Costs of maintaining organisation}}$$

If they are successful, the union balance sheet is *ceteris paribus* likely to be small, and the members' share of the net benefits of union membership large.

At the other extreme is the conception of an organisation directed primarily to maximising leaders' wealth. As union collective rents are maximised, the leadership expropriates all except the small residual which, net of membership costs, provides the individual member with a margin above the opportunity cost of non-membership or membership of another union and hence an incentive to join and remain in membership. Leaders maximise:

$$\frac{\text{Share of monopoly rent}}{\text{Total costs}}$$

If they are successful, the union's balance sheet is sizeable but the benefits of union membership relatively small.

These approaches provide a useful framework for the analysis of union income expenditure and assets and, moreover, relate these to the management of the union. Members are seen as buying union services and the costs of union organisation are, for members, the transaction costs involved in the assertion of monopoly power. For leaders, something close to the managerial theory of the firm is implied: enhanced resources are not directly appropriable, but offer numerous benefits. However such models were devised to analyse bargaining behaviour rather than union organisation and several points need to be made about their characterisation of union organisation.

The first is that there is no reason to accept, from the available UK evidence, that membership or leadership domination is the crucial distinction on which to base predictions about differential financial structure or performance.

The objection is, essentially, empirical. However, no counter-theory exists, hence the marshalling of evidence could be a lengthy process. It may be useful to illustrate matters at the outset with a simple, hypothetical, example. Imagine a simple, relatively small, and homogeneous association of employees. They bargain with a single employer over terms and conditions of employment. 'Office' is rotated and involves simply the maintenance of records and the function of representation. There is no 'leadership' to speak of. A primitive democracy obtains. We cannot predict, from these data alone, its financial structure. There may or may not be subscriptions depending on the risk of moral hazard. There may or may not be reserves, depending on the likelihood of a strike and the exogenously set demands for various types of benefit or subsidy. Expenditure too will depend on exogenous factors, notably the extent of employer subsidy including the subsidy of members' leisure time to pursue union activity. Similarly, we cannot predict the financial structure of a large leadership-dominated union from knowledge of its control structure alone. One needs to know the number of employers with whom the union bargains, the preferences of the membership for different types of services or benefits, the level of unpaid lay involvement, and the number of large-scale disputes the union has recently experienced.

As Pencavel (1971) has noted, unions provide three different types of membership service. They provide individual services such as death or disability benefit. They provide semi-collective services such as grievance or disciplinary representation: the mechanism for representation is collectively determined but representation itself is of individuals. Finally, they provide collective services such as bargaining representation. The balance between these three effects financial structure and policies within trade unions, but it is by no means clear that the mix of services reflects either leadership or membership domination.

The *mix* of services implies that, at any point in time, one set of union members may well be subsidising others. One bargaining unit, for example, may need very little collective support, while another requires a great deal. Some individuals may be in receipt of individual representation or benefit while others may not. The simple economics of union organisation require that most of the members, most of the time, are not a drain on union resources and that the union must hold reserves against variable levels of claim on its services.

We have shown that, in the UK, the level of benefit provision has fallen overall but it remains highly variable between unions. High levels of benefit provision are, in the print societies such as NGA and SOGAT, associated with considerable per capita wealth but also with extreme decentralisation of government structure. *A priori* there is no evidence here of leadership domination. Similar observations could be made about several old-established manual-industry unions whose wealth and benefit structure appears to owe more to the accidents of history than to any features of union government (Latta, 1972). These organisations quite often rely administratively on membership activity rather than on full-time 'officers'. Latta's study also indicated that a number of poorer unions were white collar. Several, such as BIFU, APEX (as was), and ASTMS combined the appointment rather than the election of officers with a focus on purely collective services (Heery, 1987). Such unions tended to focus on collective bargaining rather than benefits, to be financially quite lightweight per capita and to take a relatively small proportion of earnings as subscriptions (Willman and Morris, 1988). They tend to rely on full-time officers rather than membership activity.

This is rather casual empiricism, but it implies that the level and mix of service provision is not simply a function of leadership domination or its absence but reflects rather more complex influences. The link between simple dichotomies about government and the role of finances is not clear cut. It appears equally important to ask first, about the determinants of members' preferences for a particular service mix and, secondly, about the relationship between internal and external sources of funding: specifically, can the union's activities be supported by a combination of membership involvement and employer subsidy or must the union pay its own way?

The second point to be made about the models discussed above is that they fail to acknowledge that unions are not closed financial systems. One particularly important source of financial and other resources in unions is employer support: its implications for union financial management and performance are worth discussing in some detail.

Employers who recognise trade unions may subsidise their activities in several ways. They may provide offices, telephones, and time off for their employees who are also representatives of trade unions, thus effectively 'saving' expenditure on full-time officials. They may offer check-off facilities for union subscriptions, albeit at a price, which improve subscription yield. They may provide training of union members related to industrial relations and they may assist recruitment of new members for trade unions by encouraging new employees to join a union.

Successive Workplace Industrial Relations Surveys have indicated that these forms of employer support are widespread (Daniel and Millward,

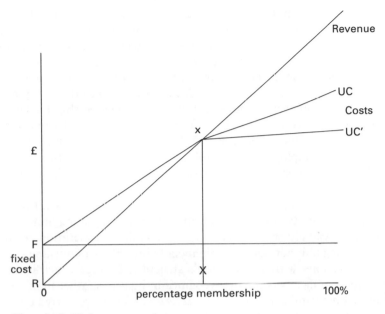

Figure 4.1. Union costs and revenues

1983; Millward and Stevens, 1986). Certain forms, such as check-off facilities, appear to have been on the increase in the early 1980s.

Unfortunately there are no data available either on the costs of such facilities to the employer nor on their value to different trade unions. Nevertheless, such support is almost certainly crucial to trade union finances, not least because it is highly likely to influence the level of lay membership activity. *Ceteris paribus*, unions without such support (or with less of it) are likely to face more financial difficulties than those with it. The corollary is that, over time, unions which gain such support will become reliant on it and thus dependent. The management of relations with employers will thus become crucial to the management of financial resources in the union. We may illustrate this using a simple example, based on Berkowitz's (1954) approach.

Figure 4.1, loosely based on Berkowitz, plots membership levels against revenue for a given bargaining unit. It sees the granting of union recognition as an inflexion point (X) on the union cost (F-UC) and revenue (RR) curves. There are fixed costs of organisation (OF) and, at low membership levels prior to recognition, costs (FX) are greater than revenues (RX). Two pressures are important here. The first is that subscriptions cannot be raised before recognition through fear of dis-affection and because services such as bargaining representation cannot yet be provided. The second is that, through lack of employer support and through membership turnover, subscription yield will be low. At X, the cost and revenue cross. Costs may in fact fall if the employer begins to subsidise union activity through provision of facilities. They may stay low if the employer encourages 100% union membership (X-UC'); they may rise with consolidatory recruitment if the cost of discouraging free-riding falls on the union alone (X-UC). Revenues will improve immedi-ately if the employer assists collection. On the assumption of constant subscriptions, they continue to rise until 100% membership is approached (X-R).

The figure emphasises the importance of union recognition for the financial viability of operations within a single bargaining unit. Of course, financial viability may not be an overriding consideration in any one bargaining unit but, logically, financially inviable ones must be subsidised by viable ones within any union's structure. Devices which increase the numbers of members in post-recognition situations rather than pre-recog-nition ones within any union will, *ceteris paribus*, be preferred on financial grounds. In fact, any device, for example a statutory route to recognition, which moves X towards the origin will assist the finances of trade unions and reduce administrative costs per capita.[2] This is a simple example, but it leads on to several observations of broader relevance to multi-unit, multi-employer trade unions.

Consider the case of union recruitment. A union which has recognition agreements with one or more employers and which is pursuing new mem-bers may seek to grow in at least four different ways. These are:

(a) Individual recruitment/recognition agreement

The union seeks to increase membership density under existing agree-ments by trying to persuade free-riders to join. Pressure from the employer may be involved. This is termed 'consolidation' by Kelly and Heery (1989). There is US evidence that such recruitment may yield benefits for all existing members, via the increased bargaining power accruing through increased union coverage (Voos, 1984).

(b) Individual recruitment/no recognition agreement

The union seeks to build up membership to the point where it can secure recognition. It cannot negotiate on the members' behalf, but may have representational rights; it may discount subscriptions in acknowledge-ment of this, in order to attract new members. In the terms used in Figure 4.1, the union operates on part RX of the membership/revenue curve.

(c) Merger or transfer of engagement

The union takes in a body of already organised employees, often with their officials, and normally with recognition agreements, either to extend their coverage of employers or to eliminate a competitive form of representation within a given firm or industry.

(d) Organising the employer

The union either initiates an approach to an employer or responds to the employers request, seeking to secure an assured membership and income stream. The employer may be non-union or a unionised employer considering a greenfield site.

The first two mechanisms involve individual recruitment. In the first case, the union directs its recruiting activities at individuals who have previously seen no compulsion to join. They may be seen by the unions as free-riders, but they are viewed by statute as individuals who have a right to remain outside unions. To succeed, the organiser must either offer attractions to membership in the form of individual benefits unavailable to free-riders – for example packages of personal financial services at discount – or must change their minds about free-riding; the alternative is to use the influence of employers to encourage recruitment. In the second case, the union organiser must encourage membership, perhaps in the face of employer indifference or hostility, perhaps with the use of inertia selling techniques, notably direct debiting of subscriptions. The union's resources are often pitted against the greater resources of the employer in communicating about the consequences of union membership.

Had both such mechanisms historically been unsuccessful we would neither have recognised trade unions nor have instances of high union density within firms. However, since only the latter two mechanisms involve the acquisition of groups of members, they will *ceteris paribus* be preferred on cost grounds. In times of financial difficulty, when cost considerations may be paramount, they may come to predominate. Where individual recruitment is pursued, consolidatory recruitment, preferably assisted by employers, will be favoured on cost grounds.

There may therefore be both cost-effective and cost-ineffective mechanisms for union growth and the role of the employer may be crucial in defining them: on such grounds, new members under recognition agreements will be preferred to those in 'pre-recognition' establishments. Moreover, the influence of employer support is not restricted to recruitment, since, as noted above, it also assists the generation of 'surplus' from existing union members.

Such considerations have, apparently, affected the calculations of union officials. Undy *et al.* (1981) discuss the cases of the 'Jones' strategy within TGWU in the 1960s. The development of a strategy of reliance on shop stewards supported by employer facilities depended on a level of – at least implicit – employer compliance. As they remark: 'Instead of the union paying for more but less efficient and expensive full-time officials, the employer could pay for more efficient and cheaper shop stewards' (1981: 99). Evidence of a negative influence – a restriction of employer support involving heavy reliance on high cost full-time officials – is available from the UK financial sector (Morris, 1986).

As this argument implies, the structure of a union's job territory also has implications for its financial requirements. Unions with few bargaining units will be financially more secure than those with many if there are fixed costs to the administration of each bargaining unit. Unions with a higher percentage of members in establishments recognising unions ought also to have a financial advantage over those with a lower percentage.

These considerations encourage a focus not simply on the role of employers in subsidising union finances but, much more broadly, on the relationship between the union and its members. The willingness of the latter to join, to participate in, and to influence the policies of the union is not easily conceptualised in terms of an economic transaction involving the exchange of subscriptions for services but is emerging as a major influence over the union's financial status and structure.

3   Sociological approaches

Any definition of financial 'health' in trade unions must be essentially contestable. Unions do not exist primarily to pursue financial objectives and their *espoused* objectives often have to do with improvement of the pecuniary and non-pecuniary conditions of the membership. If, as the wealth-maximising models suggest, some section of the union is intent on the pursuit of primarily financial objectives, then the least that needs to be said is that such objectives would need to be pursued either covertly or in the face of considerable opposition.

Many debates in trade unions concerning size, the pursuit of certain policies, and the nature of union government have financial implications. However, other debates are directly about financial matters including debates on assets, expenditure, and particularly subscriptions. These can be quite difficult for union leaders. Noting the link between financial and political control referred to above, Roberts also noted that: 'executive councils are more often defeated at union conferences on questions concerning finance than on any other matter' (1956: 343).

The management of 'net revenue' is inherently problematic. For example, a surplus of income over expenditure in any given year may be, for the union leader, evidence of good husbandry and for the activist, evidence of inadequate benefit expenditure or service provision. Again, the issue is not just a question of leader–member relationships but also of the balance between individual benefits and collective services (Pencavel, 1971). As noted above, the economics of trade union organisation require that some 'profit' is made from some members which may be disbursed to others, and the principles of this reallocation are essentially contestable, particularly if members are unsure about membership duration.

However, the broader point is that trade unions are political as well as financial in nature and that economic objectives, both for the union as institution and for its members, are not always paramount. The role of financial issues in trade unions must be understood in the context of broader debates about oligarchy and bureaucracy (Michels, 1915; Hyman, 1971; Crouch, 1982). As Crouch notes, even if one begins with the proposition that the creation of a collective organisational bureaucracy solves the essentially economic problem of interest group representation, the problem of bureaucracy remains as: 'The organisation, now seen as consisting of a staff, the "apparatus" rather than just the members, takes on a life of its own' (1982: 42).

Many would not accept that unions exist solely to represent current members' interests. Offe and Wiesenthal argue that union organisations simultaneously shape *and* represent members' interests and that, because of the problem of collective action identified by Olsen – i.e., that the costs of joining an organisation to an individual are greater than the marginal benefits of his membership – workers must 'subjectively deflate' the costs of organisation:

workers' organisations in capitalist systems always find themselves forced to rely upon non-utilitarian forms of collective action... *even if* the organisation does not have any intention of serving anything but the members' individual utilitarian interests....No union can function for a day in the absence of some rudimentary notions held by members that being a member is a value in itself, that the individual organisation costs must not be calculated in a utilitarian manner but have to be accepted as necessary sacrifices and that each member is legitimately required to practice solidarity and disicipline and other norms of a non-utilitarian kind. (Offe and Wiesenthal, 1980: 78–9)

Unions, they note, are based on members' 'willingness to act' not just their 'willingness to pay' and those which attempt only the latter will lack the resources to survive (1980: 80, 84). As Crouch notes (1982: 55), this is a rational-choice model which introduces the idea of class inequality into the Olsonian analysis. However, it also emphasises the affective link between members and their union. Union objectives, reflecting this, are likely to be complex, including organisational, membership, and wider political objectives.

Unions thus come to see themselves as both organisation and movement. As Child *et al.* (1973) note, they operate according to both an 'administrative' and a 'representative' rationality. The former emphasises routinisation, specialisation, efficiency, and speed of decision taking. It focuses on the outcomes of specific tasks. The latter emphasises democracy, checks and balances, flexibility, and the building of consensus. It focuses on the ways in which interests are expressed. Administrative rationality implies a 'unified and co-ordinated system of control, in which the prime source of authority is located at the top of the organisational hierarchy' (1972: 77–8). By contrast, representative rationality implies grass roots authority and a division of powers.

The two systems of rationality – inherently in conflict – are associated with different forms of membership attachment. Primacy accorded to administrative rationality within a union would imply passive, instrumental involvement. Primacy accorded to representative rationality implies committment and involvement. But the two conflicting rationalities must coexist. 'What is the point of a wonderfully representative system if it can never put its democratically-assembled views into practice: What is the point of a superbly efficient organisation that does not know what it is meant to be using its efficiency for?' (Crouch, 1982: 167–8).

If both coexist, they will sustain within trade unions distinctive patterns of discourse relating to the importance or otherwise of financial and efficiency considerations. At issue here is what Wright Mills (1963) has termed the 'vocabulary of motives' in trade union activity. As he points out, the avowal of motives in particular situations is essentially a social phenomenon, based on an assessment of the power and acceptability of a particular argument. He notes: 'As over against the inferential conception of motives as subjective springs of action, motives may be considered as typical vocabularies, having ascertainable functions in delimited social situations' (Mills, 1963: 439).

In any organisational context, including trade unions, some types of motive are generally and some only partially acceptable. Individual *rights* for example, are generally supported in trade unions, but individual *interests* may be difficult to articulate in the face of arguments about *collective* interests. More generally, the whole idea that the organisation has a commercial framework with minimum financial requirements may be difficult to articulate against the view that the organisation stands apart from, and attempts to restrict, a commercial, capitalist system which disadvantages union members. The use of commercial arguments by proponents of the administrative rationality to exert control over union business may appear to some members to indicate acceptance of the rules of the very system which unions are there to oppose.

The structure of discourse, including that about financial pressures, their importance and management, is affected by the distribution of, and contests over, power in the organisation. Motive avowal is affected by social position: 'The choice of a motive which is ascribed to some conduct pattern reflects the institutional position of the actor and of those who ascribe motives to him' (Gerth and Mills, 1954: 118).

Part of the political problem of financial management in trade unions is that leadership proposals for financial change may be rationalised as proposals designed to enhance leadership control or reduce membership autonomy. In certain contexts – for example, the planning of strike action – financial arguments may be deemed at best irrelevant and at worst evidence of leadership backsliding. Members and activists have little direct financial interest in their organisations *per se* as distinct from their interests in ensuring the furtherance of its ostensible aims. They may see in other trade unions alternate vehicles for their aims, and may see their own union as founded primarily on unpaid membership activity. As noted above, the reserves of the union are generally not appropriable by departing members, hence accumulated subscriptions are, for the member, a sunk investment.[3] They may press for union monies to be spent on present campaigns rather than invested against future eventualities.

The leadership and full-time officials, by contrast, have a career and salary interest in the organisation which may give them a concern with the longer view; in practice, their employment consumes most of the union's resources. A high level of reserves may be seen as a guarantee of continued employment and as a bulwark against membership disaffection. Arguments for administrative rationality thus become tied up with other conflicts between those who control the union and consume its resources and those who provide such resources.

The avowal, imputation, and effectiveness of such motives is logically prior to, but not independent of, the interpretation of particular financial measures and standards, and will underpin the overall influence and nature of financial arguments in the determination of union policy and behaviour. Some financial arguments may be relatively easy to sustain. Those for a subscription increase when real wages are rising, for budgeting or expenditure freezes when membership falls, or for the transfer of assets from low- to high-yield investments may be justified by appeals to equity, parsimony, or good sense. However, others are, within most trade unions, unavailable. Whereas a company might be able to argue for quitting an unprofitable market, a union leader might find it difficult to deploy administrative rationality to argue that a group of members, which costs more to service than the revenue yield, should be abandoned. In some unions, it is difficult to argue in favour of overseas investment of union assets or investment in non-union or privatised firms. Expenditure on non-members – even where they are prospective members and there is the prospect of some economic return to the membership through improved bargaining coverage (Voos, 1984) – is more difficult to justify than that on services to existing members or benefits to past ones.

Given the necessity of maintaining members' willingness to act, these issues are important. The union must assemble and deploy resources from a variety of quarters in order to function. In any trade union, the resources which are *actually deployed* on union activity derive from at least four sources.[4] The first is the income derived from union dues, investment, and other income. This is the unions' 'own' money and its collection and disbursement, but not its day-to-day management, are often governed by rule book provisions. The second set of resources derives, as already noted, from employers in the provision of facilities for union representation and collection of union dues through 'check-off' from salary. Most unions are in this respect employer dependent to some degree. The third originates with government in the refund of monies for balloting, provided certain conditions have been met. The fourth originates with members, whose unpaid activities are often a substantial proportion of the labour resource available. Since not-for-profit organisations in general and trade unions in particular are often labour-intensive service businesses, such resources may be an important component of the total available. Data on the value of such resources are unlikely to be available, but their volume may relate positively to the provision of facilities by employers.

It is reasonably easy to envisage how deployment of one set of resources could influence supply of another. Refusal to prosecute a pay claim may lead to withdrawal of activists' voluntary support while vigorous pursuit of it may lead to loss of employer facilities or, conceivably, government funds. Failure to pursue the membership's preferred policies might jeopardise real subscription levels by encouraging rejection of subscription charges at conference. Conversely, financial difficulties evident in the union's own balance sheet might encourage loyal members to increase the supply of time or of funds. The overall management of resources within trade unions thus involves a delicate balancing act involving different interests and income sources and the net costs of any campaign which must be borne out of the union's own funds may be difficult to predict.

This balance is rendered more precarious in some unions by the fact that, at least among activists, administrative rationality carries little weight, even where it does not conflict with representative rationality. Many of the sentiments which underpin trade union activism in the UK have been anti-capitalist or at least apathetic to arguments based on market criteria. In some unions, for example in the NUM in 1984, rejection of commercial arguments for pit closure by the employer could not easily be reconciled with a cost–benefit analysis of the pursuit of industrial action (Adeney and Lloyd, 1985; Aston, Morris, and Willman, 1990) which was thus pursued without regard to its effects on union finances.[5] The 1984 strike, though an extreme example since strikes are generally *ex post* inefficient for both parties, is not an isolated one.[6] It may, in many cases, simply not be possible successfully to base arguments on financial grounds in the face of principled objections.

In short, financial management in trade unions is constrained by the need publicly to justify decisions in terms of a pattern of discourse which, though variable, contains substantial extra-economic elements. Because, at worst, financial matters are a necessary evil for organisations which pursue 'higher' goals, financial considerations may be ignored in the pursuit of such goals. This may affect both the behaviour of trade unions and the internal style of financial management they adopt. Any objectives of net revenue maximisation must be pursued, therefore, in social settings hostile or at least apathetic to the explicit use of commercial argument and where, at least ostensibly, democracy prevails.

Because trade unions are representative voluntary associations and are also 'secondary' or 'intermediate' (Offe and Wiesenthal, 1980) in that they require influence with employers in order to function, they are not, financially speaking, closed systems. Their resources emerge through subscription payments, voluntary activity, and, through representative success, from employers. The efficiency with which different unions secure and deploy such resources varies as does the extent to which resource considerations affect policy and practice. However, it is possible to spell out in more detail the implications of the foregoing discussion for the analysis of financial systems within trade unions before moving on to the empirical questions relating to the importance of financial considerations in union behaviour.

4   Union financial systems[7]

Although trade unions differ from each other, there are certain common features. They are labour-intensive service businesses. They are concerned with the provision of individual, semi-collective, and collective goods to often heterogeneous sectional interest groups. Such goods may be generated through collective bargaining and other forms of pressure on the employer, for example, increases in wages and improvement of conditions at work. They may also be generated through reallocation of subscription or investment income, for example, the provision of injury and retirement benefit and strike pay. The main working assets of trade unions are the people they employ directly, the willingness of their members to engage in various types of voluntary work, and the resources they receive from the employers who recognise them; such resources may include check-off of union subscriptions, physical facilities for union representatives, and time off with pay for union work.

In short, unions operate as mediating organisations between employers, who see some benefit either in the granting of recognition or in its maintenance, fearing to deal with an unorganised workforce, and employees who seek various forms of insurance and representation. It follows that, to succeed, they must appeal to both sets of interests.

This may be an obvious point. To be effective, unions must have members, but they must also engage in collective bargaining which may often result in the employer conceding not only to increases in members' wages but also to facilities for union organisation. Unions are never wholly independent of employers and indeed the necessity of a certain level of dependence is, paradoxically, acknowledged by the Certification Officer in his application of the test of *independence*.[8] However, although obvious, the dependence of unions on employers and the impact this dependence has on the economics of union organisation have not been examined in terms of their influence on union behaviour.

Economists have long emphasised that trade unions operate in the membership market, competing to provide a set of services for consumption, for which members are prepared to incur certain costs. In turn, the union will incur different levels of cost in trying to organise different groups of workers, making the organisation of some groups more cost effective than others. However, conventionally, such analysis sees the market for union services in terms of members, or prospective members, only. More recently, the Harvard School have indicated that unions may provide some benefits to employers who recognise them through their capacity to organise collective voice. However, since differences between unions are not much considered in this approach, the idea that they may compete to provide benefits for employers is not explored (Freeman and Medoff, 1984).[9]

The model of union financial systems presented here is based on the view that trade unions seek to provide services in two related markets and in order to be successful, both financially and in terms of membership growth, they must reconcile the demands of both these markets.[10]

On one hand, trade unions compete to provide representation, insurance, and other services in the membership market. They seek a body of membership in order to guarantee revenue and secure bargaining power, often in competition with other unions, or with non-union environments. Without such membership, they will exert little influence. On the other hand, they compete under similar conditions to become bargaining agents

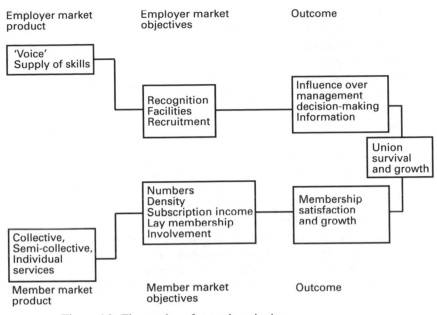

Figure 4.2. The markets for trade unionism

with employers. Without recognition, union effectiveness in any establishment is difficult to establish and membership tends to dwindle over time. In addition, pre-recognition representation is costly, since the union is, at best, only allowed individual representational rights.

With the granting of recognition and facilities, the union is able to shift some of the costs of organisation over to the employer. The two 'markets' are clearly related since, without recognition, membership is difficult to maintain and, without an adequate level of membership, recognition is difficult to secure. A successful union must be effective in both. One which relies only on the membership market cannot conduct negotiations with employers and must be able to rely on unilateral regulation for its influence. This is uncommon. Unions do exist which rely heavily on the employer market, sometimes on specific employers. Again such unions, often staff associations, are not seen as effective bargainers although they are apparently permanent features in some sectors (Swabe and Price, 1984). At the extreme, heavily dependent unions will not pass the test of independence. Successful collective bargainers must balance employer- and membership-dependence.

This two-market model is shown in Figure 4.2. The 'products' the union supplies in the two markets are, on the one hand, membership services and, on the other, collective 'voice' to employers. The former has been discussed above and is the source of considerable attention from economists. The principal addition here is to emphasise that the nature of demand for union services and benefits is highly variable across and indeed within sectors. Unions do not compete on price alone for a uniform service package, but offer distinctive service and benefit packages which may *ex ante* be difficult to value.

The level of employer subsidy to trade unions strongly implies the existence of some perceived benefits from trade union recognition. Even if these are only perceived *ex post*, it seems clear from the WIRS data and from that discussed below that in most cases employers go beyond perfunctory recognition. It is implausible to suggest they do so purely under coercion, hence it appears that some benefits arise from employer–union collusion. The Harvard School approach (based on Hirschman, 1970), provides the most comprehensive explanation of such collusion (Freeman and Medoff, 1984). Put briefly, unions provide a 'voice' mechanism to employers to assist them with remedial action in the event of organisational decline. In addition, unions may perform the more traditional function as monopoly suppliers of certain skills.

This framework may be employed to describe the reaction of employers and members to substandard union performance. Employers will initially voice objections to union behaviour by manipulating the level of subsidy and, if terminally dissatisfied, derecognise. Members will protest about leadership deficiencies though the government structure of the union and, if still dissatisfied, leave for competing unions or simply cease to be union members. Voice will precede exit but, if either form of exit happens on a large scale, the union's survival is threatened.

Political issues become relevant. Our argument here is, in effect, that unions are both dependent on and collusive with employers and that they have institutional objectives distinct from the immediately expressed wishes of the membership. This does not, of course, exclude the assertion that they provide membership benefits but does imply that these benefits coexist with and to some extent derive from policies which most or all members of some unions would resist. Political issues influence the ways in which institutional objectives may be publicly pursued as they do the description of employer-dependent activities. In short, the political environment within a trade union will influence the style of union management adopted by its leaders, particularly with respect to the pursuit of policies members might not support.

The model is thus limited to a concern with Ross's institutional goals and with what Child *et al.* (1973) would call administrative rationality. It is not a general model of trade union behaviour but rather seeks to explore the behaviour of the union as a not-for-profit organisation with a minimum set of institutional aims. Its explanatory power will be greatest where the union leadership has scope to pursue these aims, whether by its control over the membership or because it reflects in its policies the wishes of its members. Where unions pursue issues of 'principle' to the exclusion of long-term institutional objectives, it will not explain behaviour except that, we would argue, the union's survival would be threatened. Its clear implication is that unions can only survive where there is some minimum level of compatibility between the policies which yield success in the membership market and those which do so in the employers' market.

What does the model imply for financial management in trade unions? A number of hypotheses emerge. The *first* is that, since Ross's institutional objectives imply satisficing rather than maximising behaviour and because administrative rationality is unlikely to prevail, formal financial systems will be neither common nor rigorous in trade unions and that financial issues will only be to the fore in moments of crisis or where survival is at stake, for example in the course of strikes or when mergers are discussed. This broad hypothesis has implications for union income, expenditure, and assets. Since unions do not seek to maximise income but to succeed in the membership market we hypothesise, *secondly*, that unions set subscriptions competitively and avoid raising them unless compelled to do so. As a corollary, we would suggest that they would choose to improve collection yield rather than subscription levels. Since they do not seek to maximise assets, we hypothesise, *thirdly*, that unions will *not* manage their assets in order to gain a competitive rate of return and that there will be rule book constraints on asset management. On expenditure, we hypothesise, *fourthly*, that income is set to meet expenditure in the short term, rather than vice versa and that expenditure decisions are a consequence rather than a determinant of broader policy decisions. We hypothesise, *fifthly*, that employer subsidy and the prospect of its enhancement or reduction affects union decisions over finances. *Sixthly*, we hypothesise that, since this is effectively a model of the union incorporating managerial discretion, union leaders will seek to centralise the management of funds, whatever rule book provisions there may be, will seek to depoliticise income and expenditure issues, and will seek to control the activities of the finance officer: the latter is likely to be appointed rather than elected and likely to have a role isolated from the representative system of the union.

These six broad hypotheses will guide the discussion in the chapters to follow. We have developed no detailed hypothesis concerning the relationship between the financial subsystem and union behaviour other than the general, intuitive proposition that financial issues will have greater salience in times of financial difficulties. As we shall show below, there are a range of possible relationships between financial matters and union strategies which do not *a priori* lend themselves to generalisation. We shall return to this issue after presentation of the case studies.

5   Conclusion

In this chapter we have tried to bring to bear the work both of economists and sociologists on the problem of financial management within unions. Economists emphasise both the calculative attachment of workers to unions and the emergence of institutional or leadership objectives – which diverge from those of members – in the deployment of union resources. However, no systematic analysis of financial subsystems has emerged. Sociologists emphasise the related issues of bureaucracy and oligarchy, but are not primarily concerned with the economics of union organisation.

Nevertheless, both sets of literature generate insights which are directly of use in the analysis of union finances and their relationship to behaviour. From the economic work, there emerges the discussion of cost-effective organisation and of employer dependence. From the sociological literature comes an emphasis on membership influence on the politics of union finances and on the essentially intermediate nature of union organisation. We have used both to construct a model of union financial systems which will be used in the empirical chapters to follow.

5 The politics of union finances

1 Introduction

Since unions are not profit-making institutions, since the extent of managerial discretion is normally limited by ostensibly democratic government structures, and since, at least in some unions, commercial arguments are held in very low esteem, financial managers must tread carefully. Certain types of commercial argument are simply not publicly available and there is no clear maximand which might indicate good or bad financial management in the short term.

The management of finances, which, as Roberts (1956) noted, is central to the control of union activity overall is essentially contestable. The influence wielded by those responsible for financial affairs compared with that wielded by other interest groups within the union is thus important. So too is the rule book. As we noted above, public debate on financial matters will be conducted within a vocabulary of motives in which avowal of arguments about financial matters can only be justified by reference to members' interests. This vocabulary may be considered as the set of publicly available arguments about the management of the union.

In this chapter, we shall examine both the pattern of financial management in trade unions and the nature of debate over financial matters. In the first instance, we shall use questionnaire data. For examination of the debates we shall use material from the case studies.

2 The pattern of financial management

The rationale for the questionnaire and the overall response rate stratified by size are discussed in Appendix 1. In all, 72 questionnaires were returned, 46% from TUC affiliates and 54% from non-affiliates.[1] The sample included craft, general, industry, white-collar, and occupational unions as well as staff associations based on a single company. In addition, some areas of unions which submit separate financial returns also responded.

The questions covered several issues, including income, expenditure, and assets as well as the framework for managing funds and the identity of those responsible for specific decisions.[2] We shall look first at income, expenditure, and assets, then move on to look at the framework for financial management.

Income

Overall, 80% of union members in the sample pay through check-off, by far the highest payment category.[3] The second largest category, 11% of union members, pay by direct debit. In total, only 1.3% pay by some form of standing order. Under 8% of members in respondent unions pay by cash or cheque. Overall, then, the subscriptions of 87% of union members in this sample are collected by mechanisms which either require regular monitoring by the union or are employer dependent.

There were clear size effects. Larger unions were more likely to use check-off;[4] smaller ones were more likely to collect by cash or cheque.[5] However, size did not appear to affect the likelihood that either subscription records or membership records would be held on computer. Fifty-eight per cent of respondents had computerised records of subscriptions, 42% did not (q9). Since 70% of respondents had a computerised membership record (q10), it appears that in some cases computerisation of financial data has lagged behind developments in membership records. It may be that compliance with the membership records requirements of the 1984 Act prompted computerisation of membership records, but that the opportunity simultaneously to automate financial records was not taken. Most due subscription income was collected (q15). Eighty-five per cent of respondents reported that over 90% of due income was collected. In 12.5% of cases over 75% was collected and in only 3% of cases did the proportion fall below 75%.

Several questions were asked about the mechanisms for changing subscription levels and the factors which would generate an increase. Most unions considered the matter annually (q14). Seventy-one per cent set subscription income only one year in advance (or less). Only 15% set levels for more than three years, usually by the employment of some device which fixed subscription levels as a fraction of some measure of negotiated rates or earnings. In 85% of cases, the new level to be applied would originate in the finance officer's recommendation to the EC. Surprisingly, the approval of members for a change in subscription levels was required in only 62.5% of cases (q12 and q13).

Table 5.1 *Responses to q16*

Please rank the following factors in order of their importance in the planning
of raises to subscription levels.

Factor	Av. rank	Standard deviation
Meeting expected administrative costs	2.0	1.31
Subscriptions charged by other unions	5.2	1.22
Range or level of benefits to members	3.5	1.57
Earnings of members	3.8	1.37
Maintaining union reserves	3.6	1.51
The subscription level your members will accept	2.9	1.45
N = 72		

Respondents were asked to rank six factors in terms of their importance
in generating rises in subscription levels. The results are given in Table
5.1 above. For finance officers, the two most important factors are the
level of administrative costs to be covered and the political acceptability
of an increase. Competitive pressures are not perceived as important.
Since subscription levels are reviewed annually in many cases, we may
characterise the problem for the finance officer where subscriptions need
to be changed as having to 'sell' an increase to the membership which
will both cover the exogenously set level of expenditure in the short term
and prove acceptable at Conference.

There were significant size effects on some items. Larger unions were
more likely to rank subscriptions charged by other unions as an important
consideration.[6] It is likely that they feel that they compete on price rather
more than do some smaller unions with restricted job territories. They
were more likely to give a low ranking to the range of benefits offered to
members and to the need to maintain union reserves; presumably, in
larger unions the range of benefits is wider and the level of reserves higher,
hence neither prompts subscription increases.[7]

Unions differ in their allocation of subscription income. In some case
study unions, all incomes were centrally collected and subsequently disbursed. In other cases, branches either retained collected subscriptions
or were entitled to a proportion of subscription income by rule. In the
questionnaire sample, 53% of unions had a rule entitling branches to a
proportion of subscription income (q17). In general, the proportion so
remitted was less than 25% of income; 43% allowed branches less than
20% and 10% allowed between 20% and 40% (q18).

Table 5.2 *Responses to q17 and q32: Subscription Retention and Bank Accounts*

		Do branches retain subscriptions?		
		Yes	No	Total
Do they have				
bank accounts	Yes	30	9	39
(q32)	No	8	21	29
	total	38	30	68

Expenditure

Questions 27 to 45 dealt with management of expenditure. Two thirds of respondent unions had a system of budgeting to manage expenditure. There was some evidence of a size effect, smaller unions being less likely to have one (q27).[8] In the subset which did have such systems, budgets were likely to be set by the General Secretary (mentioned by 26% of all respondents), the finance officer (22%), and the EC (22%) (q28). The pattern of responses indicated that in many unions the two officers and the EC would work together on budgets.[9]

However, monitoring was likely to be the function of the General Secretary (28%) and the finance officer (32%). The EC was less likely to be involved. Whereas the finance officer was generally responsible for the day-to-day management of expenditure, he was unlikely (77% of respondents) to be involved in major capital expenditure decisions (q34); we shall return to this point below. Where budgeting systems did not exist (33% of respondents), the most common mechanism for checking expenditure was simply to refer to bank balances (25%). These were predominantly small unions, several of which had no full-time employees, and little administrative apparatus to speak of.

There were fairly strong correlations between membership levels and the size of this administrative apparatus, measured by the number of full-time employees. In addition, there was a clear relationship between membership and the number of full-time officials, even though, within a given size band, there might be variance in the number of full-time officials and lay representatives.[10]

Fifty-four per cent of unions allowed their branches to have their own separate bank accounts. Of these, over half let the branch go overdrawn on these accounts without prior permission from headquarters (q32 and q33).[11] It is of some interest to compare responses to question 17, on branch retention of subscriptions, with those to question 32. Table 5.2 shows the cross-tabulation.

Table 5.3 *TUC membership and investments*

Are there any forms of profitable investment you would avoid?

	Yes	No	Total
Non-TUC	18	18	36
TUC	31	2	33
Total	49	20	69

Eight unions (11%) allow branches a proportion of subscriptions but no account in which to bank them. The mechanism used here appears to involve the branches indenting for funds prior to expenditure. Nine unions (12.5%) allow bank accounts but do not guarantee branches a proportion of contribution income. The monies in such accounts may often represent the results of branch voluntary activity or local levy.

Assets

We asked several questions about the management of the union's investments. Sixty-eight per cent of respondents said that there were forms of profitable investments which the union would avoid (Q19). Typically, undesirable investments were in South Africa or in recently privatised industries. This pattern reflects TUC policy and, as Table 5.3 indicates, TUC-affiliated trade unions were much more likely to have restrictions on investment.

Similarly, TUC affiliates were more likely to have an investment policy. Three quarters of TUC affiliates had such a policy, compared with 42% of the non-affiliated unions. There may be a political influence on the development of financial management initiatives.

Respondents were asked (q21) to identify who was responsible for managing the union's investments. Forty-three per cent mentioned the finance officer, 39% the Executive Committee, 38% the General Secretary, and 29% the union's specialist advisers. Only 20% mentioned Trustees and less than 10% mentioned the delegate conference (or equivalent). The Executive emerged as the most likely locus for decision making about new investments (49%). Of those unions which had an investment policy, 63% identified the Executive as the main decision-making body (q24). A picture emerges of a highly centralised system for the management of assets, even in those unions which remit contribution income to branches.

Table 5.4 *Responses to q25*

In terms of the union's investment policy, please rank the following in order of importance.

Item	Av. rank	SD
Maximise income	3.2	1.1
Maximise capital growth	3.3	1.04
Provide income and capital growth	2.4	1.18
Provide security for members' funds	1.8	1.13
Generate funds for new projects	4.2	0.93
N = 41		

We asked respondents to rank several factors in terms of their importance for the union's investment policy. The results are shown in Table 5.4. By far the most important item was the security of members' funds. Income and capital growth were less important and the idea of generating money for new projects was ranked lowest. It may be that funds for new projects come from increases in contribution income through levy or subscription increases, rather than from investment income.

Once again we tested for scale effects in the rankings. These appeared significant only in the third item. Large unions were more likely to see the provision of income and capital growth as important.[12]

3   The role of the finance officer

Several questions were asked about the role of the finance officer and its relationship to financial decision making within the union. Overall, only 18% of union finance officers were qualified accountants. Eleven per cent were part qualified but the overwhelming majority, 68%, were unqualified. The likelihood that the finance officer had accountancy qualifications increased with union size.[13]

Thirty-nine per cent of finance officers were involved in only day-to-day administration rather than longer-term planning or giving expert advice to the General Secretary and the EC (q46). Only 19% reported to the General Secretary weekly or more often (q47). For the majority (62.5%), the reporting period was between one week and three months. Regular reporting to the EC or finance and general purposes committee was also normal: 35% reported monthly and 46% quarterly (q48).

A picture emerged of the role of finance officers in the union sample. The majority (67%) felt that financial factors were very important in the general pattern of decision making within the union. Sixty-four per cent felt that the job of the finance officer ought to be concerned with long-term planning; this compares with the 46% who felt that such long-term planning was actually part of their job (q46 and q50). Seventy-one per cent said that the finance officer was involved with the Executive in decisions with financial consequences (q51). In turn, this compares with the 82% who felt that the finance officer should be so involved.

From the examination of union rule books and from our case study interviews, we found that finance was formally defined as an administrative function even though it was important to union survival and achieving policy goals. We also found in our case studies that the role and responsibilities of the finance officer varied and that their influence over financial decisions differed. Some claimed strong involvement, while others simply saw their role as involving carrying out policy decisions.

We identified two dimensions along which the job could vary. One was over the *scope* of influence of the job. On the one hand, the finance officer could be concerned with operational matters, principally to do with gathering in expected income and paying creditors, wages to officials and staff, and other routine expenditures. Here the scope of the job would be relatively narrow. On the other hand finance officers could have a broader remit including the planning of capital expenditures, investment decisions for surplus funds and other significant cost items such as campaign expenditures, recruitment, and new benefits and services. This involved a longer-term planning role.

The second dimension concerned the input of the finance officer into policy decisions. We distinguished between a strict advisory function to the policy-making bodies when called for, and a broader role in which the officer was actively involved in the formulation of policy in conjunction with the General Secretary and EC (or a subcommittee of it) as well as the monitoring of expenditure for financial control purposes. Three roles emerged and they are termed Administrator, Manager, and Expert.

Administrators are concerned only with day-to-day affairs. This group is concerned particularly with expected income from subscriptions and administrative expenditure, but are not expected to have a great deal of influence over or involvement with decision making in the Executive, and to report frequently to the General Secretary. The Administrator was not expected to be closely involved in investment or capital spending decisions. Also, the Administrator was less likely than other roles to work with sophisticated control systems and less likely to be qualified. In these unions, financial administration is distinct from and subordinate to policy making: the function is principally to execute policy decisions and to maintain the operating position of the union in a steady state.

The role of Manager combines long-term planning and short-term management and is akin to that of a finance controller in a firm. The Manager is likely to be involved with the Executive in decisions with financial consequences and to have greater influence over decision making than the Administrator. Managers are likely to report less frequently to the Executive and General Secretary and to be involved in investment policy, setting of subscriptions, and large capital spending decisions. They are more likely to be qualified accountants and to have developed or introduced budgetary systems for control purposes and do not dichotomise policy and administration in the same way as Administrators.

The Expert is primarily an advisory role, being less involved in decisions with the Executive. Like the Administrator, the Expert distinguishes between policy making and administrative decisions, seeing the latter as deriving from the former. The Expert is likely to be a qualified accountant; he or she will favour the use of budgets but not set them. Setting of subscriptions and investment policy are likely to be areas where the Expert will provide advice but is unlikely to take decisions on capital expenditure. It is also unlikely that the Expert will report very frequently to the General Secretary or EC because the job is more concerned with planning and/or the evaluation of policy options. The Expert scores low in terms of involvement in policy decisions but higher in terms of systems of financial control and planning. Questions 46–53 were designed to test out whether these roles were generalisable to a larger sample and to examine their distribution. We also asked questions about what the respondents thought finance officers *ought* to do. The roles of the finance officers in our case study unions are shown in Figure 5.1.

Size effects

We had made no prediction about the correlation between size of union and the role of the finance officer but expected specialists such as Experts or Managers to be employed in larger unions with more complex financial systems and greater resources. The results did not entirely confirm this.

Administrators are more common in small unions: 50% were in very small ones, under 2,500 members and 20% in the 2,500 to 10,000 size range. On the other hand, 45% of Administrators were in the largest unions, above 100,000 members. Managers were more evenly distributed across the range but 54% were in the range up to 10,000 members. They were more common than Administrators in mid-sized unions, with 11 in the range 10,000–100,000 (36%); in the largest unions 33% were Managers. The number of Experts was small (n = 9) but, surprisingly, they were distributed across the whole size range with two in the smallest band (less

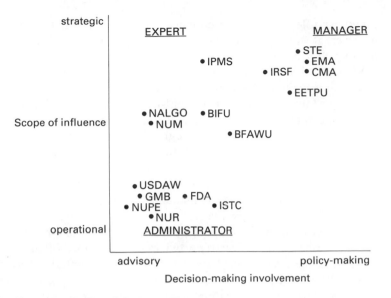

Figure 5.1. Roles of finance officers

than 2,500 members). For our case study unions, the distribution of finance officer roles is given in Figure 5.1.

Role and qualifications

The majority of finance officers are unqualified. There was no positive correlation between being a Manager as opposed to an Administrator and the possession of qualifications: in fact, Administrators were qualified or part qualified in 33% of cases and Managers 24%. Similarly, the Experts were qualified in only three out of nine cases. The definition of finance officers' jobs is set independently of their qualifications.

Involvement in policy decisions

Managers were involved in all decisions with financial consequences in 87% of cases and Administrators in 67%. No Managers said they were rarely or never involved but 11% of Administrators did so; 14% said they were 'sometimes' involved. Experts/planners were completely involved in 56% of cases but 33% only 'sometimes' and 11% 'rarely'. Controlling for size, Administrators in smaller unions were closely involved, those in larger ones were not: this is one piece of evidence to suggest that a more generalist role exists and is common in small unions. In most unions, however, it appears that financial decision making is closely linked to broad policy making.

We asked how important financial factors were in the general pattern of decision making. Two-thirds felt financial factors were important or very important. Sixty-five per cent of Managers perceived financial factors to be important and 61% of Administrators thought so; 25% of Administrators and 32% of Managers thought they were neither important nor unimportant. All Experts saw financial factors as important. The perceived importance of financial factors in general patterns of decisions is, therefore, independent of the role the finance officer plays.

It might be expected that, if financial factors are generally important and the officers are closely involved in decisions with financial consequences, contact between them and the Executive of the union would be frequent. Formally, no officer reported weekly or more often to the EC, presumably because so few Executives meet that regularly. The majority reported between every month and every quarter (81%), but Managers were more likely to report within that period (96% doing so) than Administrators (59%). The remainder of the Administrators reported half-yearly or annually (52%). The majority of Experts/planners also reported fairly frequently (i.e., monthly to quarterly) with only 12% reporting annually. This was an intriguing finding: it suggests either that Managers and Experts are more closely controlled by the EC or that they have more opportunities to influence the EC than the Administrators.

Overall, finance officers reported more frequently to the General Secretary than to the EC, as one might expect: 22% reported weekly, 33% reported monthly, and 37% reported quarterly on a formal basis. By role, 27% of Managers reported weekly and 30% monthly, while the corresponding figures for Administrators were 12% and 36%, and for Experts 33% and 22%. Again this suggests Managers are either more tightly controlled or more influential than Administrators. It is also noticeable that Experts report as frequently as the other types, even though they mainly provide advice.

Systems and responsibilities

The computerisation of membership and subscription records was not related to the degree of involvement of the finance officer with the EC in decision making, nor was the existence of budget arrangements.[14] Authority to make capital expenditure decisions was given to finance officers in only a minority of unions, but there was a greater likelihood that if the officer was closely involved with the EC he/she had the authority to purchase, i.e., they were drawn into areas of decision making beyond immediate operations.

Budgeting systems were less likely to exist in unions with Administrators (46%) than with Managers (71%). Those with Experts were most likely to have budgets (78%). Managers were also more likely to be able to take decisions on capital purchases (29%) than Administrators (16%) and Experts (22%). However, there was no difference between Managers, Administrators, or Experts in the likelihood of making a recommendation to the EC on subscriptions: a majority made a recommendation in each case (Administrators 86%, Managers 81%, Experts 89%), but only for up to one year in most instances (66%): 68% of Administrators fixed subscriptions for less than one year, 74% of Managers did so, and 56% of Experts did so. However, 21% of Administrators were in unions planning somewhat longer term, that is more than two years: 44% of Experts and 10% of Managers were in such unions. Either finance officers do not choose to fix their income stream longer term or they cannot influence the decision, which in most cases is fixed by conference rule.

Recruitment campaigns had recently been run in just over half the unions (57%) in our sample. It was more likely that these were unions with Managers (70%) than Administrators (50%). Experts worked in unions which were very likely to have undertaken a recent campaign (78%). Whether this means that Administrators work in unions which are generally less proactive than Managers or Experts, or whether Administrators work in unions which have less *need* to campaign is unclear.

For those unions which did campaign, there seemed to be little difference in the extent of assessment of effectiveness between unions with different types of finance officer. While 37% of Administrators assessed costs and benefits of campaigns, 54% of Managers did, but 31% of Administrators checked either costs *or* benefits compared to 21% of Managers. The sample of Experts was too small (n = 5) for a breakdown to be meaningful.

Role preferences of finance officers

Finally, we asked some questions which were designed to examine whether the actual job scope matched expectations; was there a certain type of role to which all finance officers aspired? First, we asked whether officers felt they should be actively involved in decisions with the EC which have financial consequences. Regardless of role, most officers felt they should be closely involved: 90% of Managers, 75% of Administrators, and 67% of Experts saying so. However 14% of Administrators and 11% of Experts did not want to be involved, while no Managers disagreed with the principle of involvement. These findings point to the possibility that involvement means different things in different unions.

There seemed to be great congruence between actual and preferred levels of involvement: only 6% were significantly mismatched, all of whom indicated that they wanted much closer involvement with the EC. But involvement can mean a number of things: we therefore compared answers on whether the officer's job should be primarily to give advice to the EC and whether the officer should be actively involved with the EC in all decisions with financial consequences. The majority saw no distinction here. Only 7% saw the role as advisory and *not* policy making and only 3% saw the role as a policy-making one and *not* an advisory one. In 5% of cases the respondents were undecided as regards one role but not the other: half of these were undecided as regards the policy-making role but strongly in favour of the advisory one. The others were neutral over the advisory role, but either strongly favoured a policy-making role or strongly disagreed with it. In 10% of cases, officers were opposed to the role being either an advisory or a policy-making one with the EC, but broadly it seems officers saw no contradiction between advice and policy making: the formal organisational distinction does not hold up in practice. This may explain why, when testing by specific roles whether officers agreed that their job should be advisory to the EC, there was little difference in the scores. Of the Administrators, 74% agreed and 76% of the Managers agreed, 89% of the Experts did so as well. Disagreement was registered by 15% of Administrators and 10% of the Managers.

The findings of the survey were surprising in some respects because of the amount of overlap between the different roles in terms of involvement with the EC in decision making, the range of responsibilities, and role preferences. This suggests that the job of the finance officer may vary considerably between unions but, as far as we can tell, not systematically in terms of job content or responsibilities. Finance officers do not appear to distinguish between administrative functions and policy making. They may not be very influential on a number of important issues or believe financial considerations are uppermost in the minds of decision makers, but they do, on the whole, believe financial factors are taken into account in decisions.

The role of the finance officer made little difference to the time horizon for financial planning, most unions being relatively short term. Managers and Experts were more likely to have budgeting systems to control expenditure than Administrators, but the differences here were less clear cut than expected. Overall, the pattern of financial management seems to be set independently of the officer's role, presumably reflecting the preferences of the General Secretary and EC.

To summarise, the questionnaire data reveal a variable pattern of financial management. There are several interesting size effects. The relationship between size and the sophistication of expenditure controls, the use of check-off, and the size of administrative staff are predictable. However, small unions in this sample do not appear to be dominated by financial concerns nor, to judge from their management systems and priorities, to be in financial difficulty; several, indeed, were more relaxed about branches becoming overdrawn than larger unions. Nor do they appear to be less sophisticated in their record keeping; many had computerised records. There is no *prima facie* evidence here for the scale economy argument nor for the proposition that small unions will disappear.

Unions in this sample pursue investment policies relatively free from membership surveillance. This is perhaps less so in TUC affiliates – one of several differences to emerge between TUC and other unions – where there were concerns to avoid South African links and privatised companies. Investment policies were defined by the EC rather than the finance officer, but it appeared the case that operationally the finance officer, perhaps with outside help, would manage the portfolio on a day-to-day basis. Overall, *security* was important in fund management, rather than capital growth or income maximisation, which perhaps explains the historically low rate of return on UK trade union assets illustrated in Chapter 2.

Similarly, income, particularly membership income, is set by a process which the finance officer can influence but not control. However, the evidence is that collection methods are increasingly moving away from potentially unreliable cash payment towards check-off and direct debiting. This *inter alia* alters the role of the branch in income generation, and few unions allowed the branch to retain more than 20% of income. In fact, the evidence on budgeting and the monitoring of cost centres indicates that local branches and areas are, with the move towards more sophisticated payment methods, increasingly likely to be seen as possible sources of unecessary cost rather than sources of income. This has implications for union government which we shall discuss in the conclusion.

We may examine the pattern of financial management in more detail in the case study unions. Two issues are important here. The first concerns the importance or *centrality* of financial matters in union decision making. The second concerns the level of *sophistication* of systems of financial management. We discuss each in turn.

The identity of the case study unions is indicated in Figure 5.2. The vertical axis indicates their net worth at year end 1989. In that year, the average for all unions was £62.50; roughly half the case study unions are thus above average per capita wealth on this measure, and half below. The x axis attempts to locate them in terms of the centrality of financial concerns in the management of the union. Based on responses to three common questions concerning the importance of financial factors in decision making in general and in the most recent campaign specifically and on the role of the finance officer in decision making, the scale runs from right to left; low scores indicate high centrality and vice versa.[15] As one might expect, the richest unions, ISTC, STE, and NUR score low on concern with financial matters. Their wealth is, after all, the result of long-term stability rather than the result of more recent financial concern. The poorest, by contrast, such as BFAWU and AEU, are extremely concerned with finances. This is perhaps less surprising than the high centrality of financial matters at EMA, IRSF, and IPMS and, particularly, the lack of centrality at USDAW. While there is some support, therefore, for the idea that unions are as concerned with finances as their wealth, or lack of it, demands, there are unexplained differences between unions of similar wealth. There are other issues. The position of NUM in 1989, for example, implies an increase in concern with money since the strike; as we show in Chapter 8, one must distinguish the wealth of the Area unions from the financial controls operative in the national union.

We asked also about the sophistication of financial management within the case study unions. Again an index was compiled based on four common questions concerning the qualifications of the finance officer, the control of subscription income, the existence of budgetary controls, and on investment management. Once more, low scores indicate high levels and the sophisticated unions cluster to the left of Figure 5.3.[16] Whereas ISTC and NUR are both unconcerned and unsophisticated, USDAW once more an outlier and the other poorer unions as sophisticated as their concern might seem to warrant, there are some notable differences between Figures 5.2 and 5.3. BIFU, for example is sophisticated in financial management but less concerned, AEU and BFAWU concerned but less sophisticated. If union leaders are concerned about finances, but the mechanisms available for financial management are unsophisticated, it may be that the leadership is simply unable to install financial controls. The presence of sophisticated financial management but a lack of leadership concern may indicate, as in BIFU, the past success of financial controls in redressing a difficult situation. We discuss this in detail in Chapter 11.

5   Financial debates in trade unions

Formal debates over finances in trade unions may occur at rule-making conferences, at meetings of branch, regional, or national executive committees or be conducted in the pages of union journals. They may concern

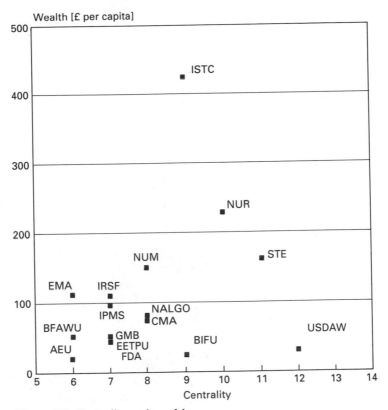

Figure 5.2. Centrality and wealth

income, expenditure, and assets, but it is seldom the financial issues themselves which originate discussion. More frequently, it is a question of
resourcing a particular campaign or assessing the financial consequences
of certain policies.

It is logical to begin with debates about income, the most important
component of which is subscription income – in the aggregate, 82% of
total union income. Subscriptions in the UK tend to be low, on average
only 0.4% of average manual earnings, but they vary substantially
between trade unions. For example, 1989, AEU raised just under £31
per member while NALGO raised £60. There is obvious scope for coercive
comparisons to be drawn particularly within sectors such as education,
health, and finance where unions compete.

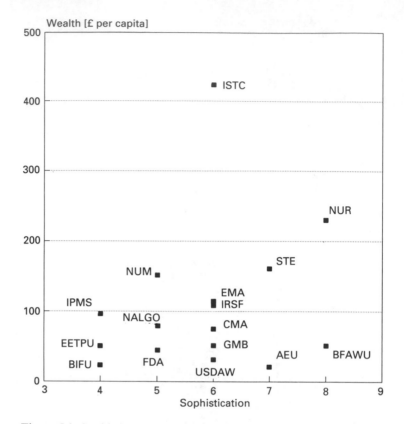

Figure 5.3. Sophistication and wealth

These comparisons are likely to come into play when the union leadership seeks a subscription increase. Such increases in nominal subscriptions have been frequent in recent decades for two reasons. The first is that periods of high inflation require frequent changes to nominal subscription rates. The second is that, because unions are labour-intensive organisations, periods of sustained real wage increases raise the cost base, further pressurising nominal subscription levels.

Union leaders have thus frequently sought increases from conferences, offering the membership the chance to deliver a verdict on the management of the union. Such appeals can put union leaders on the spot. In FDA, for example, the Executive is now required by rule to circulate to all members, in advance of the subscription debate, a document specifying planned expenditure, income projections based on several different assumptions about subscription levels, and the current subscription rates in other civil service unions. Changes must be approved at annual conference by a two-thirds majority. On several occasions, the Executive has been defeated on this matter.

Seven case study unions – FDA, NALGO, GMB, EETPU, IPMS, USDAW, and CMA – required conference approval for increases in subscription levels. In all of these unions, there was a desire on the part of financial managers to move towards indexation. In one, ISTC, the Executive Committee has the power to alter subscription rates.[17] The other eight unions had solved the subscription 'problem' by indexation. From 1990, for example, AEU subscriptions are indexed to the nationally agreed time rates; the skilled section contribution, for example, will be 1% of EEF skilled rate. BFAWU is allowed to levy a subscription equal to half of the lowest basic adult rate in the national agreement; in practice, its subscriptions are slightly lower than this. These arrangements, and similar ones in IRSF, NUM, NUR, EMA, and STE allow the leadership to avoid annual debates on subscriptions which may disrupt financial planning. Increases in subscriptions are in effect based on the union's bargaining performance, thus guaranteeing members a return on subscription changes. In BIFU, a slightly different arrangement ties subscriptions to the retail price index.

An increase in subscription income may be achieved both by increasing subscription rates *and* by increasing the percentage of subscriptions collected (i.e., improving subscription yield). The latter option, if sufficient on its own, avoids political debate, but is not without political consequences in some unions. As Table 5.5 shows, all case study unions relied heavily on 'automated' payment methods, i.e., check-off of subscriptions by employers, direct debits, or standing orders. In all save EETPU and BIFU, there was heavy reliance on check-off. In all cases, it was stated both that the proportion of members paying by automated methods had risen substantially in the previous decade and that this had improved subscription yield. In many unions the aim was to move totally towards automated payment. This has two political consequences, which relate to employer-dependence and leader–member relations respectively.

A heavy reliance on check-off payments requires the union to consider the prospect of employer-induced interruptions to the income stream during negotiations or strike activity. Where, as in the public sector, the union deals with only one or two employers, this concern is reflected in the maintenance of a high level of liquidity. Control by the employer is reflected in the experience of both IRSF and FDA where both the size and timing of agreed subscription increases have been affected by the demands of the employer's computer systems.

Table 5.5 *Income data: case study unions*

Union	% Automated payments	Branch retention	Branch accounts	Shortfall subs./exp.
BFAWU	95	Y	Y	Y
FDA	95	N	N	Y
IRSF	99	Y	Y	N
NUM	95	Y	Y	Y
ISTC	98	N	N	Y
NUR	99	Y	Y	Y
NALGO	95	Y[2]	Y	Y
BIFU	94[1]	N	Y	Y
GMB	95	Y	Y	Y
EMA	95	Y[2]	N	Y
EETPU	79[1]	N	N	Y
IPCS	98	Y	N	N
USDAW	94	Y	Y	Y
AEU	72	Y	Y	N
CMA	99	Y	Y	N
STE	90	Y	Y	Y

Notes: [1] BIFU figure includes 44% on direct debit. EETPU figure includes 22% on either direct debit or standing order.
[2] NALGO and EMA branch retentions are above 20% of total subscription income.

However, even where membership is dispersed, as in AEU and EETPU, check-off systems deliver information on union membership and turnover to the employer. Several unions were seeking to move away from check-off to direct debiting, but the fear was that the friction involved would lead to membership loss. Automated payment methods are in effect a form of inertia selling of trade unionism and there is some concern that members may leave if encouraged to reconsider their decision. Since annual reconsideration is proposed in the 1991 Green Paper, there is a concern that statutory changes may inhibit membership retention. We return to this in conclusion.

Leader–member relations are affected by the impact of automated payment systems on the role of the branch. This is particularly important in AEU and GMB with a long tradition of cash collection by branch officials working on commission. In both unions until the mid 1980s, branch officers were paid commissions on branch subscriptions or branch membership. This had several consequences. First, the branches 'delivered' income to the centre, which was thus dependent on them; branches had a very important role in the management of the union. Second, branch officers could not vote in a disinterested way on subscription levels, since a change would enhance their own commission payments. Third, it was very difficult for the centre to assess underpayment or control arrears. Fourth, as check-off spread, there emerged the inequity, particularly in GMB, that some branch officers were paid commission on income collected by hand and some for income remitted by check-off, with no effort involved.

In both unions, the growth of check-off has led to the reform of such commission systems. However, as in several other unions, it has led to a questioning of the role of the branch; if branches do not generate revenue, are they simply cost centres and, if so, what do they do? As Table 5.5 reveals, most unions allow branches to retain a proportion – normally less than 20% – of their subscription income and to have their own accounts. However, the old system of branch collection and retention has, in many unions, given way in practice to a system of head office collection and disbursement, often under tightly controlled budgeting arrangements, back to branches. Many unions, notably IRSF, have been concerned to build up their branch network in the interests of recruitment, but spending *by* branches has given way to spending *on* branches.

Naturally enough, unions facing financial problems are reluctant to relax expenditure controls. A motion to decentralise the substantial funds of the shrinking ISTC to branches in 1982 was defeated by the leadership who argued: 'it could lead to money being spent indiscriminately and might weaken the union which currently pays out more, pro rata, on services for members than any other union'.

Of interest here is also the underlying view that in ISTC, one of the richest unions per capita, there were financial difficulties. Bill Sirs, then General Secretary, had previously remarked: 'we are not getting enough money in to cover all we pay out. This union has been in the red for ten years'.[18] In fact, the union had registered a surplus of income over expenditure throughout that decade, and his calculation was based on the conviction that: 'ISTC was living on the assets and investments made years ago by the union's predecessors.' Again, the argument is that it is better to have money spent on members than by them.

The balance of expenditure within a union is often contentious. The basic problem here has been noted. The basic economics of trade unions requires the internal transfer of subscription income, but, if one set of members continously subsidise another, tensions may emerge. In NUM, such tensions emerged in the aftermath of the 1984 strike. The National Union, whose funds had been sequestered, suffered far worse than some of the Area Associations. In addition, some Area Associations had suffered worse than others (Aston, Morris, and Willman, 1990). The National

Union had been the vehicle for funds transfer between Areas but, in 1986, the Finance and General Purposes Committee decided, in the face of a deteriorating National financial position combined with the 'locking up' of assets in Area Associations that: 'From 25th September 1986 onwards, on a cumulative basis, it was agreed that the National Union would not pay any monies to any Area in excess of net contributions submitted to the National Union.'[19] This was part of a wide-ranging review of the National Union's financial position, which included proposals for the merger of Area Associations, the implementation of a voluntary redundancy programme for full-time officials, the scaling down of development plans for the Sheffield HQ and a subscription increase. In effect, the National Union was refusing directly to subsidise an Area or to act as a vehicle for the transfer of funds between Areas.

Decisions about expenditure are often in effect decisions about the government and policy of the union concerned. One of the key issues is the balance between lay activity, subsidised by the members themselves or their employer, and the employment of full-time officials and negotiators. Some unions, such as AEU, rely heavily for both union government and collective bargaining on the activities of members who are only refunded their expenses. In this context, as Heery (1987) has noted, a strong view of the official as representative – rather than manager – influences both the role and remuneration of officers and hence their overall cost. AEU looks financially lightweight in part because the government of the union is based on lay representation and is cheap, while full-time officials have their pay tied to that of members.

Other unions, particularly white-collar ones, are often financially less fortunate. BIFU, for example, has always relied heavily on full-time officials because a system of lay representation proved difficult to build up. In FDA also, the Treasurer lamented in 1980 the existence of a financially difficult set of circumstances, namely little lay participation and a set of officials employed on higher civil service terms and conditions. His remarks on increased administrative costs were reported as follows: 'Lay participation has been seen as a way of avoiding such an increase. He had to say that it just did not work. People who were prepared to give up a lot of time for the Association were hard to find.'[20] As Heery (1987) has further noted, officials of white-collar unions are more likely to be highly paid, as expert negotiators rather than representatives. They are also more likely to be unionised.

The implications of some recent changes in financial management may be far reaching. At the risk of exaggeration, one may characterise the disappearing system, particularly in manual unions, as one in which subscriptions were collected by activists in workplaces and branches, with fractions retained and the rest remitted up the union hierarchy. Expenditure would thus be *de facto* decentralised, and central control weak. Subscription changes would be debated at conference, and the Executive periodically defeated. However, the replacement system – based on automated payment of subscriptions, set according to an indexation formula, which are then remitted from the centre, often on an imprest system, for designated purposes – is highly centralised. Because of this, and because the level of internal financial information is now higher, the centre may be more accountable, but the member is less involved in the setting of subscriptions or in their payment.

A similar picture of centralisation emerges in the analysis of asset management but, in debates about the level of assets and their management, very different approaches emerge. Consider the following rather divergent views from the respective BFAWU and BIFU Treasurers.

I suppose it is the desire of every treasurer when making his annual report to announce a massive surplus, the bigger the better, but I'm afraid I've never gone along with this theory as far as the trade union movement is concerned.

Of course our union must always remain viable and to remain viable we must show a surplus, not a deficit, but if achieving a large surplus means a reduced service to our membership, then the very purpose of trade unionism is defeated.'[21]

On the other hand:

With an income in excess of five million pounds per annum, we must regard ourselves as a 'medium sized business'; and take financial decisions in a similar way that businesses would take such decisions.[22]

On the one hand, is the view that unions are financially distinctive, membership-centred charitable organisations with a need only to remain solvent. On the other is a cost-benefit approach to unionism which draws direct parallels with the operation of the firm in language conventionally used to describe commercial enterprises.

The appropriate size of union reserves *is* essentially contestable. As Table 5.5 shows, few unions actually cover expenditure through subscription income. Most fill the gap with investment income or – at worst – sale of assets or running down of reserves. In ISTC, as we have seen, there was a concern that living off high levels of investment income was in some way unhealthy. In FDA, when plans for major investment in union infrastructure were approved in 1979, the Treasurer remarked that: 'it will be for ADM to decide how to apportion the costs between an immediate increase in subscriptions and running down the reserves.'

The target level of reserves changed over time. In 1978, the Treasurer remarked that: 'the new level of reserves is near the "norm" for a trade union, of one year's subscriptions'. Later, this target was discarded. In 1981, he remarked: 'There was no hard and fast rule about reserves, although it had been suggested that perhaps they should stand at one year's subscription income. This was a rule of thumb and had no intrinsic merit.'[23]

One central problem for the leadership in the management of assets is to appear to be competent at financial management, and thus avoid membership concern over viability, but not to appear too rich, thus losing the possibility of further membership income. One commonly used device in unions is the timing of asset revaluations. Most union assets are tied up in property which is, following accounting conventions, listed at book value and depreciated at, say, 1% per annum. The 'real' (i.e., break-up) value of most unions is thus substantially greater than their declared net worth. If the property assets are revalued, therefore, the financial position of the union may be transformed. For example, EMA has revalued its assets in 1981, 1983, and 1987, thus indicating throughout the 1980s a healthy surplus of income over expenditure despite flat real subscription income levels and rising costs.

Overall, all 16 cases revealed a highly centralised pattern of asset management. With very few exceptions, including AEU which sold equities in crisis, and NUM which liquidated its quoted investments to fund the move of HQ from London to Sheffield, our case study unions moved investments into equities across the 1980s and, given the general upward movement in share prices, they benefited from doing this. Rule books and union conferences appear to put few obstacles in the way of union investment policies. The main objections among TUC affiliates are to investment in companies with South African connections or in recently privatised operations. NUM, in addition, will not invest in competitive forms of energy. However, the equity portfolio is often managed on a day-to-day basis by an agent employed for that purpose, without regular monitoring by the Executive as long as a reasonable rate of return is achieved. The objectives of union investment policies were described by finance officers as security and stability rather than the maximisation of return on assets and it is probably unusual for a union to trade its equity portfolio daily. Unlike subscriptions or expenditure, union asset management is rarely the stuff of political debate.[24] To the membership, it is invisible.

These trends need to be seen in terms of the shortfall of subscription income over expenditure in 12 of the 16 cases, shown in Table 5.5. Centrally delivered investment income effectively covers this shortfall and allows union leaders some scope to increase expenditure levels. Effectively managed portfolios allow the union to keep a lower subscription level –

or a higher service level – than might otherwise be the case and are a source of power for union leaders since they provide resources without recourse to the membership. A poorly managed portfolio is, however, a liability, particularly since, as one finance officer noted, many members currently handle their own share portfolios and have some knowledge of the market.

6 Conclusions

Certain types of financial reform have been common in UK unions. There has been increased automation of subscription payment leading to improved subscription yield. Constraints on centralised asset management have been removed or attenuated. Management information sytems have improved, giving the prospect of closer cost controls; several of these changes have been prompted by legislation. The role of the finance officer is variable, but many have substantial influence over union decision making.

These changes have had three political consequences worthy of note. First, they have centralised control over financial resources. Second, they have, to some extent, depoliticised the management of finances in unions by reducing the need for debate. Third, they have probably increased employer dependence. Overall, the vocabulary of motives in the discussion of finances has altered. It appears now to be easier for those concerned with the management of union finances to use arguments based on administrative rationality emphasising the need for organisational viability in the medium to long term in order to affect union policy and decision making. The combination of high inflation followed, in many unions, by membership loss raised the salience of financial considerations. The subsequent success of financial management policies in raising real income and reversing the decline in union assets has given credence to financial arguments in union debates.

Some interesting questions are raised. Above all, will the management of unions as businesses lead to the success of 'business unionism', by which is meant a narrowly economic conception of the union as service organisation competing with others to attract and retain members, pursuing purely institutional goals? One can imagine ways in which it might. Improved management information systems give leaders better knowledge of the costs and benefits of retaining or recruiting particular groups of members. A true 'business' union might seek both to shed members and to restrict recruitment in unprofitable areas, and perhaps focus efforts on higher income groups which can be profitably managed. The internal transfer of funds which is the premise of union activity could be managed on a cost–benefit rather than a principled basis; shifting resources from the poor to the rich might have greater benefits to the organisation than vice versa. More specifically, the membership and revenue effects of particular campaigns, disputes, or conference motions could come to determine their adoption or prosecution.

Such a form of trade unionism would require substantial leadership dominance. This may be more difficult to achieve where there are legislative controls over internal union democracy, but the evidence from our cases is that, compared, say, to the period analysed by Roberts (1956) there *is* substantial centralised control over union income, expenditure, and assets. It is not simply that control has shifted from branches to the centre or from activists to the membership in general, rather the imposition of financial controls and good husbandry in what were previously rather chaotic circumstances has given power to those in financial control and, more fundamentally, economic pressures have forced a shift in the acceptable vocabulary of motives in trade union decision making.

A second requirement is probably inter-union competition. If the union which uses financial criteria to effect its policies is able to offer a more cost-effective level of service than its competitors and thus to secure new members, it may well be imitated by others. Under such competitive conditions, the largest or most successful unions might be those whose management vocabulary focuses on the administrative issues of efficiency and effectiveness rather than on the representative issues of principles and politics.

We shall return to these considerations in the concluding chapter. However, two issues have arisen which require further discussion. The first concerns the relationship between competition and growth. Many unions wish to grow and compete with others to do so, but the financial benefits of growth, either to leaders or to members, are unclear. We look more closely at this in the next chapter. The second concerns the consequences of strike activity. For some unions, involvement in a major dispute has been the most important determinant of poor financial performance, while for others the effects have been neutral or positive. We focus directly on the finances of striking unions in Chapter 7.

6 Union size, growth, and financial performance

1 Introduction

The literature discussed in Chapter 4 and the data in the last chapter both suggest that there may be financial benefits accruing to unions by virtue of size. Larger unions can distribute fixed costs over a larger revenue base and are likely, *ceteris paribus*, to have more influence on employers. However, the material reviewed in Chapter 4 also suggested two other propositions; firstly, that there may be institutional or leadership benefits from growth but that, beyond a certain size, there may be no advantages to members themselves; secondly, that there may be circumstances in which growth is not cost effective in that recruitment costs outweigh subscription returns. Growth may, it appears, produce returns to all members in the form of scale economies, to leaders in the form of greater revenues, or to no one at all.

Empirically, disaggregated growth through recruitment or merger has been pursued by most large unions and concentration of membership has resulted. In 1950, 84% of union members were in the 50 largest trade unions. Since then, these unions have grown more rapidly than unions as a whole (Buchanan, 1981: 234). By 1985, they accounted for 94% of total union membership.

In this chapter, we shall examine the financial implications of growth and specifically the proposition that there are economies of scale in the provision of union services. Section 2 looks generally at theories of union growth and at the mechanisms through which unions grow. Section 3 looks directly at scale economies; in particular, it seeks to discover whether such economies can be said to exist and at the major elements of unions' costs. Section 4 then examines empirical data from the UK; it also looks at the effects of other factors on cost, notably inter-union competition. Section 5 looks specifically at mergers; Section 6 concludes.

2 Union growth and union recruitment

The subject of union growth has been approached from several different perspectives. The most powerful explanations of *aggregate* union growth are econometric (Bain and Elsheikh, 1976; Booth, 1983; Carruth and Disney, 1988). Broadly speaking, they seek to explain some measure of union membership or density, or changes in such measures, in terms of macroeconomic variables such as prices, wages, and unemployment, or rates of change thereof. They typically do not concern themselves with the factors which motivate trade unionists or their leaders to seek higher membership levels. This may be because the view is held that unions can themselves do little to affect aggregate membership levels (Bain, 1970), or because it is assumed, on theoretical grounds, that unions seeking a monopoly in the supply of labour will pursue membership growth until very high, historically unobserved, levels of density are achieved.

Such models are typically not deployed to explain *disaggregated* patterns of growth and in fact would be ill-equipped to do so. The approach to the explanation of such patterns has tended to be qualitative, reliant on case studies of particular unions which do or do not seek growth, and the mechanisms used in pursuit of new members (Undy *et al.*, 1981). The motivation to grow is seen as important, particularly the motivation of union leaders. Other important factors include the nature of the union's job territory and the structure of the union. On the one hand, unions will tend to 'receive' growth where employment expands, on the other, federated structures are seen as advantageous in the pursuit of merger partners. This approach is particularistic and overtly avoids any general theory of disaggregated growth. It does, however, emphasise the role of leaders in pursuing growth through recruitment and merger (Crouch, 1982: 120–61).

The work of Voos (1984, 1986) offers one avenue towards a more general theory based on the behaviour of individual unions. Voos observes a relationship between increased union coverage and returns to existing members in the form of union wage gains. On the basis of this argument, union leaders fund recruitment in order to gain greater financial returns for members in the form of wage gains through improved bargaining leverage. The applicability of this approach outside the USA is unclear. However, it can only explain 'consolidatory' recruitment which improves density under existing collective bargaining coverage. It cannot explain expansion into new areas where recognition for collective bargaining purposes has not yet been obtained, nor the pursuit of merger with non-competing unions. As we have shown in Chapter 4, certain forms of recruitment potentially involve very high costs, particularly those which involve approaching individuals where the employer is hostile. *Ceteris paribus*, 'market share' unionism involving mergers and consolidatory recruitment ought to be financially more rewarding in the aggregate. The relationship between wealth and membership in the aggregate, outlined

Table 6.1 *Union replacement ratios; case study unions, 1987*

Union	Membership (000)	Ratio (%)
BFAWU	35	14.2
FDA	7	5.0
BIFU	166	13.4
GMB	803	15.0
EETPU	369	12.0
IPMS	90	8.3
USDAW	387	28.4
AEU	815	10.0

Source: Interview Data

in Chapter 2, supports this. By definition, where unionism in the aggregate is expanding, it must be by individual recruitment much of which is likely to be in pre-recognition situations; it is likely to be cost-ineffective in the short term. However, as the disaggregate analysis showed, the experience of individual unions may be more varied.

A consideration of the costs and benefits of recruitment is not complete without consideration also of union wastage rates. Recruitment or, as we shall see below, merger, is in many cases not a measure taken to promote growth but one taken to arrest contraction. Absent recruitment activity and unions have a natural tendency to contract as existing members depart the labour force or that part of it covered by them. A certain level of recruitment activity is thus necessary in order to stand still.

Table 6.1 shows, for the cases in which such data were available, the *replacement ratio*, i.e., that level of recruitment (as a percentage of membership) which is necessary to ensure stable membership levels. For those with low replacement ratios, recruitment may be considered a luxury in the short term. For those with high replacement ratios, it is a necessity. Unions such as ISTC and FDA may regard recruitment as a low priority – they are in any event assisted in recruiting new members by employers operating check-off systems. However, for GMB and USDAW, security of tenure in several of their job territories is such that constant recruitment effort is essential.

The motivation for union expansion is, however, often unclear. From the financial standpoint, new members seldom bring in capital, and their subscriptions may in the short term be less than the expenditure required to secure their allegiance, particularly where there is employer hostility and where subscriptions stay low to encourage recruitment. A corollary of this has relevance for the internal political issues influencing recruitment activity. Such activity consumes resources which must be generated internally; it follows, therefore that recruiting unions must generate a 'surplus' in some parts of their organisation in order to spend it in others; current members must subsidise the acquisition of new members and must, presumably, see some benefit in so doing. Phrasing this in terms of the two product market model of Chapter 4, one might say that, for recruitment growth, those parts of the union which operate in both product markets must subsidise those parts which do not. The political problem for the union leadership committed to growth – for whatever reason – is to make sure that this is acceptable to the majority of members.

The problems facing recruiting unions in the 1980s in the UK were thus considerable. Not only was there a smaller surplus available for such activity, but the statutory climate was less favourable for its deployment. The Employment Acts of 1980, 1982, and 1988 and the Trade Union Act of 1984 have progressively introduced rights for individual employees enforceable against trade unions of which they need not be members. Union members may now inspect and query the union accounts and, while the majority of union rule books allow the Executive considerable discretion in the deployment of union funds, members may come to question financial decisions. The Green Paper of 1991 imples the possibility of more such measures in the 1990s. However, it may still be the case that union leaders seek expansion through recruitment in order to increase net revenue or for status-related reasons rather than to enhance membership services.

Figure 6.1 is based on a calculation of the margin of income from members over administrative cost for all unions with over 20,000 members for a sample year, 1989. This margin gives a crude indicator of the surplus generated from existing members available for recruiting new ones. This margin was small in most unions; most 'made' or 'lost' only a few pounds per member in 1989. Old, craft or manual-industry unions have the largest per capita margins – in 1989, these were FBU and NGA – but only the largest unions, whose scale translates small margins into large surpluses, look to be able to fund large-scale recruiting exercises. Many of the largest unions made no surpluses of this kind in 1989.[1] Only AEU, of the largest ten unions, registered a 'profit' of over £1 million in 1989: GMB, NALGO, and MSF registered a loss. Most unions in the size range above 20,000 members have much less than £1 million and, within this size range, there does not seem to be a relationship between size and net retained profit. Some asset-rich unions which lose money on membership servicing might be even richer if their membership declined further. The financial impetus for leader-prompted growth is not in evidence here.

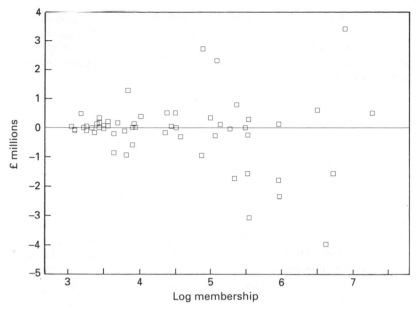

Figure 6.1. Profit and size, 1989

Data from our questionnaire sample encourage caution about attributing economic motives for growth, or at least recruitment. Fifty-seven per cent of sampled unions had been involved in a recruitment drive in the previous 18 months. Large unions and TUC affiliates were more likely to have done so than small unions and non-affiliates. Sixty per cent of unions with less than 5,000 members had not engaged in recruitment activity over the period. Fifty-two per cent of non-TUC affiliates did not recruit.[2] Less than half of recruiting unions (26% of the total) had monitored both the costs and benefits of it; 15% of *all* unions had monitored neither. Our cases indicated that commitment to recruitment could be sustained not only in the absence of but in defiance of financial information. The rationale for recruitment is essentially political and the issues involved are those discussed above in Chapter 5.

Nevertheless, membership growth remains a priority for the majority of larger unions. One possible explanation, which deserves consideration, is that unions do have economic motives for expansion, but that such motives refer to membership benefits rather than institutional ones. There may be distinct financial advantages to growth. Unions are labour-intensive service organisations with a high fixed-cost base. They may be able to provide such services more cheaply where these fixed costs can be spread across a larger membership base; in short, there may be economies of scale in union organisation. This is a rather different argument from that of Voos (1984). The suggestion here is that growth may improve service provision rather than generate wage gains. It thus applies to other forms of growth than consolidatory growth.

3   Scale economies in union services

The idea of scale economies

For economies of scale to exist, the average price of production of a particular good or service must decline as output increases. For example, in the motor car industry, the average cost of a unit falls as output increases, and the average cost of issuing a life insurance policy is similarly scale dependent. Three questions therefore arise. The first is: is there an analogous product or service 'produced' by all trade unions? The second question is: if so, what factors other than size are likely to affect its average cost? The third is: can its average cost be measured? We shall look at each in turn.

Unions provide a variety of services to members, some of which are collective and some individual. Pencavel's (1971) distinction between *collective*, *semi-collective*, and *individual* goods is relevant here. The first two categories depend on collective bargaining activity. They include the services of union full-time officials, information on employment rights and industrial relations matters, representation in collective bargaining, and the exertion of pressure to pursue members' interests. In some unions, they may include the provision of training and retraining. The third category includes benefits for sickness or bereavement and unemployment pay. Such benefits are, as we have shown in Chapter 2, in decline, falling from 31% of total expenditure in 1950 to under 13% in 1989. However, they remain very unevenly distributed, with craft societies remaining far more generous than many white-collar unions.

The 'core product' for all unions is thus administrative support for collective bargaining which generates the provision of both collective and semi-collective goods. It accounts for the bulk of union expenditure throughout the post-war period. Although unions may organise the provision of such support in different ways, it represents the distinctive and dominant service currently offered by all unions. It excludes benefit provision which is offered by relatively few.

It is true that individual union members may receive more or less than this standard support. Benefits aside, some union members receive more semi-collective goods than others. Free representation at tribunal or disciplinary hearings, the cost of which is far in excess of their subscriptions, can, logically, only be offered to a minority of members. Other members, working in establishments where unions are not recognised, cannot receive collective bargaining representation and perhaps receive fewer services than the average. However, unions normally pursue recognition and collective bargaining and are financed on the assumption that most of the members, most of the time, do not require semi-collective goods, even though their provision may be a factor in the member's decision to join. Representational services may thus be regarded as the core 'product' of trade unions and the cost of servicing the average member may be regarded as the average output cost. We turn now to an examination of the factors which influence this average cost.

Determinants of union administrative costs per capita

Since unions are labour-intensive businesses, the cost of servicing members over time is likely to depend on such factors as the number of members, their real income, and the real labour costs involved in service provision. In this section, we shall focus on the sources of variation in per capita administrative costs at one point in time, thus controlling for membership and time trends in real earnings. We shall return to the size effect below.

The major components of union administrative costs are officials, premises, the costs of communication, and the costs of meetings and travel, including conference costs. Underlying these, and perhaps most important of all, is the level of employer support for union activity discussed in Chapter 4. However, here we focus primarily on the items which appear on the union's own balance sheet.

Officials. It is important to separate out the determinants of the *number* of officials and the determinants of their *unit cost*. A high ratio of full-time officials to members is often associated with an absence of strong lay representation. In some unions, such as BIFU in the 1970s, heavy reliance was placed on full time officials in the absence of a network of office representatives and to avoid the charge of employer dependence (Morris, 1986). The union was in fact criticised for this (CIR, 1973). In other unions, notably AEU and TGWU, much of the day-to-day activity of the union, at least in well organised areas, is conducted by lay officials either working in their own time or supported by their employer. The level of employer support, therefore, either directly through provision of check-off and facilities or indirectly through the acceptance of a high level of lay trade union activity, is an important determinant of administrative costs.

A second consideration is the *number* of employers or, more precisely, the number of agreements which require servicing. A large number of agreements each covering few members is more likely to require a high level of officials' time (unless shop stewards look after them) than one agreement covering a large number of members. Even if the rate of grievance and disciplinary activity is a simple function of membership numbers, more agreements require more negotiating time. Decentralised bargaining will *ceteris paribus* require more officials.

A third consideration is the nature of membership and the level of recruitment activity. Some unions recruit, and employ dedicated recruiters, others do not, or have the employer do it for them; the replacement ratio is a key factor here. Often, high turnover is associated with an absence of employers' support for unionisation, since such support in the tangible form of check-off arrangements will itself reduce turnover. The recruitment must, therefore be conducted by full-time employees of the union rather than lay officials. In the UK, as we have seen, recruitment activity is seldom separately itemised by trade unions either for their own purposes or for the statutory returns. Such activity may be undertaken by recruiters, by existing members, or by negotiating officers.

The factors affecting *unit costs* of officials in several unions have been analysed in detail by Heery (1987). He distinguishes between, on the one hand, manual unions which elect their officials and in which the official is seen as a representative and, on the other, white-collar unions which appoint their officials who are in turn seen as negotiating experts. In the former case, the level of pay of members, or its rate of change, often determines officials' pay. This is particularly true in craft societies. In SOGAT, the branch secretary's pay is determined with reference to the area top rate, while the pay of the President of AEU is determined with reference to the rates in the National Engineering Agreement. In white-collar unions, the pay of negotiating opponents may be more important and, as a consequence, the levels of salary and thus the unit costs of officials may be higher. Unionisation of officials, more common in white-collar unions, may further raise salaries.

The regional distribution of officials may also be important. Salaries tend to be higher in the south and south-east than in the north hence, *ceteris paribus*, the unit cost of an official ought to be lower outside the home counties. The distribution of officials is distinct from the distribution of membership since the majority of large unions employ head office staff in London irrespective of the distribution of membership. GMB, for example, has moved *within* Surrey, despite the regional bias of its membership distribution towards the north and north-east. It appears to be important to remain in or close to London, and this also affects the cost of premises.

Premises. Several unions, such as NALGO, GMB, and IPCS, own London property which is a source of revenue; they have low premises costs. Others, such as MSF, have high property-associated costs although these do not necessarily appear as items under administrative costs. Yet other unions, such as NAS/UWT, USDAW, and NUM have substantial properties outside of the London area with a minimal London presence. Such properties may fulfil all union requirements but may be of lower value on the asset return than similar ones in the London area.

For most large unions, premises costs are associated with heating, lighting, etc. rather than rent. Although some smaller unions subsist in rented accommodation, most unions have sizeable property portfolios which restrict premises costs.

Communications. Unions vary in the extent to which they communicate with members, in the methods they use, and in the extent to which they pay for such communication themselves. In the past, the prime avenue of communication was via the workplace or branch, since few unions had membership lists with home addresses on them. The prime mechanism was the union newspaper or journal, containing news about negotiations, conference motions and progress in their implementation, elections and other personnel changes, and discounts for union members.

Several factors have contributed to an expansion in the overall level of communication with current and prospective members. The legislation on balloting has increased the importance of reaching individual members who do not attend the branch; union policy towards such legislation, particularly that enabling reclamation of expenditures, will have affected average unit costs. The compilation of accurate membership lists as required by the 1984 Trade Union Act increased communication costs for many unions but also put a valuable resource – a marketable membership list – into the hands of union leaders. Membership loss and the perceived need to recruit new members placed an emphasis on union 'image'; expenditures on video production, polls of current and prospective members, and 'image building' campaigns are not always separately itemised but have undoubtedly risen in real terms in the 1980s.

However, there are differences between unions. The rule book is often important in defining the level of expenditure on various forms of communication. For example, where elections are frequent, the costs of balloting – or currently the amounts of money for ballots which may be claimed back – are high. In AEU, for example, where all officials are elected, balloting costs per capita are higher than those in many other unions which appoint officials.

Conferences. Similarly, the rule book will affect the costs of meetings and conferences by spelling out the size of regional or executive committees, the frequency and perhaps location of their meetings, and the size and frequency of their conferences. The biennial National Committee meetings of AEU, for example, involving relatively few delegates, will come cheaper than that of BIFU, involving annual conferences with delegates from each branch and section, or than the even larger delegate conferences of TGWU.

Overall, then, there are a number of factors, other than size, which might affect the level of administrative costs per capita at any given time. Key factors include the reliance on full-time officials, the level of employer support, the dispersion of the membership and its turnover, and the provisions of the rule book; other 'chance' factors such as the ownership of premises are occasionally important. Given the complex interaction between these factors, it is surprising that, with the data available, a clear relationship between administrative costs per capita and size does emerge.

4   Empirical evidence

Data are available on the aggregate and unit costs of providing various services to members contained in the annual statutory returns (see Appendix 1). In addition to the requirement that unions account for income and expenditure from specific funds, the return requires that the category 'Administrative Expenses' be completed, under a range of subheadings.[3] Interest on loans, depreciation, tax, benefit expenditure, political expenditure, and affiliation fees (for example to the TUC) are specifically excluded.

A complete record exists for each returning union. An aggregate figure, separating out the administrative component of *all* unions, was published in the Annual Reports until 1987 (i.e., it exists for data up to and including 1986). It is thus possible to examine the variance in the cost of provision of basic union services in the aggregate and by union. This section will analyse aggregate data from 1950 to 1986 and pursue a dissaggregated analysis for three selected years: 1975, 1980, and 1985 using the sample of unions with over 20,000 members.

The scale effect can be analysed in several ways. There is no simple negative correlation in the aggregate between membership level and the

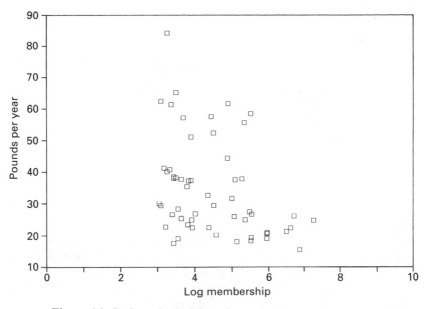

Figure 6.2. Scale and administrative cost, 1985

level of administrative cost per capita for all unions in the post-war period. In fact, the correlation is positive; real administrative costs per capita, being determined to a large extent by labour-related costs, have risen steadily across the post-war period, even though union membership was static or rising to 1979 and sharply declining thereafter. However, the partial correlation for the period 1950 to 1986, with the level of real weekly pay held constant, is negative ($r = -0.3566$). There is thus some limited support for the scale effect in the time series data.

Given that unions of vastly different sizes have continued to exist, and comprise this aggregate figure, it is difficult to know what to make of this negative relationship. If economies of scale in union organisation exist, they ought to show up in a *disaggregated* analysis. Data for the years 1975, 1980, and 1985 enable some limited assessments of the scale effect. For all three years, there are significant, negative correlations between union membership and administrative costs per capita (1985: $r = -0.3252$, 1980 $r = -0.3162$, 1975 $r = -0.2636$, all significant beyond $\alpha = 0.001$). Figure 6.2 shows the scattergram for 1985,[4] using a logarithmic scale on the x axis for presentational purposes.

We can also look at the relationship between changes in administrative costs per capita and membership across the decade. There is no significant

Table 6.2 *Size and change in administrative costs per capita, 1975–85*

Change in real administrative costs

	1975–80	1980–5	1975–85
Membership 1975	−0.3235		−0.2895
Membership 1980	−0.3403	−0.2281	−0.3091
Membership 1985		−0.2383	−0.3248

All correlations significant beyond $a = 0.0001$

relationship between changes in administrative costs per capita and membership change for the 56 union sample across the period.[5] However, there are significant, negative relationships between changes in administrative costs per capita and membership *levels*. This is the case both for the period as a whole and for two subperiods; the correlations are shown in Table 6.2. Between 1975 and 1985, the largest unions had the lowest increases in administrative costs per capita.

The significant negative relationships are common across the period for most of which union membership was increasing (1975–80) and the period of rapid decline (1980–85) as well as across the entire decade. If these are economies of scale, they are not sensitive to the observed changes in union membership. As we have shown elsewhere, both the levels of administrative cost and changes in such costs are highly and positively correlated with subscriptions per capita and changes in subscriptions per capita respectively during this period (Willman and Morris, 1988). It is thus not merely the cost of production which is size dependent, but also the price of services.

In summary, there does seem to be some quantitative evidence for the existence of economies of scale in trade union organisation, at least for unions with more than 20,000 members, i.e., our measure of the average unit cost of membership service is significantly and negatively correlated with size. But one might make several objections to the argument so far. The first is that small unions survive. Why do they not disappear, either through membership loss or merger? A second is that large unions survive and compete with each other in the same firms and industries; why do they not merge?

Could there be any other explanation for the observed pattern? Several occur. One is that the observed differences in unit costs do not reflect pure scale effects, but rather the fact that a lower quality of service is provided by larger unions than by smaller ones, simply because large

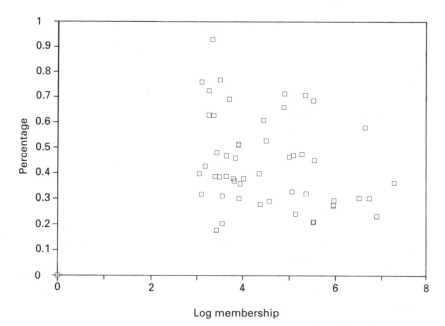

Figure 6.3. Administrative costs and earnings

unions tend to be composed of unskilled manual or lower-ranked clerical workers whose pay, subscriptions, and therefore administrative costs per capita are low. On the other hand, there are smaller, craft or industry unions whose costs and subscription charges are higher because the earnings of their members are higher. The scale effect thus conceals an underlying segmentation in the market for trade union services. High earners pay more because they can afford more; the lower costs of the large unions reflect a lower standard of membership service.

Unfortunately, the data necessary to take this further – on average member's earnings by union – do not exist. Whereas for some single employer unions, particularly those in the civil service, one might make a heroic assumption about the earnings of an average member, one cannot do so for the majority; what, for example, might be the average earnings of a member of MSF? In many cases, variance within unions is likely to match variance between them. It *is* the case that in 1989 there were considerable differences between unions in the proportion of average earnings they spent on administrative costs. Figure 6.3 shows the details.

Several unions whose members are probably relatively poorly paid, such as NUPE, COHSE, and USDAW, cluster to the base of the figure.

However, unions with a high proportion of craft or technical workers, such as EETPU, ASTMS, and some of the banking unions do also. Intuitively, there does not appear to be any simple relationship between members' earnings and the costs of administrative service provided.

A second, rather different argument relates to *type* of organisation. Latta (1972), for example, argued that white-collar unions were financially very different kinds of organisation from the longer-established manual-craft and manual-industry unions. The former were low on assets, heavily dependent on subscription income, and thus concerned very much with the relationship between per capita income and cost. The latter had substantial assets, were long established and more solvent. It might be the case in 1985, therefore, either that unions with greater assets were prepared to incur higher unit costs, or that one might still distinguish between white-collar unions on the one hand and manual on the other; the propositions here would be that there are no economies of scale in union organisation, but that (a) smaller manual unions are asset rich and thus 'overspend' per capita, and (b) white-collar and manual unions are offering different types of product to members; the observed scale effects arise because within the sample white-collar unions predominate among the larger unions. We can look at each in turn.

Net worth per capita is weakly (but significantly) negatively correlated with size in all three sample years.[6] Within this sample, smaller unions tend to be richer per member. Wealth per capita is positively correlated with administrative costs. It may well be, then, that richer unions subsidise membership services out of reserves and that, because the richer unions tend to be smaller, this shows up as a scale effect when, in reality, no returns to scale exist. However, controlling for the effect of size, there is a positive partial correlation between net worth and administrative costs per capita in 1985 ($r = 0.4075$).

Does this also relate to the manual–white-collar divide? It appears that it does not. There are no significant differences between white-collar and manual unions in unit costs, nor is the interaction between union type and size significant.[7]

A third possibility is that the observed scale effect actually reflects differences in inter-union competition. The argument here is that, since small unions are craft or industry unions – often 'closed' – while larger ones are general manual or open white-collar unions, the latter experience greater competition for members and thus will have lower unit costs irrespective of size. Consider Table 6.3. It presents the average unit cost and the range of costs in three 'competitive' sectors, namely education, health, and finance, one 'cartelised' sector, the civil service, and for the sample as a whole.

Table 6.3 *Union competition and costs 1985*

Sector	Unions	Av. Cost £ per year	Range £
Education	AMMA,NUT,NAS/UWT NAHT	22.90	8.57
Health	GMB, NALGO,NUPE RCN,COHSE	22.80	5.55
Finance	ASTMS,BIFU,BGSU NWGSU,LGSU	23.74	8.56
Civil service	CPSA,IPCS,SCPS	44.87	25.90
Whole sample	N = 56	34.50	68.70

Competitive sectors are characterised by low average costs, and a low range of costs, compared with the sample as a whole. It may be the case, then, that the market for unionism is imperfect, with cost pressures only operating on some unions. Since these tend to be the largest, the negative correlation between size and unit cost emerges.

In order to test this proposition, unions within the sample were classified as 'competing', 'intermediate', or 'sheltered'. The terminology is borrowed from Undy *et al.* (1981). This is not quite the same distinction as that between 'open' and 'closed' trade unionism, since unions might have a delimited job territory as, for example, NUT, yet compete with other occupational unions for membership share. Hence it does not refer to the existence of or level of recruitment activity, rather to the existence or absence of a major competitor for the job territory. Unions which do not compete in their main job territory such as NUM, NUR, and the civil service unions are thus referred to as 'sheltered'. Unions which compete in all areas of recruitment are classified as 'competing', such as BIFU and USDAW and the general unions. Those with an established heartland and some competitive areas, such as TASS and EETPU are classified as 'intermediate'.

The results of a multi-factor analysis of variance using this coding on 'shelteredness' and a membership coding show the greater significance of the level of competition.[8] It seems to be the case that the level of competition is a greater influence on average unit costs than size. The results of a simple least squares regression are shown below in Table 6.4. Although the R^2 value is low, 'shelteredness' again appears as a more significant influence on administrative costs in 1985 than does size. It is possible, then, that, since larger unions tend to be competitive rather than sheltered and since competition appears to drag down administrative costs per

Table 6.4 *Regression results: the influence of competition and size on unit costs*

Variable	Coeff.	SE	t	Sig. Level
Constant	28.181	4.107	6.86	0.000
Membership	−0.122	0.007	−1.88	0.099
Shelteredness	6.577	2.347	2.80	0.007

$R^2 = 0.1918$
$SE = 13.72$
$DW = 1.989$
$F = 7.53$

capita, the apparent scale effect observed in the three sample years is at least in part the effect of inter-union competition.

In summary, the interpretation of this observed negative correlation between size and administrative costs is difficult. There is a highly skewed size distribution of trade unions in the UK with, in 1985, only five unions above half a million members but 23 with a membership between 20,000 and 50,000. There is substantial size-independent variance in the mechanisms for provision of services, particularly in the degree of employer and lay-member subsidy and in the cost generating provisions of union rule books. Given the factors which *could* introduce size-independent variance, the consistency of the relationship is marked.

Several different explanations, other than the existence of scale economies, are available. Not all can be evaluated. It may be that the larger unions simply offer a lower level of service to members. Since they tend to charge lower subscriptions and their members in many cases earn less than those of smaller craft and occupational unions, this may be the case. It is difficult to envisage systematic quality of service measures. It may be that larger unions can elicit greater employer subsidy than smaller ones and thus reduce their cost base, although this explanation is counter-intuitive. Again, there are no data. However, one effect, that of inter-union competition, can be assessed and appears significant. Unions which compete for members appear to have lower unit costs than those which do not. As we have seen from Chapter 3, they also tend to have lower subscriptions and net worth per capita. The direction of causality cannot, of course, be assessed.

5   The financial consequences of union mergers

Mergers or transfers of engagements are two ways in which unions may secure relatively rapid growth. They may also help to solve financial difficulties. As both Buchanan (1981) for the UK and Chaison (1986) for the USA have noted, financial issues may be important in the decision to merge, if not in the choice of merger partner. In the 1970s and 1980s, the rate of union mergers has increased. Merger activity thus persists despite major shifts in trade union membership overall.

Buchanan, (1981: 43–5) has shown that, across the post-war period, large unions have tended to acquire small ones, which thus disappear. However, as the size distribution of UK trade unions in 1989 reveals, the process has not resulted in the eradication of very small unions. As we have seen from our questionnaire evidence, many small unions do not compete for new members; many are sustained by involvement in collusive bargaining arrangements with larger unions. Financially, many small unions may be unattractive merger partners.

This has not prevented larger unions from seeking to acquire them. Aston (1990) found that, of her sample of 63 acquired unions, the vast majority were small (less than 5,000 members), had declining membership, declining resources, and low levels of assets per capita. Nevertheless, they were acquired, mainly by large unions, which presumably saw non-economic benefits in doing so.

The questionnaire data support these findings. In all, 40% of respondent unions had been involved in merger discussions in the previous three years. Since, on average, only 2–3% of unions are involved in completed mergers in any given year, the pattern of response implies that many such discussions are protracted and, perhaps, ultimately fruitless.

There was an interesting pattern of response by size and by TUC affiliation which are, of course, related. Large unions were more likely than smaller ones to have been engaged in merger discussions; over 73% of unions with less than 5,000 members had *not* been involved in merger talks, whereas 75% of unions with more than 100,000 members had been. Related to this, TUC affiliates were substantially more likely to have been involved in merger discussions than non-affiliates.[9] In short, the current pattern of merger discussions appears likely to leave extant a large number of small, non-TUC unions, whatever their effects on membership concentration among TUC affiliates.

Only 10% of the sample had become involved in merger discussions because of the state of their own finances. In such discussions, the state of the finances of the prospective merger partner was often more important (20% of cases). This may indicate that, while trade unions are not driven to merger by financial considerations, financial discussions become important in the course of merger negotiations. However, as Table 6.5, based on only 40% of all questionnaire respondents, implies, bargaining power and membership are seen, even by finance officers, as the most

Table 6.5 *Reasons for seeking a merger partner*

Reason	Average rank	SD
Decreased membership	2.9	1.99
Bargaining power	2.5	1.68
Improved membership services	3.3	1.70
Declining reserves	4.5	1.57
Expenditure growth	5.2	0.97
Income problems	5.0	1.25
Political position of the union	4.6	2.07

important reasons for the decision to seek a merger partner. It may, then, be wrong to expect that successful merger negotiations will result in economies of scale. Certainly, the available data do not support the proposition

The relationship between pre-merger and post-merger administrative costs can in fact only be tested for a small number of mergers, simply because data undistorted by subsequent merger activity are rare. Table 6.6 shows the joint average administrative costs per member of the amalgamating partners in the years immediately preceding their merger and those of the post-merger counterparts. The data are standardised at 1985 prices; averages are taken over as long a period as is appropriate to avoid the effects of unusual items on administrative expenditure.

The data must obviously be treated with some caution since they are not in any way corrected for the impact of exogenous factors. Administrative savings do appear to have occurred with the formation of EETPU, ASTMS, and NGA 82. No change appears to have occurred with the formation of NUSMWCH&DE. Savings do *not* appear to have emerged with the formation of SOGAT 66 (from which NATSOPA withdrew in 1970), of SOGAT 82, GMBATU, BETA, and after the merger of TASS with NUSMW.

We may look at the effects of mergers on the costs of union services by looking at the careers of two acquisitive unions, TASS and ASTMS, through the 1980s until their eventual merger as MSF in 1988. The cost of services in MSF on formation was somewhere between those of its predecessors in 1987 (Figure 6.4).[10] ASTMS was a relatively cheap union, experiencing only a 32% increase in real administrative costs per capita over the period covered to 1987. Most of its mergers were with much smaller unions which were, in effect, absorbed with little increase in real administrative costs. Indeed, three small unions were absorbed in 1985 and in the following year administrative costs fell, rising substantially only immediately before the merger forming MSF.

Figure 6.4. MSF administrative costs and earnings

The experience of TASS is very different. Mergers with NUMSCHWDE and the NSMM in 1983 and 1985 respectively both took place near the year end and, at the year end, real per capita costs fell on each occasion. However, the subsequent increases reported at the next year end were considerable. Taking the first example, the merger with NUMSCHWDE, the immediate year-end results following merger on 20 December showed a 20% *fall* in costs, but the following year end, after the merger with the Patternmakers, there was a rise of 60%. The pattern is repeated with the NSMM merger.

There is evidence here, then, of both cost-neutral and highly costly mergers. What is missing is any substantive evidence of the realisation of cost savings through merger. This may not be true of the MSF merger. The average real administrative cost per capita, weighted by membership and at 1989 prices, was £34.87 in 1987. The figure at year end for MSF was £37.22, a 7% *real* increase. However, by the following year end, a nominal fall had been achieved.

Of course, it may be in general that, where administrative costs increased after merger, the range and quality of services available to

Table 6.6 *Mergers and administrative costs per capita*

Period	Pre-merger Unions	Average £	Period	Post-merger Unions	Average £
1962–7	PTU & ETU	18.4	1969–76	EETPU	16.1
1962–79	ASSET & ASW	20.0	1968–75	ASTMS	18.1
1962–5	HDE & NUSMW	21.0	1967–9	NUSMWCH&DE	21.0
1962–5	SOGAT & NUPBW	22.95	1966–9	SOGAT 66	24.8
1974–81	NATSOPA & SOGAT	32.3	1983–87	SOGAT 82	56.3
1974–81	NGA & SLADE	42.2	1983–7	NGA	35.8
1974–81	NUGMW & ASB	19.4	1983–7	GMBATU	26.3
1974–83	NATKE & ABS	40.65	1985–7	BETA	54.3
1974–83	TASS & NUSM	23.5	1984–7	TASS	29.1

members also increased and, conversely, that where costs declined there was some fall off in the level of service provision. Data do not exist to test either proposition. It also might be argued that the time periods considered subsequent to merger would not allow the economising effects of mergers on administrative costs to filter through; however, the further one gets away from the merger point, the more difficult it is to attribute changes in financial variables to the effects of merger.

Several factors are likely to make mergers costly in these terms. Trade union mergers take place under very different circumstances from those involving firms. They are negotiated between officials with a stake in the outcome. They are subject to approval by the membership in ballot; in cases of transfer of engagements, members of the transferring union have the right of veto, and in the case of amalgamations both sets of members vote. There is no equivalent of a takeover and the expectation is normally not that a more efficient management team will supplant a less efficient one. In fact, since the initiative for merger almost always originates with the union leadership or leaderships, security of tenure is often of a high priority. Add to this that there is competition among acquiring unions for merger partners and the explanation for the apparent generosity of many sets of merger terms emerges.[11] For example, in most transfers of engagements involving white-collar unions the usual form of words adopted is that: 'no permanent official or member of staff will in any way be prejudiced by the transfer and will be employed on terms and conditions no less favourable than those they already enjoy'. The influence here of the unions' own policies in the negotiation of transfers of undertakings is clear; redundancy protection terms have transferred over to the unions' own employ.

Moreover, in the larger amalgamations, the division and duplication of senior posts is rarely in proportion to the relative sizes of the unions involved. NUSMW was twice the size of the H&DEU on merger in 1966, yet both General Secretaries and Assistant General Secretaries were to carry on in the merged union for a period of eight years or until retirement. Bureaucratic duplication probably would not be a matter of major significance if both of the merging unions could be described as financially healthy; in practice, as we have seen, mergers rarely take place between such unions.

Many merger agreements are so framed that the rule book, together with the branch, regional, and district structure of the acquired party, is left intact. For example, in the merger of NUGMW and ASB, the former members of NUGMW were to form one section of the union and the former members of ASB another. The property and assets of both unions were to be integrated, but the members were to maintain their own sectional identity and continue to be administered by their own Executive Councils within existing branch structures. The two divisions were to be controlled by an overarching Central Executive Council.

Similarly, in many of the transfers involving white-collar unions, the usual format has been for the acquiring union to assume the assets, future income, and employment responsibilities of the acquired party, while the latter remains a separate section of the merged body, usually with its own Executive and rule provisions.

In fact, the process of merger negotiation and settlement is, as Undy et al. (1981) noted, likely to prevent economies being realised. Those unions which have been successful acquirers have tended to be those whose rule book allows the maintenance of sectional identity to incoming organisations. The most successful acquirers are thus the least likely to make cost savings because overheads will not be reduced in this manner.

What, then, are the motives of acquiring unions? Mergers may be a way of expanding the occupational or industrial base, simultaneously moving the union's centre of gravity out of declining and into expanding areas. The move of manual general unions into white-collar recruitment may be an example. Mergers may lead to enhanced voting or representational rights within the TUC or Labour Party. Thirdly, they may lead to a shift in or a consolidation of the balance of political power within the union; for example, the abortive discussions between AEU and EETPU in 1989 were seen by some as an attempt to cement 'right wing' power within a merged body. In GMB, as we show in Chapter 9, mergers may be used to alter the governmental structure of the union.

Mergers and transfers of engagements are essentially leadership initiatives. They may be endorsed by the membership or vetoed in ballot, but they do not originate in grass roots opinion. In fact, it is very difficult to identify any effect of merger activity on the bargaining power or relative pay of union memberships. Disaggregated data do not exist but, *a priori* it is difficult to see how such benefits could emerge. Merging unions in the UK are either unrelated in bargaining (GMB and APEX) or already collude for bargaining purposes (TASS and ASTMS).

6   Conclusion

The largest unions in the UK are generally the richest, generally involve themselves in recruitment activity and merger discussions, and, with all the reservations already expressed, appear the cheapest. However, with all of these data, it remains difficult to make generalisations about the effect of size alone. Inter-union competition, differences in the level of service provision, and differences in the choice of governance structure affect the level of costs independent of size. In addition, the level of employer support for union activity is quantified neither by unions themselves nor, in general, by employers. It may be that larger unions get more of it per capita, thus explaining the observed correlations.

Most unions, at least most large unions, do seek to grow. In many cases they seek to replace 'lost' members and revenue. However, from both the questionnaire and case studies it emerged that expansion was felt to be something unions 'ought' to pursue, irrespective of short-term costs and benefits. Such cost and benefit information was often either unavailable or deemed irrelevant. As we shall see in the next chapter, a similar approach to financial data appears in the deliberations of unions about strike activity.

7   Strike activity and union finances

1   Introduction

Strikes continue to puzzle economists in part because they are, *ex post*, often inefficient for both parties concerned, particularly for union members who typically cannot shift their consumption patterns over time in the way that employers can shift production schedules. Whereas, overall, the costs of strikes for employers appear to be low, those for union members may be high (Hirsch and Addison, 1986: 76–8, Gennard, 1982).

Few economic models of strike activity explicitly consider the institutional interests of the union and the impact of strike activity on union organisation. Several models simply posit profit-maximising behaviour by firms confronted by non-rational behaviour from union members: the strike acts to bring member expectations in line with market pressure. These which do include a role for union leaders see them either as passive or narrowly self interested. Ashenfelter and Johnson (1969) assume no independent leader interest; they simply act as rational agents for irrational principals, going along with the strike simply to avoid challenge to their tenure. In other models, such as Swint and Nelson (1978, 1980), they pursue personal interests, again subject to some minimum gain from the strike below which they lose office. The institutional interests of the union and the organisational effects of strikes are otherwise excluded.

The proposition that unions as institutions may actually *benefit* from strike activity is of some interest. Both on logical and empirical grounds we might not expect it. Looked at financially, strikes involve an interruption to revenue and, possibly, higher organisational costs. Employer subsidies are likely to be withdrawn and the union must rely on its own reserves. For many unions, such reserves would be quickly exhausted. Empirically, there are well-publicised cases, such as that of NUM discussed in detail in Chapter 8, where large national strikes have debilitated a union in this way.

However, as Chapter 2 indicated, strike activity *per se* has not been the most important factor in the financial debilitation of UK unions. Moreover, as Willman and Morris (1988) have shown, some public sector

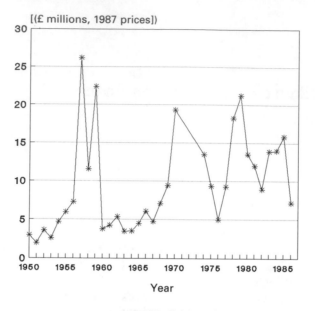

[(£ millions, 1987 prices])

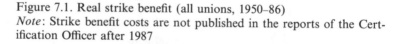

Figure 7.1. Real strike benefit (all unions, 1950–86)
Note: Strike benefit costs are not published in the reports of the Certification Officer after 1987

unions in the UK in the 1980s have emerged from large scale disputes in
good financial health. There may be institutional purposes to be served
by strike activity, irrespective of the outcome in terms of members' earnings. In this chapter, we shall look more closely at the financial implications of strike activity. In the first instance, we shall look at the aggregate
picture in more detail. Subsequently, we shall examine disputes with
differing financial consequences: the 1981 civil service dispute and its
impact on FDA, IRSF, and IPCS, the 1980 steel strike and its impact on
ISTC. Finally, we examine the effects of asset sequestration, on NUS,
SOGAT, and NGA.

2   Spending on strikes

In the aggregate, as Figure 7.1 indicates, union real expenditure on strikes
has varied with the occurrence of large disputes, often in the public sector.
Recently, the 1979 'Winter of Discontent' and the large mining and teaching disputes in 1984–5 have raised overall levels of expenditure. A contrast

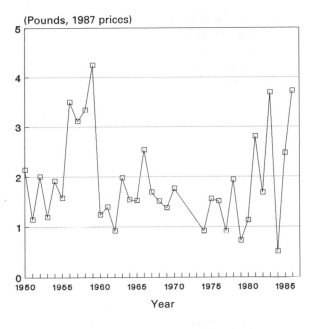

Figure 7.2. Real cost per working day lost (all unions, 1950–86)

may be made with the 1960s when a more fragmented pattern of often private sector industrial action incurred lower strike costs. Here, of course, is a clue to the dangers of relying solely on this series of data. It may underestimate real expenditure on disputes not only because unions themselves might either misallocate expenditure or subsidise strikes from other funds, but also because the pattern of strike activity itself will influence benefit provision and thus the balance of costs between members' and union funds in subsidising strike activity.

Nevertheless, Figure 7.2, which controls for the overall level of strike activity, is of some interest, mainly for the contrasts it provides with Figure 7.1. Figure 7.2 shows union benefit paid per working day lost, giving some idea of what it costs unions to support a strike day. The interest here is that, more recently, the highest real costs were incurred, not in the high strike years of 1979, 1984, and 1985, but in 1981, 1983, and 1986. By comparison, each day supported during the 'Winter of Discontent' came cheaply, as did each working day lost during the miners' strike. In these three years, highest levels of strike benefit expenditure were incurred by the civil service unions during their 1981 dispute, particularly CPSA and (then) SCPS, by the (then) POEU in the Mercury dispute of 1983 and during the dispute at News International in 1986.

However, in the aggregate, these expenditures are a small part of the total. Total expenditure on strike benefits has been less than 5% of total union expenditure, and often less than 3%, since the Winter of Discontent. The record highs in percentage terms in the post-war period are incurred during the national shipbuilding, printing, and engineering disputes of 1957 and 1959.

The problem of financial debilitation through strikes is best studied on a disaggregated basis. Some unions have managed to get into financial difficulties during long strikes – though some others have fared better – but this has not affected the financial health of the movement as a whole. It is thus necessary to focus on specific cases, but initially some general considerations are relevant.

3   Managing strikes

Unions may be required to fund strikes in a variety of circumstances. These include the situation where, perhaps because of some form of employer action which the union deems unacceptable, a group of workers strike, and the union deems it necessary to offer support. The strike does not result from union policy, its costs, duration and extent are unforeseen. At the other extreme, a strike may result from the planned execution of industrial action in order to implement a conference decision which has been costed as fully as possible in advance. The union typically targets selective action, pays strike pay and benefit, and, perhaps, plans and implements a levy on the general membership. It is likely that the costs of strike activity will be more fully assessed in the latter case and it may be that they will be more successfully controlled.

There may, of course, be strikes which only minimally affect union finances. Small unofficial strikes, such as those typical of certain manufacturing industries in the 1960s (Durcan et al., 1983), may involve no benefit expenditure and only minor disruptions to income. However, since 1984, it is likely that such smaller disputes, without ballots and often without union approval, have diminished in number. Unions are currently liable in the majority of circumstances for strike action taken by their members and, if the action is unlawful, unions may incur substantial costs in the form of fines or sequestration fees: we discuss this further below.

On the other hand, certain unions have experienced large national disputes affecting all or the majority of members. This is typically a misfortune – at least financially – suffered by industry or occupational unions who deal only with one employer or for whom the employer is dominant – the NUT and NUS, the civil service unions, ISTC, NUM, and NUR all fall into this category. All have experienced at least one national dispute in the 1980s and such disputes are particularly threatening. It is worth examining the process involved in some detail.

We refer here to the approach presented in Chapter 4. When a union strikes, it is operating only in the membership market. Even if there is some collusion between negotiators and employers either about the timing or the duration of the strike, it is fair to say that the union as an institution has sided with members in order to compel some kind of settlement. Not only, therefore, is income from members disrupted since unpaid members cannot pay subscriptions, but employer subsidy is withdrawn: check-off will, typically, be suspended. The full cost of running the union and, moreover, running the dispute, will fall on the union: as we have shown, this is untypical.

However, there may some substitution between member and employer resources. In a dispute, members suffer enforced idleness and they may, if the dispute is widely supported, be prepared to invest effort and savings into its prosecution. In addition, further revenue sources may be available through inter-union loans, as in the miners' strike, or in the form of public support, as in the recent ambulance workers' dispute. The net fall in union revenue in the course of the dispute is thus an empirical question. There may be a net increase in revenue though, of course, not all of this need show up on the balance sheet.

Expenditure is likely to rise. There are few costs which can be cut during a strike and the organisation of meetings, travel, special conferences, and the like may raise administrative costs. Benefit expenditure will almost certainly rise. In severe disputes, sympathetic organisations such as the Labour Party, TUC, or other unions may defer affiliation fees or loan repayments: nevertheless, striking unions are likely to incur higher costs.

If expenditures are higher than revenue, even the richest unions will hit trouble in a long dispute. As Chapter 2 indicated, union reserves are generally illiquid and, in per capita terms, low. The key to successful management of lengthy or large disputes is thus either the establishment of large reserves in advance or the maintenance of income in the course of a dispute. We shall examine how unions manage these problems in the next section.

4   Empirical data on large strikes

Our most general data, from our questionnaire, indicated that financial considerations did not dominate strike decisions or the pursuit of strike objectives. Fifty-five and a half per cent of respondent unions had been involved in industrial action in the previous five years. It did not seem sensible to ask respondents to assess the costs and benefits of such action, hence question 39, which asked how important financial considerations had been in the decision to take such action. The vast majority (44% of the total) felt that financial considerations had not been important. Only 3% felt they had been very important. A more general question (q40) asked about the role of finances in the union's most recent campaign on behalf of its members. Over 70% felt such considerations had been in varying degrees unimportant; only 5.5% felt that they had been very important.

Nevertheless, our cases revealed more varied examples of financial planning. The FDA, IPCS, and IRSF consciously planned for the onset of industrial action, or at least the prospect of more hostile relations with the main employer in the late 1970s. They have fared quite well in the aftermath of the 1981 dispute. On the other hand ISTC and NUM experienced disputes in the 1980s which were, to an important extent, turning points in the history of the two unions. ISTC, together with the civil service unions, is discussed in this chapter. We postpone consideration of the more complex case of NUM to Chapter 8.

The civil service unions and the 1981 dispute

The decision of the government in September 1980 to suspend the Pay Research Unit method of determining civil service pay prompted the Council of Civil Service Unions (COCSU) to plan a broad strategy for industrial action encompassing its nine constituents. As the disputes escalated in 1981, a one day strike in March was supplemented by a pattern of selective strike action, notably in computer centres. Throughout, despite calls for all out action by CPSA, this pattern of selective action continued. Eventually, the campaign was called off on 30 July 1981, as the unions, with the exception of IRSF, accepted a government pay offer prior to the report of the Megaw inquiry. The dispute involved the loss of 1.12 million working days, approximately 26% of the total for 1981.

Although by no means a victory for the unions, the dispute did mark a step forward in being the first major coordinated campaign by civil service unions, through COCSU. Substantial extra funds were raised by the main unions in dispute, and large amounts were transferred, through COCSU, from unions less involved in selective strike action to those bearing the brunt of the cost. All of the major unions involved had income and expenditure peaks in the strike year.

Table 7.1. *Financial performance of civil service unions, 1980–2*

	1980	1981	1982
Total real income £000	23,064	35,454	24,866
% change	–	53.7	−29.9
Total real expenditure £000	19610	34053	22508
% change	–	73.7	−33.9
Solvency	1.176	1.041	1.105
All trade unions			
Solvency	1.07	1. 11	1.19
% change real income	–	10.5	4.4

Notes: Figures are at constant 1985 prices.
The civil service unions covered were, at the time, CPSA, CSU, IPCS, IRSF, and SCPS.

Table 7.1 presents data for the five largest unions involved, in the aggregate. Total income for these unions increased, in real terms, by almost 54% across 1980–1. Total expenditure increased by almost 74%. In the year after the dispute, there were substantial reductions in income and expenditure. As the table shows, these figures contrast strongly with the trend for all trade unions. The solvency of the civil service unions fell substantially in the dispute year to recover thereafter but, compared to the trend for all unions, they emerged from the dispute less solvent. They also suffered lower income growth: total real income for all trade unions increased by 15.4% over the two years, but that of these five unions rose by only 7.8%.

Across the strike year, the unions fared very differently, as Table 7.2 shows. Both CPSA and CSU were insolvent in the strike year primarily because they could secure only small increases in nominal income. IPMS and IRSF were highly solvent prior to, throughout, and after the dispute. IRSF experienced massive increases in both income and expenditure due to the incidence of selective industrial action. SCPS, remarkably, entered the dispute insolvent but recovered solvency in 1981. It was the only one of the five to show a higher increase in income than in expenditure.

For the unions in dispute, there were at least three sources of additional nominal income. The first was a levy on the membership. As we shall see, several unions not only resolved to levy in the strike years but had done so in preparation for a dispute since 1978. The second was sale of assets. Net worth in CSU fell by 15% in *nominal* terms between 1980 and 1981. In CPSA nominal net worth fell by 6% between 1980 and 1982. The third source, which was extremely important for IRSF, was inter-union transfer

Table 7.2. *Disaggregated data: civil service unions 1980–2*

				% Change in			
	Solvency			Income		Expenditure	
Union	1980	1981	1982	1980–1	1981–2	1980–1	1981–2
CPSA	1.24	0.98	0.97	22.4	−5.4	55	−4.5
CSU	0.94	0.66	1.12	21.1	21.5	72.3	−28.3
IPMS	1.30	1.09	1.22	50.1	−29.6	78.5	−37.0
IRSF	1.52	1.15	1.55	304.3	−63.2	436.7	−72.7
SCPS	0.97	1.11	1.12	114.2	−18.0	87.2	−18.9

of funds, through COCSU, to support strike action. In all cases, these offset losses to normal subscription income.

Expenditure increases were incurred through direct campaigns, payment of strike benefits, and transfer of funds to other unions. Nominal expenditure may well have risen also through withdrawal of employer support for union organisation. In general, the civil service unions were well supported by the employer prior to the dispute through check-off and premises facilities supplied by the various government departments. These are not normally centrally costed and are difficult to quantify. Usually, during a dispute several such facilities are either curtailed or withdrawn, and the effects of this may be evident in expenditure figures.

Of course, the strike was not the only event affecting union finances across this period, even though it may have been the most traumatic. Policy developments and financial planning unrelated to the strike had an impact. In order to understand rather better the place of the dispute in these matters, it is necessary to proceed on a case by case basis. Three of our case study unions, FDA, IPMS, and IRSF were involved. We shall look briefly at each.

Although not directly involved in strike action, members of FDA subsidised the action in two ways: firstly, by contributing half a day's pay in lieu of participation and, secondly, by payment of union funds to COCSU. However, the strike, the first the Association had funded, had very little effect on the finances of the union. By far the greater effect emerged from the adoption of 'Standing Alone', a policy of organisational growth and change, at conference the previous year.

The background to Standing Alone lay in FDA's concerns about size and viability. Recurrent merger discussions in the 1970s, mainly with IPCS, had their roots in FDA's concerns about the prospects for an independent existence. Concern with the terms of any proposed merger with IPMS were voiced at the 1979 ADM, which passed the following motion: 'This Conference believes that the FDA is capable of continuing to operate as an independent trade union and instructs the EC to produce a discussion paper on the steps which need to be taken to achieve this aim, including, if necessary, an increase in the level of subscription.'[1] The Report, endorsed the following year, recommended further expansion in the number of officials and the range of membership services. A journal was established and a new General Secretary appointed. In all, a doubling of salary costs was envisaged, because it was felt that a viable union had to rely on full-time officials.

In 1975, the union had employed only a full-time typist. By 1988, it employed 11 staff including four full-time officials. To pay for this, regular increases in nominal subscriptions were necessary and the Executive was required to argue the case in some detail at Conference. The union always pursued tight cost controls and motions to Conference were costed in some detail. Such a motion, and ballot, was required before strike action. The union also had a policy in the late 1970s of building reserves, to a sum of one year's subscriptions. Although they occasionally fell short of this, the unions *real* end of year funds grew steadily, by over 200% from 1976 to 1979, fell markedly as *Standing Alone* was implemented, then resumed growth in the 1980s.

IPMS was rather more centrally involved in the dispute, and its financial fortunes are of some interest. In 1981, the union raised over £2 million in a membership levy to fund involvement in the dispute. In 1979 and 1980 it had already raised over half a million pounds for the same ends. As a result, it was able to remain solvent during the dispute. However solvency in the year *prior* to the dispute had been maintained only by an unusual income item: there was in fact a shortfall of membership income over administrative costs, but a revaluation of property took place. In 1981 the massive rise in real membership income covered the unusual level of benefit and after-strike related expenditure.

As with FDA, then, the strike 'hit' a union which was growing financially as a result of earlier decisions. In 1976, Conference imposed on NEC the requirement to save £50,000 in real terms each year for campaigning and £100,000 for office accommodation. In addition, it was required to save the equivalent of 10% of expenditure annually as part of a conscious policy to build reserves. Real end of year funds grew by over 250% between 1976 and 1983, uninterrupted by the strike.

IRSF was for many years regarded pejoratively as a staff association by many TUC affiliates, but it played a key role in the 1981 dispute in undertaking a disproportionate number of selective strikes. Over 3% of

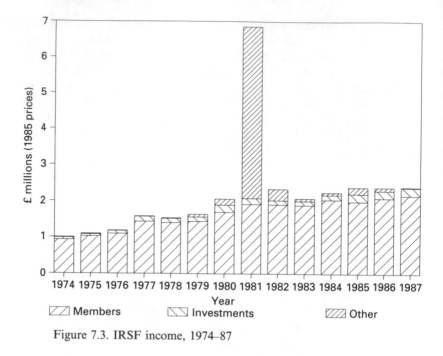

Figure 7.3. IRSF income, 1974–87

Inland Revenue employees struck, compared to 1% of all civil servants. It was helped by other COCSU unions by transfers of funds.

In 1981, such transfers accounted for the greater part of union income. Between 1978 and 1981, the union collected over £420,000 for its own disputes fund, but this was swamped by the millions received in 1981 from COCSU. In 1981, £2.5 million (at 1985 prices) entered the disputes fund from COCSU and a further £2.5 million from voluntary donations and other sources. Although most of this was spent directly on the dispute, it enabled IRSF to maintain solvency during the dispute. Figure 7.3 shows the substantial rise in real income for the strike year, and the subsequent reversion to a more gentle pattern of growth.

The role of the dispute fund in the growth of the union's assets is of some interest: once again, we are dealing with a union which was in any event planning financial growth. In the early 1970s, IRSF faced three financial problems. The first was the explosion in staff salaries due to high inflation, the second was a shortfall in the provisions for the staff superannuation fund, and the third was the knowledge that there needed to be provision for headquarters accommodation since the lease on existing premises expired in 1988. Throughout the 1970s, by continual increase

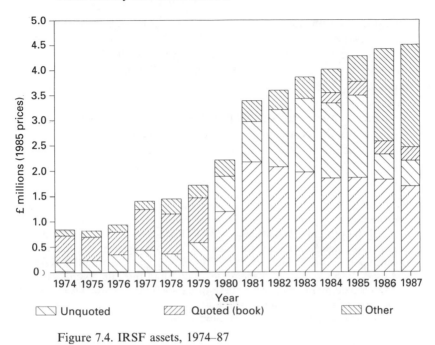

Figure 7.4. IRSF assets, 1974–87

in nominal subscription rates the union's assets grew (Figure 7.4). In the 1980s, the union supplemented this strategy with levies for specific purposes, such as the purchase of accommodation, in order to avoid taking on debt.

The purchase of new accommodation in 1980 altered the composition of the union's assets, but so did provisions for the strike. Although income from other sources such as COCSU flowed straight in and out in 1981, the value of the disputes fund has grown considerably, from approximately £275,000 in 1978 to nearly £1.5 million in 1987 (both at 1985 prices). At the establishment of the strike fund in 1978, by transfer of £35,000 from the general fund, the General Secretary apparently:

saw no point in pretending that with the way the Federation was currently financed or, indeed, might ever be financed that it was going to be in a position in the foreseeable future of establishing a strike fund which would permit it to finance a significant strike across the membership.[2]

However, after the dispute, the fund continued to grow.

A disputes fund needs, above all, to be liquid and the union thus sought to use the money markets in order to gain a return on large cash deposits. This proved to be highly profitable. By 1986, the Treasurer was able to

defer a proposed motion for subscription increase because of this investment success; he announced that: 'the EC would not be seeking a
subscription increase. There had been a big rise in dividends as a lot of
money was in the money market.'[3] Much of this money was from the
disputes fund. The success of the union's investment policy is evident
from Figure 7.4.

A further consequence of the preparation for and experience of the
1981 dispute is the power given to the Executive to protect the union's
funds from use in disputes. The rule book gives the Executive Council
the authority to make a distinction between 'protected' and 'unprotected'
funds:

All the funds of the Inland Revenue Staff Federation shall be specified as protected
or unprotected. Any property which is or has been comprised in a protected fund
is and shall be precluded from being used to finance strikes or other industrial
action. The protected funds are the General and Management Funds, and the
following Special Funds: The Accommodation Reserve, The Building & Equipment Reserve, The Leasehold Redemption Fund and the Life Assurance Fund.
All the funds held by Branches other than those financed from the Disputes Fund
shall be protected. The Executive Committee shall have power at any time to
declare an unprotected fund, or a new fund, to be protected.

Overall then, the 1981 dispute does not appear to have interrupted the
financial growth or unduly hampered the financial performance of the
three case study unions. CSU and CPSA may, of course, be rather different. In the case of IRSF the provisions the union has made for disputes
and, more specifically, the financial arrangements for funds' transfer in
1981 appear quite beneficial to the union's financial well being.

Attribution is quite difficult, since it is difficult, even with disaggregated
data, to be sure about the precise effect of the dispute compared with
other contemporaneous factors. However, it does seem to be the case that
the supply of resources for union activity may expand considerably during
a dispute and that a union's financial position can be transformed by a
large dispute. In other circumstances, particularly involving an all-out
national strike, the outcome may be very different.

ISTC and the 1980 steel strike

ISTC has been amongst the richest, in per capita terms, of British unions.
It has for many years lived beyond its means at least in terms of membership income, subsidising expenditure from investment income (Willman
and Morris, 1988). As a result of its wealth, it has been able to fund
relatively generous benefits: because of its investment income, it relies less
on subscriptions. However, it is also a union in financial decline. Since

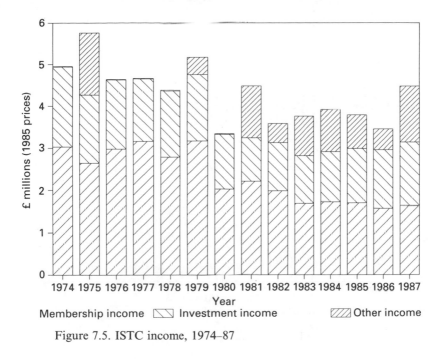

Figure 7.5. ISTC income, 1974–87

the current reporting requirements began in 1974, and probably for some time before that, membership and measures of real income, expenditure, and assets were in decline. In 1980, decline was accelerated by the first national steel strike since 1926.

The strike began on 2 January 1980 and lasted approximately 13 weeks. Although the main dispute was with British Steel Corporation, which employed the majority of ISTC members, for a period ISTC attempted to extend the strike to the private sector, thus encompassing practically all members. Eventually, a jointly agreed inquiry established the terms of a pay settlement which supported a return to work. However, after the dispute, the rate of membership loss accelerated as BSC rationalised capacity and employment at a greater rate.

Figures 7.5–7.7 show income, expenditure, and assets for ISTC. They reveal a financial structure in which surplus was maintained through investment income and they illustrate the financial impact of the 1980 strike. In 1980, expenditure rose to £6 million, but the union was unable to maintain income, which fell to £3.5 million. In the strike year, therefore, ISTC suffered a massive shortfall of income over expenditure. The strike and subsequent membership loss have encouraged a situation where ISTC

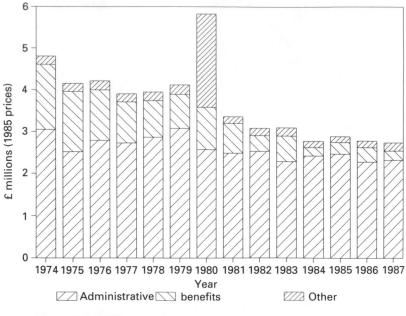

Figure 7.6. ISTC expenditure

maintains solvency through asset sales rather than merely through investment income. The financial burden of the strike is evident both in the
'other expenditure' category for 1980 and the large benefit expenditure
for that year. Subsequently, the union has failed to cut administrative
costs in line with membership loss or with benefit expenditure. To 1987,
real administrative costs fell by only 24%, whereas real benefit fell by 86%
and membership by 43%.

By 1986, the General Secretary was reporting to conference the drastic
economies made in head office staff over the previous two years. A motion
at that year's conference called for a balancing of subscription income
and total expenditure to enable a reduced dependence on 'stocks and
shares'. Although it was defeated, the Executive acknowledged the argument in its justification for a subscription increase the following month:
'In arriving at the decision to increase contributions, consideration was
given to the relationship between overall income and expenditure and in
particular upon the continued dependence on our investment income.'[4]
Despite this concern and despite continued asset sales, ISTC assets continue to grow in real terms (Figure 7.7), particularly since 1981. It appears
that the union may have been the beneficiary of an investment policy

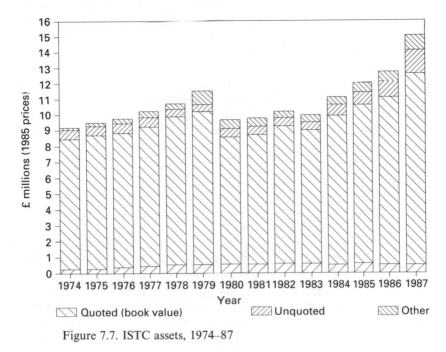

Figure 7.7. ISTC assets, 1974–87

focusing on quoted stocks and shares in the favourable climate of the early 1980s. In fact, ISTC may be richer than appears from the figure, since its extensive properties are almost certainly not valued at market rates.

Much of the assessment of the financial impact of the strike depends on the linkage of the strike to subsequent employment loss. The latter factor has been more important than the strike in changing the financial structure of the union since it was sufficiently rich to ride the financial consequences of a long national dispute. Paradoxically, ISTC was probably better equipped in 1989 to ride a dispute than in 1980, since suspension of subscription income would then have caused loss of only about one third of revenue.

Strikes and sequestration: NUS, NGA, and SOGAT

NUS is an example of a union already in long-term decline pushed to extreme financial embarrassment and merger by the consequences of a national dispute. Unlike ISTC, recovery was not possible, not least because, following the dispute, several employers chose to derecognise the union.

The strike began as a 24 hour national protest over the sacking of 161 NUS members at the Isle of Man Steam Packet Company. There was, however, a long-running dispute with P & O at Dover over the employer's revision of terms and conditions of employment. On 1 February 1988, the day after the stoppage, P & O and Sealink obtained an injunction on the grounds that NUS was involved in secondary action. NUS initially defied the injunction, and subsequent compliance did not include the dispute at the ferry ports. The legal action was thus pursued, and a protracted and interrupted set of sequestration hearings concluded in May 1988 with the union being fined £150,000 and its assets sequestered. The union subsequently called off its action, in May, and the assets were returned in August. P & O, having dismissed strikes in March, resumed normal services by September 1988, although picketing by dismissed NUS members continued well into 1989.

The financial consequences of the dispute were severe. NUS had not, during the 1980s been financially particularly successful. In five of the eight years, prior to the dispute, expenditure had exceeded income. Its real net worth had fallen steadily across the period, from £4.5 million in 1980 (at 1989 prices) to £3.0 million in 1986. During the same period, membership fell by 39%. Subscription income per capita had risen by 45% across the period but per capita administrative costs had risen by over 115%. The annual deficit on membership servicing, prior to the dispute in 1987, was £19.4 per capita (1989 prices Figure 7.8). The union went into the dispute with a shortfall of income over expenditure.

As Chapter 3 indicated, the dispute led to disastrous financial results in 1988. Total income, the lowest in the 1980s at £1.32 million, did not cover even the sequestration costs of £1.36 million. £1.8 million of other expenditure had to be met from reserves. Across the year, real net worth fell by 70% to £38 per capita. The union had been among Latta's rich, industry unions but decline left it with very few income generating assets and a heavy reliance on a declining level of real subscription income: investments had declined in real terms since 1980. By 1989, NUS had over £1 million debt to other unions and a per capita net worth of only £18: it incurred further sequestration costs of £$\frac{1}{3}$ million.

The strike involved all the ingredients of financial calamity – income loss, membership loss, derecognition, sequestration, and the liquidisation of most assets. It transformed gradual decline into the frantic search for a merger partner. Union survival was threatened because the retreat from certain parts of the employer market was permanent. In September 1990 the union merged with the NUR.

The total cost of sequestration was approximately £1.7 million. Other costs in the dispute are more difficult to estimate. The union paid unemployment and dispute benefit, but its total costs fell across the strike year,

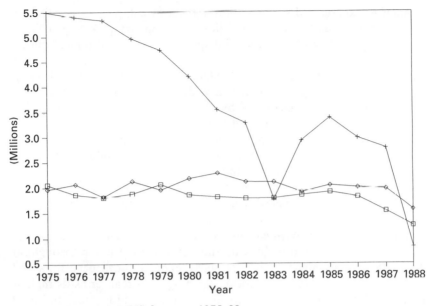

Figure 7.8. NUS finances, 1975–88

in part because of loss of members which in turn caused loss of income: 1988 membership income was, in real terms, £0.3 million down on the previous year. Over time, this represents a substantial loss of income stream but one must be wary about attributing it to the strike. The loss of members across the strike year was 11.6%: the average for the previous seven years of the 1980s was 8% *per annum*. It is likely that the union would have continued to lose members and membership income without the dispute: in fact, membership *income* had fallen in real terms since 1985.

The strike, then, perhaps hastened the end. It was described by the High Court judge ordering sequestration as 'an act of suicide', but financially speaking, the union was suffering a lingering death in any event. For a union with 20,000 members, its administrative costs were, at £71.00 per head in 1989, very high. Its asset income was negligible and subscription income static. A financially unwise strike decision was the culmination of a decade of financial difficulty.

Sequestration of assets is a serious, but not necessarily financially disastrous issue for a trade union. In the 1980s, there have been three other cases of sequestration of the greater part of a national union's assets. In 1983, during the Stockport messenger dispute, NGA were fined over £$\frac{1}{2}$ million and then suffered sequestration. NUM, described more fully in

Chapter 8, experienced sequestration and receivership in 1984. SOGAT had its assets sequestered in 1986 following secondary picketing at Wapping during the News International dispute: NGA was also fined during this dispute.

The two print unions appear on the face of it to have suffered little long-term financial damage. NGA, recently merged with SLADE, massively increased subscription income – by 300% – across 1983, so remaining solvent during the year, although net worth was static in real terms. SOGAT reported expenditure higher than income and a slight drop in real net worth at the end of 1986, but recovered in the following year. As we have shown in Chapter 3, both were financially strong in 1989.

A closer look at events in the two unions reveals that the disputes and the sequestrations placed a heavy burden on the internal financial management systems. In 1983, NGA spent 41% of its per capita subscription income on unemployment and disputes benefit. The greater part of this was on unemployment benefit, and, although the union throughout the 1980s was the highest payer of such benefit in both per capita and absolute terms (Oram, 1987), the 1983 figure is in real terms its highest so far. In fact, during 1983 subscription income, total income, and total expenditure increased massively, the main mechanism for this being the use of membership levy to fund the disputes and the attendant costs.

However, although successful in 1983, the difficulty of using membership levy in disputes was highlighted by events in both NGA and SOGAT in 1986 during the News International dispute. Both unions balloted their members on a levy to fund the dispute. In NGA, a narrow majority in May 1986 approved a membership levy of 50p: a much larger majority approved its reduction to 20p in December. In SOGAT, the introduction of a levy sought by the General Secretary was voted down. As a result of this loss, the union formally withdrew from the dispute to avoid threats of legal action. In subsequent years, it has reduced benefit expenditure as a percentage of total expenditure in each year.

Oram (1987: 20) for SOGAT and Gennard (1990: 246–9) for NGA speak of these unions having faced 'severe financial difficulties' in these years. This must be put into perspective since, as with NALGO, the *apparent* wealth of both unions is far greater than that available to leaders. Members pay subscriptions to Chapel, branch, and union and the two societies both contain branches which have accumulated substantial assets. The London Region of NGA and London Central Branch of SOGAT have substantial investments effectively outside of the control of the central leadership which then faces the difficult battle of convincing members in less well-endowed branches to fund London disputes through levy. Hence, although the SOGAT General Secretary estimated costs of sequestration, litigation, and benefits at £5 million in November 1986, this must be set against the total net worth of the union in December 1986 of £24.3 million.

Gennard notes the main difficulties involved in the use of levies by NGA. First, they needed to be pitched at a higher level than actually required, because of uncertainties about both yield and feasible duration. Second, they lacked flexibility and were unpopular, since the liability for levy and the need for it did not, even in the longer term, coincide. NGA, faced with a series of disputes in 1983, 1985, and 1986, required a more stable basis for the funding of disputes which avoided levy and the problem to which levy was an *ad hoc* response, namely depletion of the General Fund. The solution was the establishment of a separate disputes fund in 1986 (Gennard, 1990: 237–49 and 484–514).

The final point to make about this series of disputes is that a major item for both unions was the funding of unemployment benefit, particularly following disputes, rather than disputes benefit itself. In 1983, for example NGA spent over £3 million on unemployment benefit but only £289,000 on dispute pay.

5   Conclusion

Unions spend a variable amount on strike activity, depending on its incidence, predictability, and duration. They seem not to assess the value of strike activity *ex ante* in terms of its effects on union finances but this observation does not exclude the further proposition that strikes may be managed well or badly by the union concerned.

There is obviously a clear distinction to be drawn between lengthy national strikes of all members and selective action, often of short duration. It must be doubted whether *any* union can endure a prolonged strike of all members without financial debilitation. Those which have tried have been, by British union standards, very rich. However, it is also the case that some unions foresee, and make specific provision for, action which results in revenue loss. Strikes which enjoy the support of the majority of members – expressed through their support for voluntary levy – may result in substantial financial growth for the unions concerned, irrespective of the outcome for members' salaries. There are thus, from the institutional point of view, cost-effective and cost-ineffective forms of industrial action.

For strikes to lead to the long-term debilitation or disappearance of trade unions, it appears that three ingredients are necessary. The first is that the strike must be lengthy and involve the majority of members, thus increasing expenditure and reducing income. The second is that, from the employer's point of view, the union is seen as an inappropriate bargaining partner, so that full or partial derecognition ensues. The third is that asset sequestration occurs. Both NUS and as we shall see, NUM, suffered all three.

The NUM case is presented as the first of five chapters in which we analyse more closely events in five case study unions across the 1970s and 1980s. The five case studies are designed to do rather more than merely describe five types of union financial management. Our argument throughout is that financial matters do not simply concern discrete subsystems of union government but that the overall policy or strategy of the union interacts with financial issues. In some unions, finances influence policy formulation, in others policy concerns prompt changes to financial management. Our concern in the cases is to document this interaction between financial management and union strategy.

To this end, all cases share a common structure. We describe the recent history of the union initially, with a view to accounting for the main strategic issues each union faces. We then describe the systems of union government, which indicate how the union spends its money and how policy is formulated. Two sections then follow on financial performance and financial management and, in conclusion, we seek to relate financial matters to union behaviour.

8   The National Union of Mineworkers: strike and financial disaster

1   Historical background

More than any other union, the finances of NUM have been subject to public scrutiny since the year long dispute with the National Coal Board in 1984–5. The dispute proved to have major consequences for the union because of the size of funds involved, the loss of almost all membership income for such a long period, the protracted nature of the litigation which the union faced, and the publicity shed by the Lightman Inquiry, set up by the NEC to investigate financial management in the union during the dispute (Lightman, 1990). As we shall see, the federal structure of NUM affected its capacity to respond to financial crisis even after the dispute was over. While the leadership of NUM has responded to this with a number of important reforms, it remains clear that even extreme financial pressures have not altered the industrial policies of the union.

The National Union of Mineworkers (NUM) came into being in 1945, following the effective wartime nationalisation of coal production in 1942. It was formed out of the Miners' Federation of Great Britain, set up in 1888 and comprising some 40 separate local organisations. NUM is often regarded as an industrial union and, to the extent that its members are confined to coal and coke production, it is, but it shares the industry with three other unions. The British Association of Colliery Management (BACM), which came into existence in 1947, represents all those engaged in professional, technical, and managerial grades in the mining industry or associated industries and the National Association of Colliery Overmen, Deputies and Shotfirers (NACODS) organises those who have statutory qualifications as colliery deputies. In addition, the Union of Democratic Mineworkers, established after the 1984 dispute, competes directly with NUM for mineworkers' membership, particularly in Nottinghamshire and Derbyshire.

Membership of the union has declined with employment in the industry since the war but decline accelerated in the 1980s (Figure 8.1). The economic background to this was that total demand for energy in the UK had contracted because of the recession in heavy industry (1979–82), and energy conservation initiatives and new fuel efficient plant had reduced the worldwide demand for oil, leading to lower oil prices. Moreover, the fall in the US dollar during the 1980s encouraged consumers (particularly the CEGB) to import low-cost coal.

These adverse market conditions put tremendous pressure on the industry to restructure itself quickly in order to bring about real reductions in the cost of extracting deep-mined coal; this pressure was reinforced by government policy. In 1983, the government instructed the National Coal Board (NCB[2]) to achieve commercial viability (i.e., 'achieve a satisfactory return on capital while competing in the market place') when appointing Ian MacGregor as chairman. As an outsider to the industry and a man with a reputation for strong management in the pursuit of profitability this signalled a clear change from previous appointments. The Monopolies and Mergers Commission also undertook an investigation into the industry.[3] Apart from pointing out that surplus production from high-cost, low-productivity pits must be eliminated by closure, a proposal which subsequently became NCB policy, the Commission made various recommendations involving changes in procedures, systems, management style, and structure, which would promote more effective management decision making and accountability.[4] In particular it recommended that Areas should be operated as business units, and increased use should be made of efficiency audits. Prompted by this external pressure, the NCB underwent substantial organisational change in the early 1980s. Areas were merged, while headquarters departments and their structure were rationalised and streamlined.

These reforms were strongly resisted by the new leadersip of NUM which was elected in the early 1980s. Arthur Scargill was elected President in 1981, with 70% of the vote, marking a major shift in union policy towards the left. This was followed in 1984 with the election of Peter Heathfield, a close ally of Scargill, as General Secretary. Scargill's policies contrasted strongly with those of his predecessor, Lord Gormley, who had sought a series of pragmatic compromises over wages and output and kept the union broadly out of political decisions concerning the size of the industry. Scargill, from his political base in the Yorkshire coalfield, consistently called for the rejuvenation of the coal industry. His policies have been described as those of an idiosyncratic marxist (Campbell and Warner, 1985) insofar as he opposed workers' control and supported proportional representation, but in leadership he has consistently called for reexpansion of the industry with the restoration of high wages to all mineworkers.

In his address to the 1982 Annual Conference, Scargill laid down a radical programme for NUM. He insisted that the union was entering a new era, and that there would be a sharp break with the principles and practice of the recent past. The primacy of Conference was emphasised, and NUM leadership undertook to make itself more accountable to the membership. The new era would be one of resolute resistance to closures, militant wage campaigning, and a demand for a massive expansion of coal output. Various unfulfilled Conference resolutions were also resurrected and pressed on the NCB once more. Thus a demand for retirement at 55, for higher severance payments, and for other benefits would be added to the negotiating agenda in all future bargaining. These plans to revitalise NUM suffered a setback when a ballot on strike action in pursuit of an improved pay offer failed to endorse action in November 1982.[5] Three weeks later, the NCB announced it intended to close 60 collieries over the next eight years, giving exhaustion of reserves as the reason.

The disputes over pay and pit closures came to a head in 1984. In September 1983, the NCB offered NUM a 5.2% increase on grade rates. The NUM rejected the wage offer and began an overtime ban, asserting that the wage offer was conditional on pit closures, though the NCB denied this. At the beginning of March 1984 there were a number of strikes in Yorkshire and Scotland. On 1 March the NCB announced that Cortonwood should cease production, subject to discussions within the Colliery Review Procedure. On 5 March 11 out of 16 pits were on strike in South Yorkshire, and the following day NUM decided to call a strike across the whole of Yorkshire. Following a meeting with the Board, the NEC of NUM then decided that, in view of the strike in Yorkshire, they should endorse the decision of the Yorkshire NUM to strike, and that they would also endorse the actions of any NUM Area deciding to support the Yorkshire strike.

No national ballot took place, despite attempts by NUM to get all Areas out on strike. There then followed mass picketing throughout the coalfields which was so intense at some pits that no safety cover was possible. Pits in Nottingham, Leicestershire, South Derbyshire, Warwickshire, Cumbria, and the open cast mines continued working as did a few pits in Lancashire, North Wales, and Staffordshire, but those in Scotland, Northumberland and Durham, Yorkshire, South Wales, North Derbyshire, and Kent all closed.

Following the emergence of mass picketing, NUM in South Wales had their assets sequestered for breaching an injunction (restraining picketing at Port Talbot and Llanwern steel works) and refusing to pay a fine.

Subsequently, NUM's national funds were sequestered for breaching an injunction (restraining the leaders of NUM from describing the strike as 'official') and refusing to pay a fine. This led to elaborate international litigation and negotiation in attempts to locate and obtain possession of these funds, some of which had been transferred abroad before the strike. A group of working miners then started a case which led the Court to remove the Trustees of NUM's funds and place control of their assets in the hands of a Receiver appointed by the Court[6]. The strike lasted a year. There was no negotiated return to work but miners on strike began to drift back to work in early 1985 and, on 5 March, NUM instructed all those still on strike to return to work.

British Coal estimate that the strike cost the industry £1,750 million, about 70 million tonnes in lost coal production, and £10,000 in lost earnings for each miner. For NUM, the costs of the dispute were also severe; the national union is estimated to have lost over £6 million, and NUM Areas in excess of £10 million.[7] Moreover, during the strike, Nottinghamshire and South Derbyshire miners broke away from NUM to form the Union of Democratic Mineworkers (UDM). UDM has subsequently been recognised by British Coal.

Since the strike, industrial relations within the industry have not improved markedly. About 1 million tonnes of production were lost through strikes in both 1985/6 and 1986/7, and 4.5 million were lost in 1987/8. The high 1987/8 figure was the effect of an overtime ban called by NUM (between September 1987 and March 1988) as part of a campaign against the Code of Conduct and Disciplinary Procedures for Mineworkers which British Coal revised following the emergence of UDM. NACODS was also involved in a short strike (January to February 1988), and there were 329 other short stoppages.

There are various reasons why these poor relations persisted. The first follows from the support given by British Coal to UDM. British Coal recognised UDM when the strike ended, and terminated the existing conciliation machinery set up in 1946. In 1986 British Coal attempted to reach agreement with all unions to a new conciliation arrangement which would include both UDM and APEX before negotiations took place over the 1986 wage award. UDM agreed to the new scheme, but NUM refused and still refuses to agree the basis on which any wage offers for miners might be negotiated. No wage negotiations between NUM and British Coal have taken place for those units where NUM miners are in a majority, and British Coal has unilaterally applied the terms of UDM negotiated settlements to all miners for the time being. Additionally, British Coal has implemented its closure programme and taken other measures to raise productivity which in some cases appear to have been unpopular (Richardson and Wood, 1989).

2   Structure and government

The unusual feature of NUM is its federal structure which has its roots
in the Miners' Federation of Great Britain. Basically, NUM was grafted
onto numerous older local unions or Constituent Associations (CAs) and
mineworkers given dual membership of the national union and their local
CA. NUM's Constitution defines the spheres of authority of each part of
the union, but the CAs are registered separately as trade unions with the
Certification Officer and hold their own funds. Most of the CAs are
organised as Areas of the union, but some are not.

While the rule book provides the National Executive Committee with
considerable powers over these Areas, it has no authority over the separate funds of either the branches or the CAs. Hence, although Areas and
branches are subject to the authority of 'the Union and shall comply at
all times with the directions of the NEC and Conference' (NUM Rules)
it cannot use the 8% of weekly contributions levied by branches, nor can
it force any CA to merge.

The principle of federalism is therefore reinforced by contribution
arrangements. The national union receives a set fee per member (0.75%
of average earnings of face workers) and the CAs levy a separate subscription at a rate fixed by its members. As many of these CAs are the descend-
ants of old mining unions and had sizeable memberships for long periods,
substantial funds have been built up in a number of cases. This has been
further aided by the division of financial responsibilities. These require
the national union to meet many of the administrative costs of the Areas
including salaries of officials and staff, and office expenses including rents,
rates, and other running costs. Much of the union's total income is spent
in the running of the Areas by the national union. In the past this gave
the Areas little incentive to be concerned with cost efficiencies. Meanwhile,
they use their own membership income and that generated through social
clubs to provide welfare facilities and generate their own reserves.

The NEC also appears to have very little authority over organisational
structure, the rule book simply saying 'The NEC shall keep under review
the organisation of the Union and shall make appropriate recommendations to Conference from time to time.' The Area structure of NUM dates
back to 1943, when it had a membership of 750,000, and it is now rather
out of date. Ideally, the NEC would like to reduce the number of Areas
by amalgamations from 18 to six in line with contraction in the industry
and decline of members. However, some CA's have been unenthusiastic
about organisational change because, amongst other things, they would
not agree where a new Area office, which would now have to be shared
between several CAs, should be located. Each CA had become accus-
tomed to having its own Area office. According to the rule book 'Conference shall have the power to create, dissolve, merge, combine, or amalgate

Areas and the NEC shall prescribe the rules of any new Areas so created. . .', but it has no authority to force CAs to merge.

In recent years there has been some agreement in principle to a reduction in the number of Area Associations. For example, the five CAs in Northumberland and Durham (Durham Area NUM, Durham Mechanics Group 1 Area, Durham Enginemen Group 1 Area, Northumberland Mechanics Group 1 Area, Northumberland NUM) have agreed to the formation of a new North East Area Association, but concomitant proposals to merge into a single CA could not find agreement. The two Scottish associations (Scottish Area NUM and the Scottish Colliery Enginemen, Boilermen and Tradesmen's Association) also agreed in principle to share a new single Scottish Area office, but formally rejected a merger in a ballot in 1988.

3   Financial performance

Given the formal division of financial rights and responsibilities it is not surprising that the CAs have performed rather differently from the national union in financial terms. Three sets of figures are presented here, one set for the national union only, another set for all the CAs, and an aggregate for NUM as a whole. The figures referring to the CAs have been calculated by subtracting data for the national union from the aggregate data published by the Certification Office.[8]

It is worth noting that variations in accounting practice over time and between CAs mean that the accuracy of the figures may be disputed. Furthermore, aggregate data are not available for 1984, thus no figures for the CAs can be calculated; only the national union submitted a set of accounts to the statutory authority in that year.

The membership of NUM has declined dramatically since 1982 but the scale and extent of the decline is difficult to assess from the data supplied by the national union. Figure 8.1 shows two sets of membership figures, one supplied to the Certification Office, and the other to the TUC. The TUC series records the decline in full members while that supplied to the Certification Office includes Retured, Limited, Associate, and Honorary Members. The membership structure of NUM is more complex than that of other unions, and retired members (some of whom are the spouses of former miners) or unemployed members have traditionally played an active role in the union. This is no doubt because historically the CAs have always provided attractive benefits for those who are either retired or unemployed. According to the TUC series, membership in the union has declined by more than half since 1982 from approximately 245,000 to 53,000 in 1989 while over the same period the number of pits worked

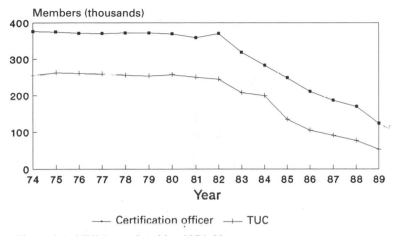

Figure 8.1. NUM membership, 1974–89

by British Coal has fallen by over 50%. The key break point on membership is 1982, but because of the importance of the 1984 strike for union finances it is useful to consider the periods before and after the strike separately.

The position to 1984

Figure 8.2 shows that the national union and CAs both experienced declines in income during the mid 1970s, but then were able to recover. Contribution income fell in real terms because it was not index-linked and, to rectify this, contribution levels were linked to basic pay in 1977. Real income per member rose from an average of approximately £30 between 1974 and 1977 to £41 in 1979. Membership stability up to 1982 meant that the national union was able to cover its largest item of expenditure – administration – out of membership income and that income consistently exceeded total expenditure between 1976 and 1984.

Because the CAs were less dependent on subscription income, membership trends were less important for their finances. While 90% of national union income came from members, only 61% of that of the CAs came from that source between 1975 and 1982. During the period up to 1984 the CAs generated surpluses each year except 1978 when a negligible loss was incurred. It is also notable that their total income frequently exceeded that of the national union.

Figure 8.3 confirms the disparity in wealth between the two. The bulk of NUM's wealth was held by the Areas which had accumulated the

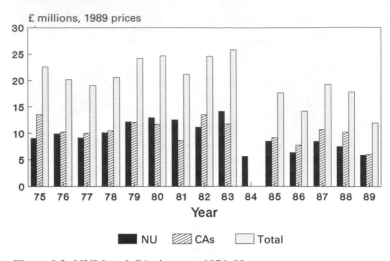

Figure 8.2. NUM and CAs income, 1974–89

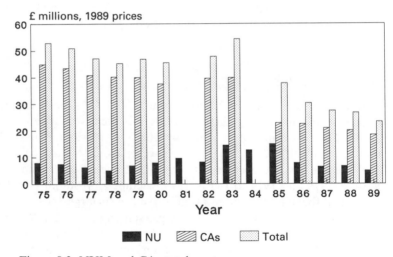

Figure 8.3. NUM and CAs total assets

contributions of past generations of miners and held these mainly in investments. By contrast, the national union's wealth had been built up since the war. At the beginning of the 1970s NUM was, in aggregate, one of the wealthiest unions in Britain, measured in assets per member (Latta, 1972) and it remained well-cushioned up to 1984. The breakdown of

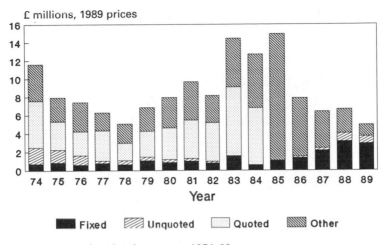

Figure 8.4. National union assets, 1974–89

national union assets is given in Figure 8.4. It can be seen that the unions quoted assets disappeared during the dispute. The large amount of 'other' income in 1983 came from the sale of London property. In that year also, the union sold all of its equities, subsequently compromising its capacity to increase investment income.

The position since 1985

From the onset of the dispute, the financial position of NUM began to change dramatically. Principally, this was because of the loss of virtually all normal membership income during the strike, followed by the pit closure programme which led to a rapid loss of membership: between 1985 and 1988 membership declined by over 50%. The creation of UDM has also deprived the union of income. At the end of 1988, UDM claimed 20,000 members, and, although this figure is disputed by NUM as an inflated one, it remains the case that all UDM members would have been NUM members prior to 1985.

The net result is that the national union ran a deficit for every year after the dispute until the end of 1988 (Figure 8.5). The deficit would have been much greater but for certain extraordinary items including donations, a rebate from the Mineworkers' Trust in 1985,[9] and a settlement in excess of £1 million in connection with a breach of trust action from certain banks in 1987. In 1987 also, the national union received a tax rebate of over £1 million from the Inland Revenue which accounted

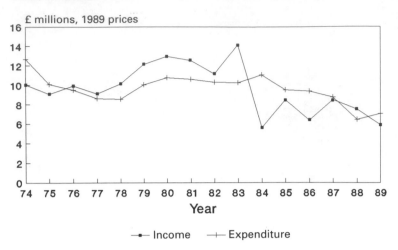

Figure 8.5. National union income and expenditure, 1974–89
Note: Quoted assets at book value

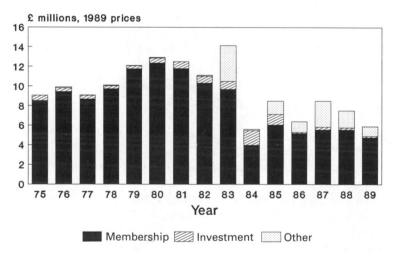

Figure 8.6. National union income, 1974–89

for much of the 31% of total income from 'other' sources in that year. Figure 8.6 shows a breakdown of the components of income for the national union.

The deficits recorded by the national union would also have been much worse but for the success in controlling expenditure from 1982 onwards.

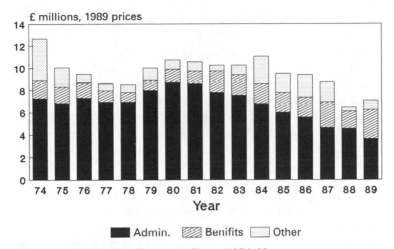

Figure 8.7. National union expenditure, 1974–89

This is shown in Figure 8.7. The key to this was the control exerted over administrative costs, principally in the running of the head office and the Area offices. Many of the measures designed to tighten expenditure control were introduced by Scargill on becoming President, including the introduction of new accounting systems and the appointment of a new finance officer and chief executive.

For the Areas, the effects of the dispute were also considerable, but because of the federal division of funds they were able to recover more quickly than the national union. The dispute appears to have cost the Areas in the region of £14 million at 1985 values, or approximately 50% of their pre-strike wealth. However, they were not subject to the litigation which led to the national union being placed in receivership and this, as we show below, enabled NUM to continue to prosecute the dispute despite the court action. Since the dispute, the Areas have also been proportionately less affected by the loss of membership income and did not experience the same pressure to reduce administrative costs as the national union. While the wealth of the Areas has declined since the ending of the dispute, they may be better off in terms of assets per member than in the early 1980s because of the dramatic fall in membership.

The picture since 1983 has therefore altered dramatically. Despite reducing spending by nearly 30% in four years, the national union has suffered a major liquidity problem through the loss of almost all income during the dispute, protracted difficulties created by the receivership until 1986, plus the sustained fall in membership from 1983 onwards, particularly after the end of the strike. Only at the end of 1989 was it able to report a small surplus. While it had assets worth over £5 million, this was mainly in property and could not easily be used to solve its cash-flow difficulties. It was also not easy to resolve the difficulties because of the national union's responsibilities under the constitution for the running of the whole union, including the Areas. Nor could it gain access to the still considerable wealth of the Areas. Meanwhile it faces a future where continuing membership losses are likely and hence persistent pressure on the operating finances are likely.

4   Financial management

In discussing the arrangements for financial management within NUM, one is aware, because of the publicity during and since the strike, of the difference between the formal systems embodied in the constitution, rules, and practices of the NEC and the less formal financial arrangements which arose prior to the strike and which have continued since – at least until the Lightman investigation. Since the formal arrangements provide necessary background for understanding the informal, we begin there. Throughout, we focus on financial arrangements in the national union except where clearly specified to the contrary.

The NEC is formally responsible for the financial management of the national union, but the Finance and General Purposes Committee (FGPC) of the NEC is more intimately involved. The NEC however has no authority over the money of the constituent associations, and in fact the national union knows nothing of these funds except what is disclosed to the statutory authority since the constituent associations are not required to report their financial position to the national union.

The President of the union is chair of the FGPC and the General Secretary acts as secretary. The office of General Secretary includes that of Treasurer, which carries with it the formal responsibility for preparing balance sheets for the NEC and the auditors. Under the authority of the NEC there is a finance department employing a fully qualified accountant and four other members of staff. The finance department uses a computer and off-the-shelf spreadsheet packages for account management. It is the only computerised deparment of the union; it is also the only non-policy-making department. Additionally there are three Trustees, appointed by Conference who are subject to the direction of the NEC and ultimately Conference.

Upwards of 95% of income from working miners comes into the Area offices through check-off. Check-off arrangements have been in operation since 1949, and the costs to the union are now small (£11,100 p.a). This fee was fixed in 1949, and has not been changed since. About 3,000 limited

members, who are essentially unemployed miners, pay half normal rate
by hand to the Area office. About 92% of income from Full Membership
of the national union comes from British Coal, but NUM has members
in licensed mines, and some of these pay cash directly to the branch. The
national union experiences few instances of arrears, but when they occur
they tend to happen in the licensed mines where members are on short-
term contracts and may be in the union for only a few months. The
national union does not earn any income from Honorary members, nor
from retired members; retired members contribute to the CAs according
to the particular benefit or welfare scheme to which they belong.

NUM has no computerised membership register, but has been in negotiation with British Coal about one. Membership data are held in the
Areas, and Area offices receive a monthly exceptions list of members
and subscription payments, and a full computer printout quarterly. This
information is then handed down to branch secretaries to make manual
adjustments. Area officials are responsible for transferring the national
union's contribution income to the national union, but they can in effect
sit on this money for two months.

The contribution rate for a full member is 0.75% of the average earnings
of surface workers. On top of this contribution to the national union,
miners will pay a levy to their CA and sometimes a branch levy as well.
For example, in South Wales members pay £1.40 per week to the national
union and £1.40 per week to the CA, the South Wales NUM. For COSA
the white-collar section, the subscription is £1.40 per week to the national
union and 30p per week to the CA.

The contribution rate was linked to pay in the mid 1970s in order to
overcome the difficulties of revision. The national union has not yet
needed to adjust the subscription proportion, but it could happen should
the average earnings of surface workers go down in real terms. For the
higher paid face workers, the contribution rate is low in relation to their
earnings. Should the national union wish to adjust the contribution rate
the NEC would have to seek the approval of Conference. If the contribution rate were changed, this could be done without reference to what
other unions charge because NUM has no major competitors in the industry. The only slight exception to this is among white-collar workers.
APEX, now part of GMB, has a few members in the white-collar grades
and only charged 95p per week in 1989.

Expenditure in the national union is now very tightly controlled by a
budgeting system. This is because the losses inflicted by the strike on the
national union, and the dramatic contraction of the industry since 1983
have rendered the existing administrative structure of the national union
extremely expensive to maintain. The national union has traditionally

covered all the costs of Area administration, including staff salaries, rent, rates, lighting, and heating so that, although most offices are owned by the Areas, the national union pays to operate them. Additionally, branches receive a branch retention of 8% of their contribution. With the decline in membership, particularly since the strike, the national union has found itself in the position of having to remit the bulk of its income back to the Areas to maintain an administrative structure which is unnecessarily large for the national union's present requirements, and it began to take steps to reform the situation after the dispute.

In September 1986, it was agreed that the national union would not pay any monies to any Area in excess of the net contributions submitted to the national union. This was to remedy the problem that some Areas were, in effect, taking more out of the national union than they put in, particularly the five Area offices in the north-east. Other Areas, such as Yorkshire, were effectively subsidising them. Subsequently, the five north-east CAs agreed to share a single Area office between them under pressure from the national union. At the same time the national union began to freeze posts which fell vacant, and in 1987 it was able to lose seven officials and some 15 members of staff in the Area through voluntary redundancy. However, membership losses and reorganisation mean the union still carries more officials than it needs.

The effect of restricting payouts to the total value of net contributions for each Area simply resulted in many Areas making a zero contribution to the national union. Thus, the NEC attempted to reduce chargeability through the development of imprest accounts, but this proved inadequate, so at the beginning of 1988 the NEC imposed a budget on each Area imprest account to prevent them from spending up to the limit of their membership contributions. Some of the organisational changes that the NEC now has in progress emerged out of a report commissioned by (then) Peat Marwick at the beginning of 1983, and an internal report undertaken by the national union's accountant in 1986.

The budgeting process has also been tightened to control Area spending. The total budget is fixed by making a prediction of income, estimating expenditure based on past or historic costs, and building in an allowance for a surplus, which acts as a buffer in case income is overestimated. The budget is set by the finance department, approved by the FGPC and referred to the NEC. The national union can predict its subscription income insofar as it knows how much the contribution will be for each Full Member from the accounts of British Coal, but the union's main difficulty comes in estimating the size of the Full Membership for the coming year, and in recent years the decline in membership has been more dramatic than expected. A further set of reforms has been designed to change the federal balance of responsibilities in the national union's favour. These have included proposals to shift office running costs to the CAs, for the latter to share more resources among themselves, and for the CAs to assist with the financing of severance/redundancy pay by providing the national union with interest-free loans.

A budget is estimated for each Area of the union, and for each department within the national union. There is a separate budget for capital equipment such as computers, which covers stated items that are costed in detail, but the allocation to each department of the national union is to some extent flexible. For example, some funds allocated to the finance department, which are not needed, can be transferred to education. Each cost centre has two months to appeal before the FGPC finally agrees each budget. Areas claim against their imprest account every month, and money is transferred to them from the national union. At the same time they are informed how much is left in the budget.

The finance department monitors the budgets constantly, and the NEC reviews the situation quarterly. Areas that cannot live within their budgets have to make a very good case before the FGPC for additional funding, and sometimes they may have to make up the shortfall from their own funds. However, the national union has made no attempt to claim monies belonging to the CAs because it is a common belief within NUM that such an effort would prove fruitless. In many CAs retired members are active and, as far as they are concerned, the accumulated funds belong to them. Moreover, as the Full Membership declines and retired members die, the value of this money to each remaining member of the CA increases; for example, Northumberland in 1988 had only 12,000 members but assets worth over £1 million, and this is can be a source of resistance to merger within the CAs.

The NEC is formally responsible for investments but, since 1983 when equities were sold, the national union has suffered a serious cash-flow problem and has therefore had no surplus to invest. Most of the cash in the General Fund and in the Political Fund is invested with Unity Trust or in the money markets.

Informal arrangements arose prior to the dispute but in anticipation of it and of the sequestration of assets which might follow; receivership was not, apparently, anticipated (Lightman, 1990: 14). Informality was not the norm. Immediately prior to the dispute in March 1984, the Miners' Solidarity Fund, aimed at alleviating hardship among striking miners and their families, and the Mineworkers' Trust, intended as an educational and welfare fund, were established. The latter was vested with £1 million in NUM assets and was established by decision of the FGPC on 7 March 1984.

Informality was necessitated by the appointment of a Sequestrator in October and the Receiver in November 1984. Thereafter, any monies from whatever source, whether members, other unions, or sympathisers, designed to assist maintenance of the fabric of the union or to prosecute the dispute had to be indirectly and confidentially donated to avoid the attention of the two officials. The union's formal revenues and assets were frozen, but its expenditures remained – presumably – high.

To deal with this problem, two trusts were established by the President. The first, the Miners' Action Committee Fund (MACF), operated on an entirely *cash* basis from October 1984 to October 1989. Its sources of revenue included other unions and sympathisers in the UK and overseas, including the CGT and mining unions in Europe and elsewhere; revenue was approximately £1.2 million from these sources. The second, which did have a bank account, was an NUM/IMO Fund, established in January 1985, the revenues for which came both from the MACF and from overseas organisations, some unspecified (Lightman, 1990: 23–9, 40–6).

Lightman acknowledges the impossibility of an accurate assessment of the workings of these two informal funds. The report focuses only on the national union, not on Areas, although funds from outside the union were routed through Area accounts to the national union. There may have been external monies retained in Area accounts. A second problem is that overseas donors, such as the IMO, refused financial information on sources and applications of funds. A third is that, since many of the transactions of these trusts were cash and in secret: 'there is no way of ascertaining what amount of cash may have passed through Mr. Scargill's hands' (Lightman, 1990: 42). Lightman is able to conclude that: 'Since the beginning of the sequestration, the union has in effect operated two sets of accounts, the official accounts properly administered and audited, and the unofficial accounts operated by the National Officials [in effect Mr Scargill] with no supervision or control' (1990: 125).

There emerged a system of almost byzantine complexity. Lightman lists 70 'official' accounts of NUM and 17 'unofficial' ones disclosed by Scargill to the Inquiry. Several were overseas. Many of the unofficial accounts continued to operate until December 1989, although the receivership terminated in June 1986. Lightman was particularly concerned about the continuance and continued non-disclosure of the existence of these accounts to the NEC by NUM. His view was that, in 1989, NUM funds remained tied up and hidden in an NUM/IMO trust account, due to 'Mr. Scargill's failure to distinguish between the IMO and NUM' (1990: 43). Although he could not totally identify all revenue sources, the movement of money from the MACF and his findings concerning the intention behind donations from Soviet miners led him to this conclusion.

The terms of reference of the Lightman Inquiry focused on the possibility and subsequent use of donations from Libya and the USSR to assist the strike, as well as certain issues concerned with the repayment of home loans to national officials. Several of these issues do not concern us here and involve amounts of money so small as to have no bearing on the overall financial position of the union. However, Lightman does argue that the failure to wind up the informal accounts and return the money to the formal ones had to do with Scargill's concern to encourage the rationalisation of the union; it would not assist such rationalisation if the national union were to appear financially healthy. Lightman professes to believe that: 'one reason for the non-disclosure of the (overseas assets) was the urgent need to rationalize the structure of the union, integrate and cut costs and expenses. Only financial stringencies would persuade the union to agree to these measures and disclosure of that asset would have destroyed this impression and this scheme' (1990: 47).

On this reading of events, systems of informal financial management devised to protect the national union's funds from sequestration have subsequently performed a role in altering the political system, much as was suggested in Chapter 4.

The Lightman Report suggests that the national union may be somewhat richer than the figures given to year end 1989 might suggest. However, the amounts involved – less than £2 million – do not alter the overall picture of post-strike financial decline, nor do they alter the picture of financial differences between the Areas and the national union. Whatever the internal political or legal implications of its findings, NUM remains in some financial difficulty.

5   Finance and strategy

One can discern two phases of financial management in the period under consideration. Up to the strike, the union was amongst the wealthiest, in both absolute and per capita terms. Financial issues were dealt with on a decentralised basis. There were occasional problems, particularly with inflation in the 1970s, but the financial situation was comfortable overall. As a result, financial matters were not important influences on the strategy of the union. Typically, the union's financial matters were dealt with quickly, in private session at the Delegate Conference. There was no formal report from the FGPC to the Conference.

The change occurs in 1984, the year of the strike. However, one might argue that the financial distress suffered by the union during and after the dispute was exacerbated by the unfortunate coincidence of a move out of equities in 1983 to fund the move of headquarters, followed by the costs of the strike and sequestration. At the Special Conference that year financial matters were important. An Area Accounting Procedures manual was approved 'to provide for standardisation of accounting practice at area level and better monitoring of imprest expenditure'.[10] A new building fund was established, into which the union's realised equity assets were placed, to generate funds for the new head office.

Initially, at least, there was considerable concern expressed by the General Secretary about the costs of the dispute:

Through a prolonged strike the Union obviously has no income at all and it follows that, as employers employing 300 personnel, that during the strike there has been a substantial drain on this Union's resources, it is around £115,000 per week. It follows... that we can quite easily in a struggle of this enormity finish without any assets at all in the general fund of our union. It may well be that during the course of this year we shall have to be contemplating how we can best replenish our resources... We will have to face it realistically in order to preserve the financial viability of the organization.[11]

Subsequently, reports from the Finance and General Purposes Committee feature annually in the NEC Report to Conference. Their concerns are consistently with the control of expenditure, the reorganisation of the union to achieve economies, and the process of recovery of union monies, initially from the Receiver and subsequently from the Inland Revenue.

The two phases are, therefore, distinguished by the primacy of financial matters rather than by differences in the influence of financial matters on strategy formulation. In the first phase, financial matters are unimportant. After the strike, in the second phase, it became very important to realise economies in administration and to regularise area accounting procedures in order to maintain viability and solvency. However, in this second phase, the union's policies, for example towards the policies of British Coal or UDM, remained those of the pre-strike period. It does not appear to be the case that the union leadership would sacrifice its policies in order to maintain independent existence.

Since Arthur Scargill's election to the Presidency of NUM in 1981 with 70% of the vote, and his supporter Peter Heathfield to the position of General Secretary in 1984, NUM's overall strategy has been clearly delineated. As the leaders of the national union they have broadly pursued confrontational policies against British Coal to stop what are seen as politically inspired moves to reduce the size of the industry and reestablish managerial authority.

Security of employment is demanded through ending the closure programme of British Coal with a national pay and bonus system to unite mineworkers in different areas. To overcome the slow contraction of the industry, a four day week for all miners has been demanded and a permanent ban on overtime working. Much of this is in the syndicalist tradition of the Miners' Federation at the turn of the century.

Implicit in these policies are political objectives although NUM has tended to rely more on industrial power than political influence. NUM has proclaimed itself as in the vanguard of class action against the government's economic policy and, in particular, has campaigned for reforms to energy policy which would end the reliance on nuclear power generation. This clearly has sectional implications as it would, if adopted, result in raising coal demand once more. For similar reasons, NUM has also campaigned against coal imports.

However, despite the rhetoric, the union's failure to control the rate of contraction in the industry, changes to the pay system emphasising local variation, and recognition of UDM have driven it towards a survival strategy in financial terms. The elements of this have included cost cutting through moving to Sheffield (this was also politically desirable as it relocated the national union in Scargill's power base). The union has reduced the number of full-time officials as the number of members dropped; it has improved accounting systems and introduced budgeting with the advice of its auditors; it has tried to raise financial awareness among members by greater publicity of its position and it has tried to offload some of the costs it currently bears for Areas on to them. Most importantly, its plan to regroup Areas and reduce the total number is designed to reduce operating costs and improve the asset base of the national body through the transfer of accumulated funds.

Subscriptions pose a rather different problem. As members subscribe to Areas as well, and as Areas are the delivery mechanism for services and benefits, the national union is perceived as a bureaucratic overhead by members, even if, in practice, it funds much of the Area work. This is one factor the union would like to get over more accurately, but finds difficult, consequently raising subscriptions would meet with some resistance. In the longer term, the continuing decline in membership means the union will have to pursue merger. Although its financial strategy has improved cash-flow, the obstacles to reasserting the former degree of power it possessed and the devastating effects of the 1984–5 dispute on its asset base appear to have made continuing independence extremely difficult.

9   The GMB: merger and financial reform

1   Historical background

GMB[1] is currently the second largest union in the UK, following the merger between GMBATU and APEX in 1989. GMBATU itself was a relatively new creation, following from the merger between GMWU and the Boilermakers' union in 1982, but both unions had a much longer history. The numerically larger GMWU was founded by merger of three municipal and labouring unions in 1924, but its roots go back to the gasworkers' militancy of the 1880s. In the post-war period, GMWU membership has been concentrated in six sectors; namely, engineering, food drink and tobacco, gas, chemicals, electricity, and local authority employment. However, it also has members in the NHS, in the water industry, in textiles and, more recently, in catering and distribution. It is strongest in the north-east and north-west.

GMB competes with a wide range of both public- and private-sector unions but most notably with the Transport and General Workers' Union (T&G). The older GMWU differed in a number of respects from T&G, most notably in its attitude towards shop stewards and industrial action. During the 1960s, when T&G were decentralising activities towards shop stewards, GMWU was involved in a number of conflicts over steward independence, most notably at Ford and Pilkingtons (Eaton and Gill, 1983: 317). At the time the union had a rather staid, right-wing image and remained highly centralised.

Unlike T&G, GMWU was relatively unattractive as a merger partner, in part because of its image but more because of its strong regional structure. It was, in Undy *et al.*'s terms 'restrictive-passive' in its orientation to growth, compared with the 'positive-expansionist' approach of T&G. Comparative growth rates reflected this; between 1965 and 1975, GMWU grew by 10.9% compared with T&G's 28.6% (Undy *et al.*, 1981: 128). This reflected poorer performance in both recruitment and merger. Their description of the union before 1975 is of some interest:

the GMWU in the 1960s was 'benefit oriented' rather than 'service oriented' – it
was primarily concerned to provide substantial benefits to existing members, such
as educational facilities, convalescent and holiday home and friendly benefits,
rather than servicing existing or potential membership in the industrial sphere. . .
At times, this benefit oriented approach led the GMWU to emphasise financial
solvency at the expense of membership. . . members or potential members who
threatened to cost substantially more than they contributed were not usually
welcome. (Undy et al., 1981: 134)[2]

In an attempt to change this pattern in the 1960s, branch administrative
officers were introduced and, in 1974, the (then) new General Secretary
David Basnett introduced the grade of district officer, primarily responsible for recruitment. A higher officer/membership ratio developed and
the union analysed in some depth the factors which might support future
growth (see below).

One major change was a move towards merger activity. In the early
1970s, GMWU benefitted from transfers of membership from a number
of small unions. However, larger mergers were to follow. The merger with
the Boilermakers took place in 1982, that with the Amalgamated Textile
Union in 1986 and that with APEX in 1989. The union merged with
NUTGW in 1991. Together with the formation of a white-collar section,
MATSA, in 1972, these moves may be seen as part of a long-term strategy
to move the union out of its traditional, declining, job territories. The
union anticipates a merger a year for the next five years.

2   Government and structure

The basis of the GMB structure in 1989 was still the old regional structure
of GMWU, in which powerful regional secretaries appointed officers,
decided on branch organisation and structure and controlled finances. In
the past, they also dominated the General Council, Executive Council,
and Annual Congress, the three main governing bodies of the union.
(Undy et al., 1981: 53). Both the leadership of the union, the General
Secretary, and the lay organisations of shop stewards and branches were
heavily constrained in their activities by regional power.

Matters have, however, changed considerably recently. In 1976, the
former General Council and national executive were abolished and
replaced by the Central Executive Council (CEC), the ruling body
between annual Congresses. This CEC consisted of an elected chairman,
the General Secretary, the ten regional secretaries, and two members from
each of the ten regions, elected by the regional councils. Further reforms
took place in 1987. Currently, the CEC is composed of three GMWU

representatives, from each region, who must be members of the regional council, three representatives from the Boilermakers' section, one woman from each region elected to a reserved seat and the General Secretary and Treasurer. Elections are held every four years.[3]

Beneath this, there have been further changes. Since 1969, there have been regular industrial conferences for the major sections of membership, 18 in total. Since the merger with the Boilermakers, there have been several rule changes designed to assist the integration of the two structures. Currently there are two sections to the union, and plans exist to integrate GMWU and Boilermakers' regional and district structures; these are currently specified within the rule book (rule 45). In addition, further structural changes are planned in 1989 and 1990 to integrate the APEX organisation with the GMBATU regional structure. More mergers are anticipated in the future, which, if successful, may further alter the union's system of government. The objective is to develop a sectional structure which is 'amalgamation-friendly' and gives a clear identity to the various industrial or occupational interest groups.

In short, there have been substantial organisational changes in the period under study which, coincidentally, is the period of office of the two most recent General Secretaries, David Basnett (1973–85) and John Edmonds (1985–). A common thread throughout the period has been the General Secretaries' concern to gain membership, or reverse its decline, through recruitment or merger, both of which have – given the historical structure and culture of the union – required organisational change. The drive for growth originated, as we shall show below, partly in financial considerations but also in a concern with the union's wider influence in the labour movement. Under Edmonds' leadership, one might almost say that mergers have become a device for leveraging organisational change and that such change has involved the movement of power away from the region on the one hand to the CEC, and the branch on the other. We shall return to this proposition below.

3   Financial performance

Figure 9.1 shows membership trends since 1974. The union benefited from growth in membership from 1975 to 1979, but suffered a steep fall thereafter, only reversed (in 1989) by merger with APEX. Because of the merger with the Boilermakers, 1982 data are unavailable, but it seems likely that only a fraction of the declared membership of the Boilermakers (approximately 115,000 in 1982) found its way on to the GMBATU books. Subsequently, membership decline continued more slowly but steadily from 1983.

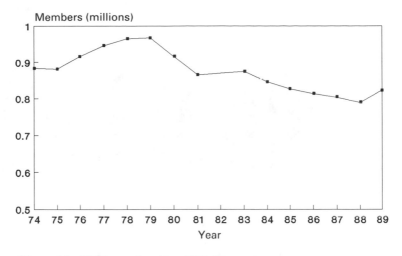

Figure 9.1. GMB membership, 1974–89

One of the problems for GMB is the membership retention ratio. On the union's own figures, it had to recruit 108,305 new members in 1987 in order to report a membership loss of just 10,000. Put crudely, then, 118,000 new members annually were needed to sustain a total of approximately 802,000; this is a turnover of almost 15% per annum. A further complication is that new members tend to be juvenile or part time, i.e., in lower susbscription categories, while departing members are 'Grade 1', high category susbscription payers. In 1987, the union gained almost 10,000 of the former, but lost over 21,000 of the latter.[4] The union defines a category of 'financial membership' which includes part timers but excludes associate and retired members; these non-payers constituted less than 5% of membership during the period in question.

This pattern of loss and change has hit the union's income, which has been broadly static across the period (Figure 9.2). GMB is highly subscription-dependent and this dependency has increased slightly over time. The fact that real membership income was static over the period of growth from 1975 to 1979 and has been stabilised in the period of contraction 1984–8 reflects changes in systems of financial management, discussed below.

Over the period in question, subscriptions for Grade 1 members increased on six occasions. The normal procedure for this required a revision of the rules, which could only occur triennially. Subscriptions are set at rule 17 of the 1987 rule book. In order to avoid such revisions, the

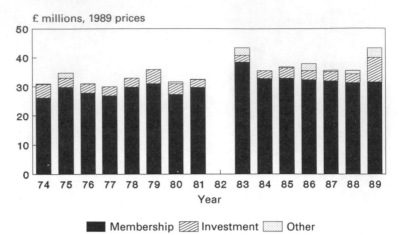

Figure 9.2. GMB income

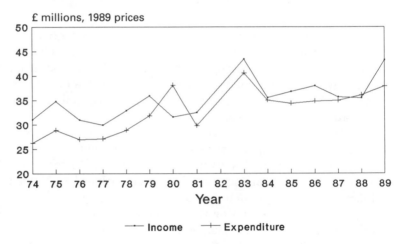

Figure 9.3. GMB income and expenditure

leadership has tried on occasion to move towards indexation of subscriptions. This has proved unpopular, and recent survey evidence indicates that it remains so.[5]

Despite this income problem, the union has remained solvent over the period, with the exception of 1980, the year of the steel strike (Figure 9.3). Expenditure was unusually high that year and income fell. In 1983, the union was rather better at managing the effects of the water dispute;

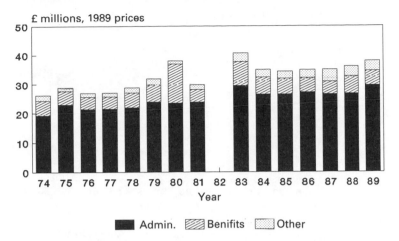

Figure 9.4. GMB expenditure, 1974–89

although expenditure rose, so did income. The higher amounts of 'other income' in 1983 and 1986 are funds of incoming unions.

Figure 9.4 details expenditure. Unusually for large unions, GMB has managed to control administrative expenditure across the period. There has been a fall in total administrative expenditure, mainly due to internal financial reorganisation, since 1983. There has also been a fall in real benefit expenditure, aided by the somewhat unpopular policy of freezing benefit levels or even removing benefit options. Benefits are financially important, because, as a service organisation, GMB has been relatively efficient in controlling administrative expenditure.

Figure 9.5 shows the surplus of membership income over administrative expenditure. Despite this surplus, the union sees itself as unusually labour intensive. The argument has been put at Conference that this follows from the adherence to a regional structure which gives good service but replicates functions. In 1970, staff costs stood at 43% of total administrative expenditure, rising to 47.5% by 1980.[6]

In GMB, total funds and total assets have, in effect, been the same. Both registered steep falls in real terms during the 1970s, and during membership loss to 1981. The influx of the Boilermakers' assets in 1982 clearly raised the overall level, but subsequent asset performance has been better. This may not be unconnected with the move into equities, shown in the disaggregated analysis of Figure 9.7, from 1983 onwards. In addition, some £4.5 million of 'other assets' in 1987 was cash, which previously sat in term deposits but now is put on to the money markets at higher rates of return.[7]

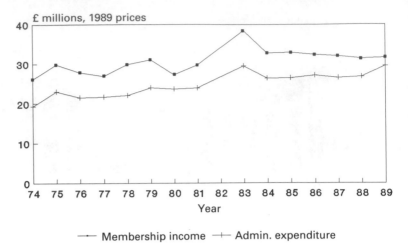

Figure 9.5. GMB membership income and administrative expenditure

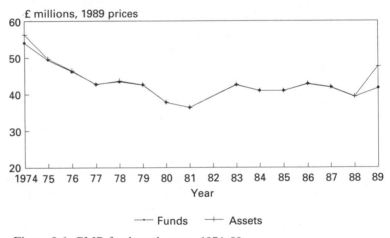

Figure 9.6. GMB funds and assets, 1974–89

The union has been reluctant to 'live off' investment income. In practice, growth in funds across this period came from growth in investment
income rather than that from members' contributions.[8] This was a source
of concern, as the Treasurer remarked to the 1977 Conference:

to maintain the true value of accumulated funds, a substantial part of interest
and dividends must be regularly added to the funds. The union's established
policy of utilizing current contribution income to meet current expenses must be

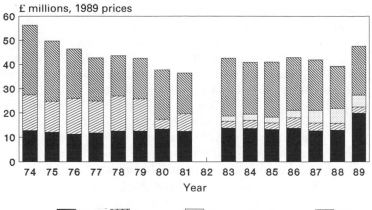

Figure 9.7. GMB assets, 1974–89

maintained and the use of investment income for current expenditures must only be used as short term expediency.[9]

It remained a concern up to 1989:

> The union must begin to accumulate funds rather than living off our investment income, our assets or our spiralling contribution increases as we have had to do in the last ten years. The challenge which has been faced was... to ensure the Union spends within the resources that our members provide for us.[10]

Overall, then, the union has shown some success at cost control and overall income maintenance, but has been less successful, at least until recently, in generating increased members' income and in the management of assets. There appear from the figures to have been changes in investment policy. The next section will analyse their nature.

4   Financial management

Financial management has been a concern of the union leadership across the period in question. The overall financial problems outlined above have set the agenda, but internally the focus has been on subscription levels and yield, the financing of branches, the costs of union administration, and the availability of funds at the centre for investment. Since there has been considerable change to systems of management, it is probably best to deal with the problem chronologically.

In 1976, GMBATU Congress considered a document entitled 'Union Structure and Financial Strategy for the 1980s'. Its concerns were the impact of inflation on union finances and the consequences of changing labour markets and new employment legislation on union policies. It focused on the relatively fragile financial situation of the union, calling for a contribution increase. It outlined the unsatisfactory nature of a nominal, 5p per week part-time contribution rate when the number of part timers was increasing. Equally unsatisfactory was the position where stewards were paid a commission on subscription income, despite the fact that 80% of members were covered by check-off arrangements. As Basnett put it: 'there is already a wide variation in practice between branches and even between regions on the payment to check off stewards for which there is no Executive authority and for which there is no authority in rule'.[11] The Report also discussed possible benefits from computerisation and the more general issue of the balance between a 'benefits orientation' and a 'service orientation'.

The immediate stimuli for the Report were the change to the composition of the Executive, the reporting requirements of the 1974 Trade Union and Labour Relations Act, and the failure of a recent subscription increase to solve the union's financial difficulties. It was not adopted in its entirety, but it provided an agenda for financial discussions in the 1970s.

Contributions were a problem. Congress regularly saw figures indicating the fall in union contribution rates as a percentage of average male manual hourly earnings. In 1964, this figure stood at 27%, but it was down to 14% in 1979 and rose only back to 18% in 1983. The leadership objective, indexation, was not attained, but subscriptions rose every other year from 1977 to 1983, despite the fact that the normal review period, under the rules revision procedure, was triennial. In addition, much of the union's income was, and remained for some time, unavailable to head office. As late as 1988, 17.5% of income was remitted to branches as commission; head office had no control over how this was spent. Fifty per cent of total income stayed with the regions. In total, then, head office saw only 36.5% of total union income in 1988.

The 1989 Conference debate on subscriptions and services indicated some of the problems. On the one hand:

The Union continues to run a substantial deficit on its contribution income... it is estimated that the contribution income deficit for 1988 will be in excess of £2 million compared to the estimated deficit forecast in last year's financial review of £1.16 million.

On the other hand, there was perceived membership resistance:

there is little point in suggesting to our members that a further contribution increase is needed when the Union still seems incapable of managing the finances of the Union even after a contribution increase has only just been authorised and implemented.[12]

The control over this expenditure at branch level thus assumed considerable priority. As the 1980 discussion document noted, trade unions tend to use one of two distinctive financial administrative control mechanisms; either the rules regulate the level of honoraria to specific named branch officers or the branch retains or is remitted a specific percentage of membership income for administrative purposes.[13]

One of the main problems perceived with the former was that it allowed branch secretaries to vote for subscription increases – and thus in effect for a rise in commission payments – at Conference. GMB has moved in the 1980s from the former to the latter. Rule 35 of the 1987 rule book states: 'a Branch shall receive a commission quarterage which shall consist of quarterly payments made by the Region to the Branch of 7.5% of all check off contributions attributable to the Branch'. From this percentage, employers' check-off costs, to a maximum of 2.5%, are deducted. Branches must spend their commissions within the quarter. They cannot use the commission for benefit or political purposes, or to finance 'activities which are intended to circumvent policies of the union'. In other respects, they are free to spend it as they wish.

However, this alone was not enough. The financial position deteriorated in 1983 and 1984 (see Figure 9.3) and a major review of the union's financial strategy and performance was put to the 1984 Conference. *Decision 84* focused on several objectives, specifically the maintenance of adequate income, cost control, enhancement of recruitment, the provision of a clear management structure within the union, and the integration of the Boilermakers' membership. The main proposals fell into the following categories:

(a) *Finances and contributions*

The concern was that membership income was not covering total expenditure. The reliance on investment income was unwelcome and the option of liquidating assets was seen as unwise. The document proposed further subscription increases, but not in part-time rates.

(b) *Cost reduction*

Benefits were to be frozen or cut, officer and staff costs reduced, the education services were to be concentrated on one site, and regional operating costs were to be reviewed.

(c) *New officer structure*

The relative failure of recruitment, the inflexibility of resources, and the need for better officer motivation prompted proposals for a new grading structure and the movement of officers between regions.

(d) *Specialist services*

The allocation of further resources to services such as education, legal, pensions and health and safety, which were seen to be an important part of the union's image and services, were proposed.

(e) *Regional and administrative structure*

The main issue here was cost: 'The regionalised pattern of financial and administrative organization in the GMB is one of the reasons why staff costs are substantially higher than other equivalent unions. There is duplication. Some concentration (not necessarily at head office) of administrative functions could save substantial staff costs in the administrative and financial area.' However, the outdated nature of regional boundaries and the lack of a management structure were also important.

(f) *Branch and workplace organisation*

The structure and distribution of branches, the role of branch secretaries and stewards, and the level of membership involvement were all considered.

(g) *Head office structure*

Once more, cost was an issue, but the question of the role of the General Secretary/Treasurer was also discussed; 'the reponsibility. . . covers far too wide a span'.

(h) *Political activity*

The union's role and expenditure within the TUC and Labour Party and internationally were reviewed.

(i) *Amalgamations*

Feeling that 'Many of the difficulties of British trade unionism have resulted from competitive unionism', and that previous merger attempts had not been successful, the document suggests a 'more determined approach to the opportunities available'.

Much of *Decision 84* was discursive rather than implementable. Nevertheless, the document was adopted in 1984, just prior to the retirement of David Basnett. Subsequently, a number of changes took place designed to address income and cost problems. The regional structure was changed in 1985. The officer structure has also been reviewed and there are moves to put head office into smaller premises. Computerisation of the membership and contribution records, both at national and regional level, has proceeded.

There has been a shift in emphasis from check-off to direct debiting. Although the vast majority of members pay through check-off, GMBATU is worried about the cost and reliability of the method. Collaboration with the Trustee Savings Bank on discounted financial services – approved at 1988 conference – will be extended to direct debiting. It is anticipated that up to 5% of 'lost' income can be retrieved this way but currently less than 5% of members pay by direct debit. However, it remains the case that contribution records and arrears information is handled at branch and regional level and that head office cannot deploy all of the funds within the union. The system remains relatively decentralised.

Budgetary control systems based on past expenditure levels have been introduced at head office. Regions have autonomy on expenditure within broad limits, but there remains variation in levels of expenditure between regions and in the sophistication of regional accounting systems. In 1989, regional accounting systems were linked to head office by computer.

The General Secretary, who is also the Treasurer, ensures that both CEC and Conference have sufficient financial information both to understand the current financial position and to cost various motions and initiatives. His responsibility includes the translation of policy objectives emerging from Conference or CEC into management objectives for the various officers of the union. He also reports back on management and financial progress.

CEC controls all major expenditure decisions, has sole power to borrow as it sees fit, protects the funds against 'extravagance and misappropriation' and appoints auditors (rule 5). It also has power to manage funds and 'to employ the funds of the union in such a manner as shall be found necessary and expedient' (rule 12). The Trustees, together with two national officers, have the more limited role of assisting the CEC and Treasurer in fund management by executing 'the duties and functions assigned to them by the CEC' (rule 10). They effectively form a finance committee. Rule 12(7) indicates that there are no restrictions on the permissible range of investments. Under rule 11(4), members have the same right of access to accounts as the auditors.

Overall, the union has been at the forefront of attempts to use accepted management techniques in the administration of trade union affairs. Its members are regularly surveyed on issues such as contributions, benefits, and union image by external consultants. Officials' activities are coordinated within annual business plans setting specified objectives. New membership 'markets' are analysed and targeted in order to gain a return on recruitment expenditure.

5 Finance and strategy

Throughout the period under study, the leadership of GMB has been concerned to reverse relative or absolute membership decline. Throughout most of the post-war period, GMWU combined poor membership performance with relatively high overheads, an emphasis on benefits, and a rather staid image. It was not an attractive merger partner.

Latterly, much has changed. The membership problem is by no means solved and the union still recruits in a set of highly competitive membership markets, but GMB has been successful at cost control and merger activity in the 1980s. It has also, through the adoption of the new 'working together' logo and image, put resources behind a change in external image.

The union has introduced policy innovations in order to gain new members. Examples include the signing of no strike deals, joint ventures with employers in bidding for privatised services, attempts to recruit the self-employed, the promotion of support for individual employment rights in sectors where collective bargaining is unlikely to be achieved, and the use of charity sponsorship to attract young people into membership.

This transformation has been achieved with a close eye on financial matters. In fact, particularly in the 1976 and 1984 initiatives, there is a close relationship between organisational objectives, structural change, and financial reform. This can be illustrated by looking more closely at recruitment and at merger behaviour.

Where GMB seeks to organise poorly organised areas, it faces several problems. Often, prospective recruits are part-time, female employees, who pay low subscriptions. They move between employers, hence check-off is inappropriate to collect subscriptions, and they often do not have bank accounts, hence direct debiting is difficult. Nevertheless, they are seen as a priority area, hence the reform of the image, of the officer structure to encourage recruiting, of the system of subscription payment and of the financial services package. In addition, the union has recently proposed alteration in its scale of subscription charges and its benefit levels, in order to target specific new groups with appropriate and cost-effective subscription/benefit packages.

In effect, GMB sees the organisation of such areas as the 'new unionism' of the 1990s. This has been explicitly articulated by the General Secretary, both in its implications for recruitment and for financial management:

The new Union of the 1990s must be efficiently managed. New unionism must be open to all, high paid and low paid, full-time and part-time. So we must never allow our contribution rates to rise to levels where trade unionism is priced out of the reach of people who need the support and dignity of union membership, every pound must be carefully spent, every service economically delivered and every initiative properly controlled. Very often Trade Unions have combined good intentions with sloppy administration. The new unionism developed by the GMB must be a byword for professionalism.[14]

Mergers set up different problems. The traditional approach to the encouragement of mergers is, as Undy *et al.* (1981) note, sectionalisation or federation so that incoming bodies of membership retain some identity. However, for two reasons, this was inappropriate for GMB. The first was cost; federation, *ceteris paribus*, introduces greater administrative overheads and the union was facing a cash-flow problem for most of this period. The second concerned control. The historic problem for the union leadership was control of revenues, hence any federation would have been doubly unwelcome in that it would have proliferated cost centres and preserved the traditional regional and branch autonomy which inhibited allocative efficiencies. The integration of incoming union organisations has taken more time, but has resulted in a more easily controlled financial structure and clearer management lines. The structural reforms have proceeded with merger in mind. One of the objectives of *Decision* 84 and of the move from ten regions to six was the need 'to be structured efficiently so as to be the most dominant partner in any future major amalgamation.'[15]

The overall policy of the current leadership is governed by the conviction that fewer, larger unions embracing all occupations and industries will come to dominate the TUC in future. The task for GMB is defined in terms of growth through merger in order to become one such. This does not require the generation of vast reserves, but it does imply surplus on the day-to-day activities in order to fund recruitment and other campaigns. The union has been keen to control 'traditional' benefits, such as death or retirement benefit, while developing new ones such as financial and legal services. However, it has sought, through the development of costly specialist departments, to enhance its 'service' image.

New merger partners, in both the public and private sectors, are being canvassed in an aggressive policy of targeted growth. This has brought GMB into conflict with other unions, most noticeably EETPU, and it is likely in the short term to exacerbate inter-union competition. Hence it seems likely that, for the foreseeable future, the union's emphasis on a combination of innovative service packages and rigorous cost control will be maintained. The objective is to form a union of between 1 and 1.5 million members, with a bias towards female, white-collar service-sector employment, with a friendly and supportive, rather than a combative, image.

10   The Amalgamated Engineering Union: back from the brink

1   Historical background

The Amalgamated Engineering Union (AEU) can trace its history back, through several changes of name but few of structure, to the foundation of the Amalgamated Society of Engineers (ASE) in 1851. Its features, much praised by the Webbs (1907) as a major development in the history of trade unionism, included craft exclusiveness, high contributions and benefits, and a high level of financial centralisation combined with the devolution of a high level of autonomy over collective bargaining matters to district committees.

Many of these original features have disappeared. The craft exclusiveness progressively disappeared with the dilution of skills in the engineering industry and the spread of union membership into other areas. By 1985, only 30% of the union's membership were in skilled categories, although the majority of officials still had craft origins.[1] The union's subscription rates, 70p per week, were in that year among the lowest of the major unions; their subscription yield was easily the lowest.[2]

However, there is a great deal of continuity in structure and government. The full-time Executive Council (EC), which runs the union, was established in 1892. The National Committee (NC), the ruling body of the union, was established in 1920. District committees relying on the activities of lay members have been the key to the union's operation for over a century.

This may be because of the relatively low level of merger activity evident in the union's history. Four episodes are relevant. The first, in 1851, established the ASE. The second, in 1920, combined the ASE with a number of smaller craft societies to form the AEU. The third, beginning in 1967 with an amalgamation of the AEU with the Foundry workers, and ending in the creation of the AUEW in 1970, also involved the Constructional Engineering Union and the Draughtsman's and Allied Technician's Association (DATA, subsequently TASS) in the attempt to found a broad based craft and technical federation. Undy et al. (1981:

154

188–201) describe this as a defensive merger, triggered by membership competition from the general unions. It was to prove abortive, a number of political differences preventing the full assimilation of the four sections. Relations between the engineering section, the old AEU, and TASS over the issue of postal ballots being particularly fraught.

Eventually, a partial demerger occurred, with TASS leaving the federation and a full merger of the three remaining partners – the fourth important episode – taking place in October 1984. The reformed AEU had, in 1985, almost 975,000 recorded members, the vast majority being in the engineering section (914,775); the foundry section numbered 39,119 and the construction section 20,582.[3] By 1989 it had fallen to 741,647. The union has membership throughout private manufacturing and in parts of the public sector such as government industrial establishments, electricity supply, and hospitals.

2   Government and structure

Constitutionally, AEU has an extremely decentralised system of government, based on the principle of separation of powers, with a complex system of checks and balances on the powers of senior officials. Government revolves at national level around the President, who deals mainly with external matters, including relations with employers, the General Secretary, who broadly speaking manages the union, the full-time EC, and the NC. Both of the senior officers, the EC, and full-time officials are subject to periodic election by postal ballot of the membership. The NC is made up of delegates from divisional committees.

The NC is the supreme governing body. It consists of 121 lay delegates from the various divisions of the union, i.e., 26 geographical engineering divisions, the foundry and construction sections and the womens' section. The NC meets annually to 'review agreements with the Engineering Employers' Federation, or other employers, and suggest any alterations or amendments deemed necessary. They shall discuss past and future policy of the union, with a view to giving the Executive Council instructions for the ensuing year and may initiate any policy which they think would be beneficial to the union.'

Every fifth year, the NC constitutes a Rules Revision Meeting 'to consider suggestions from branches for alterations of the rules and byelaws and to make new or alter exisiting rules and byelaws accordingly'.[4]

The EC and general officers have an original jurisdiction where the rules are silent, but 'in no case shall they alter the established rules and byelaws of the association.'[5] All officials are now elected for five years. In the engineering section, the EC are elected from seven geographical electoral divisions, which are not to be confused with the (currently) 26 divisions through which the NC is elected and which constitute the next tier in the union's administration. Two EC members from the foundry section and one from the construction section are elected on an industrial basis.

Below the divisions are district committees, which have wide-ranging powers 'to deal with and regulate rates of wages, hours of labour, terms of overtime, piecework and general conditions affecting the interests of the trades in their respective districts'.[6] They may also deal with admissions of new members and appointment of shop stewards. Any dispute between the EC and a district committee goes to the NC, itself composed of representatives elected through divisional and district committees. A Final Appeal Court for appeals against decisions of the EC is composed of lay members elected through the EC divisional system.

At the bottom level, AEU branch structure was traditionally organised on a geographic basis. Recent reforms have altered this by introducing industrial- or factory-based structures. By the end of 1990 total branch numbers stood at just under 1,700 and by 1991 it was the EC's intention to reduce this to approximately 100 geographic branches and designate up to 100 industrial or factory branches.

The union allows branches powers over individual matters such as contributions, benefit, and disciplinary matters. It also allows branches to hold funds (see below). However, the EC has greater powers to interfere in the affairs of branches than it does over the affairs of district committees. It may dissolve or amalgamate branches, or require surrender of funds.

AEU is an extremely democratic union. It ballots its members frequently on matters of policy, and on all elections. Since 1972, it has used postal ballots consistently. This appears to have had two consequences. First, it has affected the balance of power between left and right factions within the union, and thus the composition of the EC.[7] Secondly, until the provision of public funding, it raised the costs of the union. Subsequently, such costs have been publicly borne; for example, in 1989 the union claimed approximately £361,000 in refunded ballot costs, almost 2% of total administrative expenditure.[8]

In summary, then, although there have been numerous rule changes, the structure of the union remains broadly that of the 1920 amalgamation. The principle of the separation of powers and the regular balloting of the membership ensures limitation on the powers of full-time officials. Rule making, policy formation, and the final court of appeal are the responsibility of bodies of lay activists.

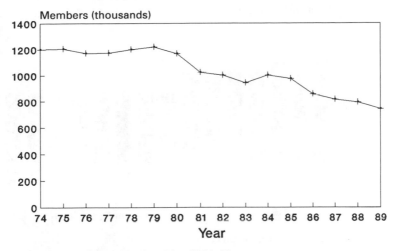

Figure 10.1. AEU membership, 1974–89

3   Financial performance

Figure 10.1 shows the membership of AEU, or its nearest historic equivalent, across the period. From 1974 to 1984 the membership noted is that
of AUEW (E); thereafter, it is the current AEU. The figure illustrates
that, aside from the absorption of the foundry and construction sections
in 1984, the union has suffered membership decline across the whole
period. Unlike many other unions, membership is static across the period
1974–9. It declines rapidly thereafter. The particularly steep decline from
1985 to 1986 is partly due to changes in the procedure for recording
membership; about 200,000 members disappear from the books in that
year.

Income has also fallen steeply in real terms since 1976 (see Figure 10.2).
The union is highly subscription-dependent and has become more so in
the 1980s as investment income has practically disappeared since 1984.
In fact, since 1986, membership income quoted in the union's own
accounts has occasionally exceeded total income due to the union's practice of calculating investment income net of expenditure on properties;
this led to a negative total throughout, alleviated in 1987 by refund of
monies to the superannuation fund.[9] The statutory return data net off this
expenditure but, even on this more conventional calculation, over 95% of
all income in 1989 was from members' contributions.

As Figure 10.3, showing the balance between income and expenditure,
indicates, the worst years for the union were 1982–6, when it registered a

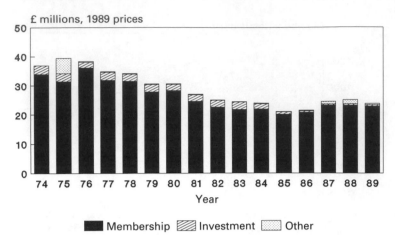

Figure 10.2. AEU income, 1974–89

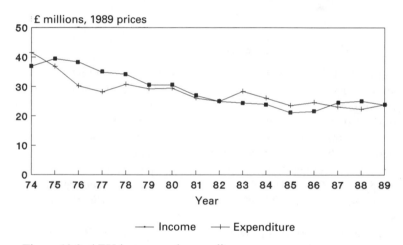

Figure 10.3. AEU income and expenditure

deficit; 1983, just prior to merger, and 1986 were the worst years. Thereafter, the situation has improved; the union registered a shortfall across
all funds of nearly £3 million in 1986, a small surplus of £826,526 in 1987,
and a much larger surplus of over £2.5 million in 1988. Nevertheless, for
most of the period in question, the union's solvency position has been
poor. In 1989 and 1990, it was again in deficit.

Expenditure has, however, also fallen in real terms. AEU performed
the remarkable feat of registering expenditure levels in 1989 which were

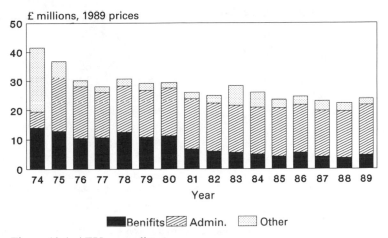

Figure 10.4. AEU expenditure

in real terms only a fraction of those of 1974. There have been two components to this. The first has been the freezing of real levels of administrative expenditure. The second has been large cuts in real benefit expenditure, particularly since 1980. The union regularly reports levels of benefit expenditure as a proportion of income. In 1985, benefits were 22.12% of income, in 1987, 18.4%; the union was still, comparatively, benefit oriented.[10] However, where income is falling in real terms, this masks the fall in real benefit expenditure (Figure 10.4).

One point to emphasise about Figure 10.3 is that both income and expenditure are relatively low for a union of this size. In 1987, GMB and NALGO had 98.5% and 93.1% respectively of AEU's declared membership. However, their income levels were 47% and 105% higher respectively and their expenditure levels 52% and 83% greater. By 1989, the membership position had changed, but AEU total income and expenditure were still low per capita.

Nevertheless, as Figure 10.5 indicates, the union, being highly subscription-dependent, has always registered a surplus of membership income over administrative expenditure; without high levels of benefit expenditure, its solvency would have been assured. The comparatively low levels of both income and expenditure per capita may be related to AEU's heavy administrative reliance on lay participation and its avoidance of certain major costs, for example a large annual delegate conference. There is every indication, then, that the union's long-established government structure, which may, as Undy *et al.* (1981) have remarked, have discouraged merger, nonetheless sustains an efficient administration.

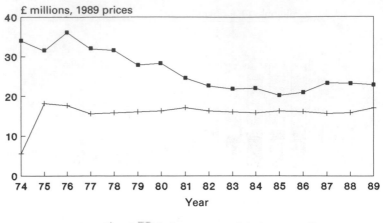

Figure 10.5. AEU membership income and administrative expenditure

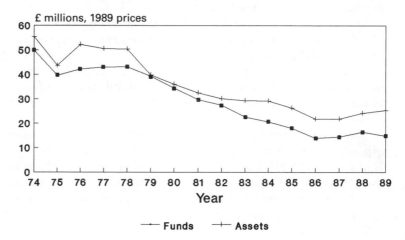

Figure 10.6. AEU funds and assets

Figures 10.6 and 10.7 deal with funds and assets. As Figure 10.6 indicates, both have declined since 1977 in real terms. The major item accounting for the divergence between funds and assets in Figure 10.6 is a provision, amounting to over £5.6 million in 1987, against future repair and maintenance of property.

As the fall in investment income and in the real value of funds implies, the union has been selling assets in order to cover the membership income

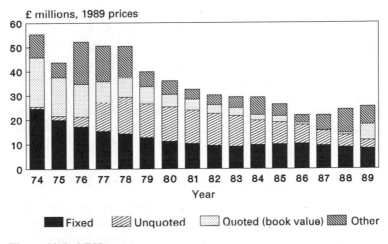

Figure 10.7. AEU assets

shortfall. This is shown in Figure 10.7. The union has effectively liquidated its quoted investments since 1985. Unquoted investments have also been sold. The union in 1989 was worth, in real terms, less than half of its gross asset value in 1974. It has contracted around the rump of fixed-property assets. This has occurred as the result of covering current expenditure from asset sales. In 1985, for example, for each week's subscription of 70p, another 5.8p was drawn from reserves to cover expenditure.[11]

A liquidity crisis was close in 1986. In that year, the union had only £721,000, approximately two weeks' expenditure, in cash (including deposits). By 1988, this had risen to over £5.5 million, or about three months' expenditure. However, these data may exaggerate the financial plight of the union. On the brink of the 1986 financial problem, the General Secretary made the point that the property portfolio was worth more than the accounting policies disclosed:

our fixed assets are shown as £8,164,240. This includes our 104 properties shown at a net book value of £5,883,504... We never revalue property. In fact, we depreciate at 1% per annum. The insurance value of our property is over £36 million. We are a large, financially sound trade union, and I am determined to ensure we stay that way.[12]

This was a candid admission on the eve of financial reform but a full property revaluation might have made it more difficult to argue the case for branch reorganisation.

In summary, then, AEU suffered deteriorating financial performance across the period, culminating in a year of considerable financial difficulty in 1986. Since then, there are signs that the situation has improved; this may relate to changes to the rules and systems for financial management, discussed below. However, the net effect is that AEU is both in real terms and relative to other trade unions much weaker financially than it was at the start of the period. Its assets are – accounting policies aside – smaller than those of several unions of much smaller membership and it remains highly dependent on membership income to remain solvent. It has been effective at controlling administrative expenditure and has also tackled the politically more sensitive issue of benefit levels.

4   Financial management

It has historically been the paradox of AEU that, whereas much decision making concerning bargaining and politics has been decentralised, financial decision making has been rather more focused on the General Secretary and the EC. Across the 1980s, centralisation has in some ways increased.

The AEU rule book is unusually explicit and detailed on financial matters. Indeed, AEU lists certain financial objectives among the overall objectives of the union. These include the transaction of insurance business, the holding, leasing, and mortgaging of land and property, and the provision of funds to support a wide range of actions 'which may, in the opinion of the union or its Executive Council, be deemed to be calculated to further the interests of the Union or of the trade union movement generally'.[13]

The General Secretary of the union is also the General Treasurer. He has a number of responsibilities under rule 15 which relate primarily to the management of expenditure and, with the Trustees and the NC, to the management of funds. He has the further responsibility for the production of the annual income and expenditure report from branch returns.

However, he has less control over income. Since income depends on subscriptions, it is influenced by subscription levels and subscription yield. Subscription levels used to be set by rule, and were thus subject in principle to annual revision. However, from 1990, the subscription level is indexed to the EEF national time rate. Under rule 22, the Section 1 contribution rate is set at 1% of the National Engineering Agreement skilled rate; other section rates are set in proportion to this.

Subscription yield is influenced partly by method of payment. The union in the 1970s used to receive approximately half of its subscriptions through check-off and half through direct cash or cheque payment through the district committees. Currently, the proportion on check-off is approximately 70% and rising by 2–4% each year. Of the remainder, about 15% is collected by branch secretaries, about 7% by hand by shop stewards, and about 7% by 'unofficial' check-off in which the employer hands a cheque to shop stewards. Few members are on direct debit arrangements, but there is a provision in rule for direct debit payers to pay only 11 months' subscriptions, and the number is expected to grow to 100,000 in the next few years.[14]

The union has had a serious arrears problem. In 1984, arrears stood at 26.5% of general fund income. By 1988, this had risen to 31.3%. Changes to collection methods and the elimination of spurious or outdated membership records will help reduce this problem in future, but the union does not yet have a clear picture of the income stream, and those in charge of expenditure cannot easily influence it.

It appears that there may have been underpayments, of various forms, but, since the computer systems for membership and for contributions were separate, it is difficult to draw a precise picture. However, this situation was remedied in 1990 with the introduction of a new computer system. In the opinion of the finance manager, the check-off system itself may be unreliable. With 3,000 employers involved, and no link between membership and financial data, the union can only manage by exception; large quarterly discrepancies are checked.[15] It was estimated that the check-off system itself may only have generated 80% of due income in 1989.

Part of the problem is membership turnover. Between January and December 1988 the engineering section had 54,000 admissions but lost 18,300 members. Crudely, then, it needed 72,500 new members a year, almost 10% of its declared membership, in order to maintain a stable membership level. This may understate the turnover problem. Data do not currently exist to map movements fully which is, in some respects, rather surprising since AEU has had, for postal balloting purposes, a full list of members' home addresses since the early 1970s.

Not all of the collected income is available at head office, although the controls over branch and district expenditure were tightened up considerably in 1986.[16] Under rule 3, the branches are allocated 10p and districts 15p per quarter per eight members paying full contributions for the Local Purposes Fund. Under rules 5 and 12, branch officers and those attending district committees are paid fees and expenses by the EC from general office.

Under the old rules, branch secretaries were paid out of retained branch funds by the branch treasurer on the basis of members less than 26 weeks in arrears. The branches' accounts were allowed, under rule 10, to be audited by the general office, but in practice only a sample audit was taken. The current position is as follows. Rule 5 specifies:

The president, secretary and treasurer shall be the trustees of the branch and signatories to the branch bank account... The president, secretary and treasurer shall be paid quarterly from the Union's General Office after the branch's accounts for that quarter have been audited.

As implied, the branch monies are now remitted and disbursed rather than retained. Financial controls have also been improved.[17]

Along with this, there has been a reduction in the number of branches and a corresponding cut in the overheads of the union. Under rule 9, the EC has the power, after consultation, to merge or close branches. Between 1980 and 1989, the number of branches was reduced from 2,700 to 1,860. The EC also has the power to group branches into districts and to merge district committees.[18] District committees have been merged over time; the 1970 rule book lists 219, and the 1988 revision lists 157. Again, this takes overheads out of the union's administration.

However, districts and branches account for a relatively small amount of the overall administrative expenditure of the union. In 1988, districts accounted for 19.8% of administrative expenditure from the general fund, by far the largest item in which was the salaries of district officers. Branches accounted for 10.4%, most of which was on fees to officers. General office accounted for 43.1%; salaries were again a major item.[19]

The control of salaries in general and general office expenditure overall is thus important. Salaries of officers are set by the rules revision meeting. Comparatively, they are low, the highest, for President and General Secretary, being £20,000 in 1988. The number of officials is controlled over time by the General Secretary and EC. AEU employs approximately 160 officials. However, numbers have been reduced, particularly at district and divisional level; between 1986 and 1987, staff and officers at this level were reduced by 25%. In addition, a number of offices have been closed; some properties have been sold.

This relatively low officer–member ratio indicates the union's reliance on lay involvement. Only 29% of overall expenditure went on salaries in 1989. Fifteen per cent went on fees to officers and the expenses of meetings. Almost 20% of expenditure went on benefits to members. Compared to many other unions, the salary fee is low and the benefit fee quite high, in percentage terms. However, for its size, the levels of both income and expenditure in AEU are low.

The day-to-day management of expenditure is the province of the General Secretary and his staff, particularly the finance manager and general office manager. They have a relatively simple fund structure to manage. They are: the General Fund, wherein are contained the bulk of the union's funds, the Superannuation Fund, sustained by investment income plus a large subvention from the General Fund, and a Political Fund. There are also smaller funds for the foundry, construction, and roll-turning sections.

Expenditure is managed without, as yet, a formal budgeting system. Many expenditure items, particularly salaries, fees, benefits, and expenses, are defined by rule. However, AEU is moving towards a cost-centre approach. Most purchasing is done centrally and branches and districts must indent for items such as stationery. The objective is to have one cost centre for each EC electoral district, in addition to those at general office which include education, research, and public relations.

The rule book also provides in detail for the management of the union's funds. One significant provision allows for the funds to be replenished by levy where they are unduly depleted:

When the General Fund is reduced to £4 per member, the contributions shall be increased by such sums per week as will sustain the funds at not less than that amount. At any time the Executive Council may take the votes of the members as to the desirability of increasing the General Fund by extra contributions and such extra contributions shall not continue in force for longer than twelve weeks without a second vote of the members being taken.[20]

This rule has not been applied, and the General Secretary indicated that he would be reluctant to do so, but it does provide a backstop against total depletion in the event of large-scale unplanned expenditure.

Rules 35–9 cover the investment and control of funds. They give relatively unfettered powers to the EC and the Trustees, particularly over investments. The Trustees, seven in number, are elected from branches in the London area by the NC; they hold office for three years. All property and funds are vested in the Trustees who 'shall, with the consent of the Executive Council, have power to borrow money, to give such security for such borrowing whether by way of mortgage or otherwise as they may think fit and to provide guarantees for borrowing by others'.[21]

Together with the EC, the Trustees form the Investment Committee which has the power to invest all or any of the union's funds 'in any undertaking of any kind whatsoever in the interest of the labour movement'; however, the NC has the right of veto.[22] Rule 38 specifies that there shall be three bank accounts, for the General, Political, and Benefits funds. Significantly, the General Fund accounts have included all branch bank accounts since 1986. Prior to this there was no mention of the location of branch funds in this rule.

In summary, then, the system of financial management in AEU is far more centralised than that for operational management or regulation of the union's collective bargaining activities. Once National Committee or

Rules Revision Meetings have specified financial rules, their operation is the responsibility of the General Secretary, EC, and Trustees.

Much of this discussion has concerned the union's rule book. This is because AEU specifies financial matters in rule to an unusual degree. Changes to subscription setting, expenditure, benefits, and fees as well as to officers' salaries and even the fines for non-performance of specified union duties are detailed in rule. As we shall show below, this means that the financial reforms of the 1980s have had to proceed through the encouragement of rule changes.

In practice, the most important rules concern income. The union has few assets to manage and has demonstrated good expenditure control. The move towards indexation of contribution rates, the continued computerisation of accounting records, the move towards relatively reliable payment methods such as check-off and direct debiting, and the collection of all income centrally before remission to branches are thus central to the return to solvency in 1987.

5   Finance and strategy

The union's financial reforms of the 1980s were less strategic than crisis driven. In examination of the union's financial management practice and financial accounts for the 1970s it is difficult to find any evidence of financial strategy at all, other than the acceptance of steady decline in both relative and real terms.

The changes after the Rules Revision Meetings of both 1983 and 1986, which may be broadly characterised as an attempt to create financial information and to centralise financial control, were prompted by large deficits on the current account. The General Secretary, Gavin Laird, sought certain reforms in order to eradicate the deficit rather than to pursue long-term objectives. Certain current policies are thus best seen as attempts to prevent the 1986 situation recurring.

Two examples may be given. The first is the concern to replenish funds from membership income. As Figure 10.6 has shown, funds fell steeply from 1978 to 1986, to historically very low levels. For a period, assets were being sold to run the union on a day-to-day basis. The current concern is to avoid any repetition of this and to aim for per capita assets more closely in line with those of competitor unions.

The second example is related. While funds declined, membership income exceeded administrative costs. The major problem area was benefit expenditure and a second current objective is to fund all benefits out of contribution income. This involves, as we have shown, a freezing of real benefit expenditure. It also involves the provision of membership benefits and services which are cost effective or income generating.

One such membership service is the joint development with Unity Trust, in a TUC sponsored scheme, of a range of financial services at preferential rates, including personal pensions, banking services, personal investment management, and travel services. The 'concern here was to maintain a level of services to members, to attract younger potential members, and, with an eye to competitor unions, to present a more up-to-date image. This package was devised by general office, but is not mentioned in the rules.[23] AEU also invested just over £1 million in 1987 in a TV production company, Hamlet, through a joint venture both as a revenue generator and as part of its general initiative to improve communications with members. This was one initiative which proved unsuccessful, however, and at the end of 1990 the union had to make a provision of £1 million against the investment.[24]

Notwithstanding this, the 1980s financial strategy consisted in getting the union back on an even keel and establishing protocols which would prevent the lapse into deficit from recurring. The General Secretary summarised the union's policies in his 1991 Annual Report:

We are determined to stay at the bottom of the league table in terms of administrative costs per member. . . What matters most to all of our members is that the Executive Council and myself as treasurer maximise expenditure on benefits to members. We are consistently at the top of the league, compared with other unions, in paying benefits out of contributions and it is our firm intention to remain Top of the League in that regard.

There were also attempts to plan ahead, but here one must take account of the relationship between systems of financial management and union government.

The planning cycle in AEU is based around the cycle of officials' elections, which come every five years. The union also has five-yearly Rules Revision Meetings. This means that it can be difficult to plan financial matters in the longer term. As Undy et al. (1981) have demonstrated, there exist separate political factions within the union and elections might result in the adoption of a different set of financial objectives or management systems if a different faction were returned to power on the EC or NC. AEU is deeply committed to its current democratic system of government. In narrow financial terms this is problematic. It has led to problems of financial control. It results in a system of checks and balances which inhibit centralised decision making. However, the commitment to the political structure – essentially unchanged since 1920 – dominates attempts at financial reform and there seems no doubt that the financial reforms will continue to be subordinated to the current governmental structure.

The union seeks to grow. It must recruit just to stand still, and the kinds of people it is recruiting, namely women, part-time workers, and non-craft employees, will continue to shift the membership composition away from the centres of power in Sections 1 and 2. However, its objective is not merely to halt membership decline, but to expand. This implies expenditure on recruiting as well as the development of new policies such as single-union deals to attract employers as well as employees. But, there is a severe limit in AEU on what can be done centrally. The union relies on stewards, branches, and districts to recruit. Its officials are negotiators rather than organisers, called in to lead in formal set-pieces such as the Ford or CSEU negotiations, and immediately accountable to the membership. It follows firstly that the union cannot centrally coordinate its recruitment and secondly that it cannot assess the costs and benefits of recruitment activity, most of the expense of which falls on lay activists.

A second route to growth, however, is the pursuit of merger partners which *is* initiated from the centre. AEU's merger history since 1920 has been unspectacular. The formation of AUEW was ultimately frustrated, and the eventual merger with the foundry and construction sections has resulted in the adoption of two loss-making sections, at least until 1988.

There are several reasons for this. In the longer term, the district committee structure, with no provision for federation or sectionalisation, may have discouraged smaller unions wishing to preserve some identity on merger from transferring into AEU. For the last decade or so AEU, with low per capita assets and an operating deficit, may have looked unattractive to other unions. The officials of prospective partners may also have looked with particular misgivings at AEU's policies of electing all officials and at their low officials' salaries.

In any event, the union did not succeed in negotiating further mergers despite courting several candidates for several years. Negotiations in 1989 with EETPU reached an advanced stage before foundering at National Committee; again left–right politics and the plans for election of officials were at issue. Negotiations were subsequently resumed and the merger confirmed by membership ballots in 1992. It seems clear that the union will approach further merger partners.

There are several reasons for this. The perceived major competitors, TGWU and GMB, have grown or slowed down decline through merger in the last decade, and AEU has slipped from second to fourth largest union. In addition, the union still focuses on declining job territories. It has few service-sector employees in membership and no white-collar section. It remains predominantly a male, manual manufacturing union and must move out of this declining job territory to maintain its position. There is also the issue of union politics. AEU is currently perceived to be to the right of two of its major competitors, TGWU and MSF. It has maintained good relations with EETPU following the latter's expulsion from TUC and the opportunity to form a major right-wing block within TUC and the Labour Party was possibly a major spur to the decision to merge with the Electricians in 1992.

11 The Banking Insurance and Finance Union: competitive unionism and financial survival

1 Historical background

BIFU's current strategy and financial position can only be understood in the context of the union's long fight for recognition against employer hostility. Founded at the end of the First World War as an all-grades union for clerks in the English clearing banks, it grew very quickly and by 1920–1 could claim 10,000 members.[1] Subsequently, this growth ceased as the banks indicated their disinterest in or outright opposition to trade unionism. In most cases, they set up rival staff associations. There then followed a long period during which the union unsuccessfully sought recognition in each of the banks. Eventually, recognition was achieved in Barclays Bank. During this time the union's membership stagnated and it struggled financially.

The banks' staff associations benefited from employer subsidy and did not need complex bargaining arrangements, hence their overheads were extremely low: in most cases they did not charge a subscription until after the Second World War. This forced the national union's operations to remain small and centralised. Nevertheless, it remained union policy that all officials had to be employed full time by the union to ensure their independence, in contrast to the situation in the company-based staff associations.

This preoccupation with independence as the means to differentiate itself from its competitors also influenced the union's structure. Branches were organised geographically rather than on a company basis and the union tried to stress the importance of industry-wide, rather than of domestic company, issues. Such a focus proved difficult to sustain. Although pay and other terms and conditions did apply nationally through informal coordination between banks, most employees did not transfer between banks and were (at least formally) offered the opportunity of a life-long career (Morris, 1986).

After the war, the union combined with its parallel body in the Scottish clearers, the Scottish Bankers Association and became the National

170

Union of Bank Employees (NUBE). Despite suffering from staff association competition and employer hostility to recognition, it raised its membership in the early 1950s as conditions of employment and career prospects worsened. In this situation, the staff associations, which stressed cooperation with employers and had no formal bargaining rights, were exposed as relatively powerless, but the union still failed to gain national recognition in the clearers.

NUBE did have more success in the small retail banks, notably the TSB and the Cooperative Bank. Recognition in the former was secured in the early 1960s by its first use of industrial action and this made a significant impact on the subsequent policies of the union. Until then it had stressed cooperation and favoured arbitration to resolve disputes. Under certain circumstances, however, it seemed that greater aggression could be both popular and effective.

These circumstances were repeated in the clearing banks in the late 1960s when a combination of inflation, pay restraint, and employer inflexibility led to staff discontent. The union successfully organised a number of disputes in 1967 which led, through government intervention, to national recognition. However, a stipulation enforced by the banks was that the associations should be recognised nationally in joint negotiating machinery with NUBE. This was to prove a severe problem for the union, as national bargaining did not work to displace the staff associations; indeed their membership rose faster than the union's in the 1970s (Morris, 1986).

This was one reason for NUBE's decision to diversify membership, moving into other areas in the early 1970s. Other reasons included the growth of new areas of employment in the financial sector, such as international banking, the beginning of deregulation of the sector, and the emergence of rival forms of representation including other TUC unions and staff associations in building societies and insurance. A further factor was the poor financial position of the union, resulting from its low subscription rate and high reliance on independent full-time officials, both of which resulted from its competition with the staff associations. Diversification provided a solution in that membership rose and income with it, but probably of more importance in the long run were the facilities the union eventually received from the clearing banks, which allowed it to strengthen its organisation and membership relatively cheaply. In other areas, NUBE struggled against rival associations and employer hostility and could often make only minor headway, as in international banking and the building societies. This sort of growth was expensive and difficult to achieve on any scale (Willman and Morris, 1986).

2   Structure and government

Diversification created structural problems. By the mid 1970s NUBE was bowing to pressure from members for what was called more 'institutionally based organisation', that is branches and sections based on occupation, employer, or employment area within the overall sector rather than on geography. Tensions subsequently developed over how far institutionalisation and sectionalisation should be extended given the traditional commitment to a geographic structure. The new forms were seen by many to be similar to the staff association practice of company-based organisations. Tension heightened as smaller unions or associations were acquired by the union (which became BIFU in 1980) and other membership groups began to acquire special powers over negotiations as well as representation on the NEC, where the clearing bank groups had dominated.

The current outcome is a compromise which overlays sectional and geographic structures. Sectionalism is apparently popular with members but stresses diversity rather than unity; it is also appropriate for attracting mergers and transfers of engagements. Sectionalism also fits with the trend to enterprise-based bargaining which has reemerged in the sector. Nonetheless, the geographic structure is still important and although only a minority of members remain attached to geographically based branches an area structure overlays the institutional branch system. Not the least factor in any decision to retain a geographical structure is the desire to avoid breakaways of any disaffected section of members. Where there are competing staff associations, particularly in the London clearing banks, no company-based group of members may be formed into a section.[2]

Membership growth has been crucial to BIFU for a number of reasons. Its asset base has been relatively low and income growth has been necessary to cover the costs of its growth in administrative overheads arising from diversification across the sector. In many cases a significant membership base has been necessary to secure recognition or to displace the rival body. BIFU has had the good fortune to operate in a sector which has grown rapidly over the past 20 years and has been able to take advantage of this. Throughout the 1980s it has not suffered from the sort of membership losses sustained by other unions and in most years made net gains in members without merger. Most recently, it has projected itself as providing security against the growing risk of redundancy in the City, an area where it has been poorly represented.

Because of the turnover levels in clerical jobs in some institutions, BIFU has to work hard at its recruitment: in 1990, for example, it lost 21,429 and recruited 22,049 members. Its recruitment activity works both through employers, as in the case of the London clearing banks where the union sends literature to new entrants, and more commonly through temporary travelling representatives as well as through 19 full-time organisers. Use of this method is necessitated by the dispersion of employment in retail finance. It is expensive but, without strong workplace organisation, it appears to be the only appropriate method.

The results have been mixed. BIFU has failed to break the majority positions of the clearing bank associations and, in particular, has come off badly in Barclays where it has faced exceptionally aggressive competition. On the other hand, Midland Bank offered BIFU sole representation in the spring of 1989, removing recognition from its rival, MSF. While formally BIFU did not seek to override the Bridlington Principles of the TUC, it did want to raise membership levels in the Midland, where it had over 24,000 clerical and managerial members at the end of 1988. It was assumed by the bank and BIFU that this would provide it with growth particularly in the technical and services grades where it was not dominant in membership terms.[3]

The pattern of membership growth is mixed because of a range of factors influencing each of its main sections. In the Scottish clearers BIFU has gained generally from growing employment and its organising efforts in the absence of recruiting competition – staff associations having been disbanded or merged with BIFU in the past. However, it has suffered from the integration of international and domestic divisions in the London clearers, because of resulting job loss. In the international banks it has been unsuccessful in overcoming employer hostility particularly in the large American banks, but has had more success in those of the Commonwealth countries.

Running the International Banks section of the union is difficult and expensive without breakthroughs in the larger banks because of the large numbers of employers involved and the generally low numbers of members in each: the International Banks total membership is only 3,550. Similarly, its building societies representation is dispersed and limited to smaller societies: growth tends to be by absorption of staff associations.[4] In Insurance it has also absorbed staff associations, notably in Guardian Royal, Royal Liver, and Sun Alliance, but still faces aggressive competition from MSF. Much the same is true in the finance houses. The net result is that over 80,000 of its members are still employed by the Big Four London clearers and to some extent subsidise the operation of other sections. On occasion, this has led to some disquiet among members. The union's objective is thus to develop a structure which reflects the different interests of its members, yet ties them together, and provides a forum for growth both through merger and organically.

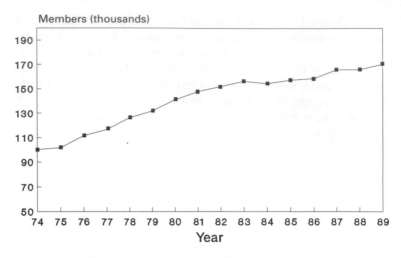

Figure 11.1. BIFU membership, 1974–89

Sections therefore tend to concentrate on setting bargaining objectives for the representatives of members in their domain. Areas, on the other hand, are the instruments through which the NEC implements decisions down to the branches, including branch organisation, recruitment, and membership. Areas also 'stimulate and foster support for any approved policies of the union'.[5] They therefore act as the vehicle for maintaining national policies.

To summarise, the history of BIFU is important in explaining its structure, government, and policies. Having faced both employer hostility – which meant it took some 50 years to obtain recognition in its core territory – and the operation of rival forms of representation, BIFU has traditionally pursued all-grades recruitment across the sector. It has broadened its job territory partly because of its failure to overcome competition in its original territory and particularly as the financial services sector has become deregulated and integrated. It has adjusted its structure to attract new members and staff associations but avoid breakaways. To cope with this diversification, it remains centralised in its decision making but has tried to extend responsibility for organisation to lay activists, funded by employers. Much of the impetus for these strategies has been to resolve its financial problems, which again relate to competitive pressure.

3   Financial performance

Figure 11.1 shows membership growth from 1974 to 1989: overall, there has been a steady rise. Although membership was static from 1983 to

1986, the union has not had to cope with the financial consequences of membership loss. As Figure 11.2, showing the union's income over the period, indicates, the union is highly subscription dependent and there is a very close relationship between membership level and subscription income. The exception is in 1987, when a larger proportion of 'other income' – from the sale of property – is recorded.

To resolve its long-standing cash-flow problems and reduce its collection costs, BIFU moved to a variety of check-off methods in the 1970s and subsequently encouraged direct debiting. Some 48% were paying by the latter method with 45% on check-off by the end of 1990. As a result the problem of underpayment which was quite serious some years ago has declined. The union's objective is to raise as far as possible the proportion of members paying by direct debit. The income is collected at headquarters and branches take no part in the administration process; membership records are also held at the head office and employers operating check-off send in hard copy or magnetic tape which is married to the membership record. Non-payers can be relatively quickly deleted from the record.

Subscriptions may only be changed at Conference, although the NEC has the authority temporarily to adjust subscriptions charged to incoming groups in order to attract them into membership. Although subscriptions have had to take the staff associations into account historically, the union is increasingly competing on its higher level of services rather than on price. A proposal to Conference to reduce subscriptions in pre-recognition areas was recently defeated because it was argued that this has not helped recruitment and there was no evidence of resignation on the basis of price. Part-time subscriptions were cut in 1985 but this has had little effect on the recruitment of part-time members.

Figure 11.3 shows that the union has consistently maintained a surplus of income over expenditure since 1975. Because of the low level of assets and of investment income, it has also managed, unusually, to cover its administrative expenditure from membership income; servicing the membership yields a small profit (Figure 11.4). As Figure 11.5 indicates, the union spends very little indeed on benefit and the bulk of expenditure, which has risen steadily throughout the period, goes on administration. This relates both to the continued reliance on full-time officials in the absence of strong workplace organisation and to the sectionalised structure which requires a rather large administrative overhead.

Because membership income has always been only marginally higher than expenditure, the union constantly seeks to control its spending. Subscription income is set to match predicted expenditure and, in the event of a shortfall, the finance committee has to decide whether to reduce

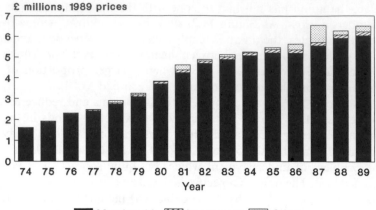

Figure 11.2. BIFU income, 1974–89

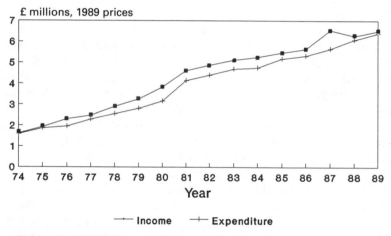

Figure 11.3. BIFU income and expenditure

expenditure or levy more: it is not likely to allow debts to incur. Disputes are not major cost items as BIFU does not pay strike pay, although it will consider individual cases of hardship. It has, however, increased its spending on recruitment and on services, particularly educational services, both of which are seen as central to the pursuit of growth. The problems of growth are intensified by membership turnover and the dispersion of employment. The union does evaluate the cost effectiveness of these campaigns and has its own formula for calculating how long it needs to

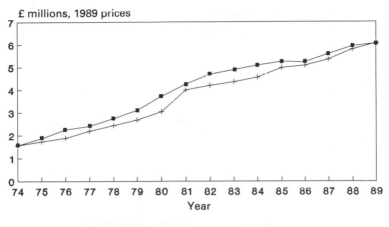

£ millions, 1989 prices

—— Membership income —+— Admin. expenditure

Figure 11.4. BIFU membership income and administrative expenditure

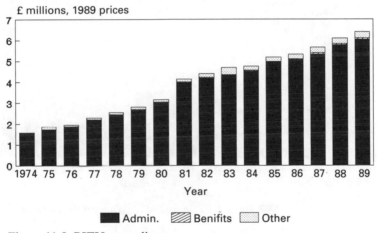

Figure 11.5. BIFU expenditure

retain a member to pay for recruitment. It does not usually target specific employers for recruitment campaigns, but will pursue mergers with company unions or staff associations.

The other area of increased spending is new benefits. The union has put together a package of holiday and financial discounts which are aimed at being more 'upmarket' than other unions' services, and it has also examined the possibility of providing discounted mortgage schemes, since

£ millions, 1989 prices

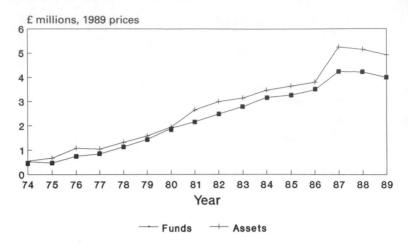

Figure 11.6. BIFU funds and assets

£ millions, 1989 prices

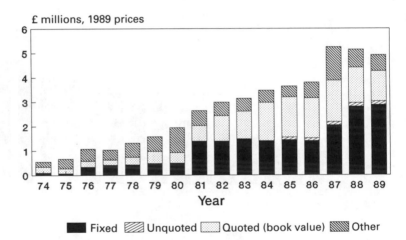

Figure 11.7. BIFU assets, 1974–89

its research shows that fewer employees are subsidised by the banks than was supposed. As a result of this activity, spending on publicity, education and administration has risen significantly in recent years but benefit spending still represents a very small proportion of total expenditure.

The union's policy is to build up capital and assets to enable it to manage expected membership growth. Figure 11.6 shows the value of funds and assets and Figure 11.7 the composition of assets across the period. BIFU had to sell assets to meet current expenditure in the 1970s but now seeks to ensure expenditure is firmly limited within current income ranges. It is the union's policy to invest in freehold property at headquarters and regional offices, and again this needs income surpluses. It recently moved its headquarters to a larger site and lets those parts it does not use, which will generate substantial income in due course. Only in the past decade has BIFU properly developed a policy for its investment portfolio, under the guidance of the finance officer, and it has moved to a greater reliance on equities with a wider spread of companies.

4   Financial management

According to the rule book, BIFU is highly centralised, the rules specific-ally stating that branches and Areas should not retain funds nor incur expenditure above the maximum of £75 and £125 respectively. Branches indent for funds which are spent through their own audited accounts: no fund accumulation is permitted. The rules tightly define the powers of the NEC, allocating substantial powers over funds, investment, and expendit-ure. It also has authority over allocation of funds to other units of the union. Delegate Conferences have the authority to determine subscription charges.

Because of competition the union is careful with money. Its long period of non-recognition was financially fraught and only when it managed to establish facilities agreements could it build its asset base, which was among the lowest of any large union in the 1960s (Latta 1972). Conference decisions to peg subscription changes to the rate of inflation during the mid 1970s (although this appeared to cause membership loss in the short term) and the shift away from payment by cheque to automated methods secured the real income stream. Today the union's leaders are still con-cerned to run what they describe as a 'rather lean organisation' in terms of staffing levels, commitment of funds to projects, and operating expendi-ture controls; they appear to be more parsimonious than the membership. Instilling a sense of financial discipline is an important theme of the Treasurer's work. He remarked to members in 1988: 'We must NOT pass motions at Annual Delegate Conferences on the basis of emotive speeches, but must apply sound business and financial sense to our decisions. Any other path would lead us rapidly into a state of financial chaos in a very short space of time.'[6]

However, one other objective is clearly important to BIFU. This is to become more market oriented in order to grow. Two aspects to this policy are of note, first the increasing amounts of money spent on recruitment and second the development of a range of services for members in order to attract or retain them.

During BIFU's period of impecunity in the 1970s, the General Secretary was closely involved in the day-to-day management of finances. Since it has sorted out its operating position, the General Secretary has been less involved. He does, however, examine the agendas of the Finance Committee and Audit committee (an internal inspection unit), all conference motions, and the financial reports of merger candidates. He sees finance as the means to achieving the growth target of 200,000 members and is keen to encourage BIFU to be more market oriented. Overall, the policy is to encourage cost consciousness but not to let this inhibit any activity which is to the benefit of members, notably providing legal services on their behalf.

The finance officer has day-to-day responsibility for the union's performance. He is a qualified accountant and has developed budgeting systems and control since coming to the union in 1981. He acts as secretary to the Finance Committee and is particularly involved in managing budgets and projects. Budget setting is acknowledged to be 'a political process' based up until this year on a 'current year plus x' basis, but consideration has been given to a zero-based budgeting experiment. This would help the fact that, although the budgeting process in BIFU is extensive and costs are allocated in detail, actual controls on expenditure are difficult to enforce. Overspends are common and subject to negotiation with the Finance Committee.

This Committee is also concerned with investment decisions, but it would normally take advice from the finance officer and two independent firms of brokers before taking any decisions. The objective is to balance capital appreciation and income and in recent years under advice from the finance officer the spread of equities has become broader and represents a larger proportion of the total.

Fundamentally, the finance officer's role is to provide an expert resource rather than to direct. If members wish to spend more money than has been allocated, it was argued that this is their right and could hardly be prohibited; it would, however, be actively discouraged. Additionally, the officer sees his role in mergers and policy making as being to advise on options and their possible consequences without being prescriptive.

To summarise, BIFU is exceptionally centralised in its financial management. It relies greatly on subscription income and has tried to move away from direct cost competition with the staff associations. It claims to run a tight organisation because of its inability for many years to accumulate reserves or change subscription rates substantially. Currently it appears to be moving towards greater spending on recruitment and benefits with the confidence that it will be able to fund this through growth, but retains a strong sense of caution over keeping spending within the limits of its current income.

5   Finance and strategy

Two factors are central to understanding the strategy of BIFU: the progressive deregulation of various parts of the finance sector which have led to a corresponding widening of the union's recruiting territory and, secondly, the competition the union has faced from staff associations and other unions for members. The search for recognition and growth to a viable level of membership under these circumstances has shaped the policies and actions of the union. The union was first established in the English and Scottish retail banks. It began in the late 1960s to pursue membership elsewhere in the finance sector; this trend accelerated in the 1970s. In the process of growth, the union consistently came up against a competitive form of representation predominant in the finance sector, company unions, or staff associations. Seeking to match the challenge of these bodies, BIFU adopted a number of strategies but usually struggled because of advantages held by their competitors. One is the preference of employers for dealing with an association rather than the union or for a policy of peaceful competition (Bain, 1970). Relatively few employers have ceded the union sole recognition rights, the most notable exceptions being the TSB and Cooperative Banks and, latterly, the Midland. A second advantage held by the staff associations is that their membership fees are usually lower. In the past this was due to employer subsidy in various forms. As legal regulation of 'independent' unions became tighter this support was removed but the staff associations can still compete on price by carrying fewer overheads and not affiliating to the TUC. They also subsidise subscription income to a greater extent than TUC unions by selling financial services to members. A third factor to the staff associations' advantage has been the apparent preference of many financial sector employees for this form of representation because of its 'moderate' image: most staff associations oppose the use of industrial action or will only very reluctantly turn to it.

These factors have led the union to adopt a number of policies for growth and to meet the charge that it is an 'inappropriate' form of representation. One is the pursuit of mergers with staff associations. Currently this appears to be the dominant strategy and the union claimed in 1989 to be talking to 22 staff associations as well as those in the main clearing banks. One major problem is that the largest staff associations are in the clearing banks and they have repeatedly declined to take up the union's offer of merger. As the majority representatives in the clearers, they are the major block to membership growth for BIFU. The union's most significant success recently was to attract the Bank of England Staff Organisation with some 3,000 members. Otherwise its appeal has been limited to small associations in insurance and the minor building societies and even here it has suffered the setback of a subsequent breakaway by one group, in Eagle Star Insurance.

A second, and occasionally contradictory strategy has therefore been to try to have associations outlawed. This was favoured in the 1970s, using the legislation passed by the Labour government. Failure to prove that the staff associations were not proper 'independent' unions led to its abandonment, although it is a charge still used by the union in its litera-ture. A third strategy used by the union has been to attract members individually. This has proved difficult and costly where the union is not recognised or where it faces strong competition from a staff association.

Expansion into other parts of the financial sector has brought the union into competition with other TUC unions, notably MSF. The result has either been compromise arrangements or fractious competition for sole rights, depending usually on employer policy. For BIFU, competition against MSF means differentiating itself, usually by claiming either greater moderation and non-political status to appeal to the assumed preferences of its potential constituents, or by claiming greater expertise as the specialists in the financial sector. Given numerous changes in employment in the sector, including spread of information technology, European competition, and continuing deregulation, it is hoped to capital-ise on this in the future.

Competition with the staff associations takes a different form. BIFU concentrates on being seen as a more effective agent by virtue of its independence, back-up, and negotiating expertise. Its problem has been to demonstrate this both to non-members (who may choose to free-ride) and to staff association members (who gain many benefits anyway). Effectiveness claims may also be inhibited by the disinclination, in the view of BIFU officials, of many members to take more then the minimum of industrial action in most circumstances.

The union has increasingly developed campaigns to influence the direction and pace of change in the sector. In particular, these cover cam-paigns aimed at women – who constitute a majority in membership and in employment in the sector – concerning career prospects, equal pay for equal value, and health. The union is also campaigning to maintain bargaining rights in the face of shift to individual performance related rewards, notably among managerial grades, and to control the introduc-tion of technology and other factors affecting conditions of employment including hours of work. By and large, however, it appears to have had little influence on employer strategies. Its long-standing problem of demonstrating effectiveness to secure growth therefore remains the obstacle to achieving the target of 200,000 members which it is believed is the minimum necessary to maintain a full range of services and functions in the future.

Strong competition has pegged back subscription income. However BIFU's advantage in recent years, compared to other unions, has been the growth in employment in its recruiting territory which has allowed it to raise its income, but attracting staff associations into the union has meant that the union has had to subsidise transferring partners. In more recent years, the union has appeared to try to compete less on price and to adjust its subscription more in terms of its costs and changes in the price index. It has also tried hard to improve its collection rate to overcome the price elasticity of membership demand. This initially involved securing check-off arrangements but now the objective is to secure more direct debit payments and move away from check-off because of the reliance on employers this involves. This should also assist membership retention as it is believed that subscription changes were a major cause of resignation in the past. Direct debiting also aids cash-flow and reduces the arrears problems which were experienced until about five years ago.

Because of continuing constraints on income, BIFU plans carefully and there are considerable efforts to instil financial discipline in decision making. Subscription income is set to match expenditure which is determined in the budgeting process in the autumn. This system is sophisticated and precisely allocates money under budget heads to head office departments and institutional committees but the controls on spending are weaker in practice. The result is a tendency to overspend at a time when the union is seeking to build its reserves, but as one of the key causes of overshoots is in member meetings there is little union leaders feel they can do to increase control, given that to do so could be seen as undemocratic. To resolve this, there is a general effort to exhort members to bear in mind the financial consequences of decisions at conference.

As growth and the reduction of competition are central to the union's strategy, increased funds have been allocated to these policies. This involves the funding of transfers by staff associations and carrying officials where necessary. So, although BIFU does assess the financial position of potential merger partners carefully, this is often a secondary factor in the merger decision. Additionally, the union spends an increasing amount on recruiting drives, both general and in specific institutions. The success of these campaigns is monitored and the costs and benefits of recruitment are calculated.

The management of recruitment therefore illustrates the interaction of strategic and financial factors in BIFU. Its medium- to long-term objective is to achieve the minimum size to operate economically given the income constraints within which it operates. This objective also reflects the need of the union to grow in order to become the dominant union in the sector and larger, at the enterprise level, than its competitors in order to have greater influence on the bargaining process.

A second aspect in which strategic and financial factors interact concerns reserves. Greater reserves would allow BIFU more scope to extend its organisation which is critical to growth. In the 1970s it achieved more cost-effective growth than previously by securing and extending representative facilities from employers but these only very rarely included closed shop arrangements. Subsequently it has found it difficult to spread these arrangements, particularly in building societies, insurance companies, and International Banks where much employment growth has occurred and the union has had to bear the costs of recruitment and subsequent servicing of relatively small groups of members. Greater reserves would therefore allow it more scope to build local organisations and pursue one-off campaigns. The difficulty is that its operating expenditure continues to rise and absorb much of income, even though BIFU rigorously retains its cash at central level and limits the amounts branches and areas may hold.

To summarise, the key for BIFU is to secure cost-effective growth. The long-standing competition from other unions and the experience of employer hostility have consistently undermined its capacity to recruit and retain members cheaply enough to build reserves, expand its organisation, and move to a virtuous circle of further growth. Its strategy now is to pursue two forms of membership growth, both of which are designed to raise its influence, and achieve what the union sees as the minimum economic size. One is through piecemeal recruitment although it knows that this is a difficult and long route. Because its operating ratio is close to unity it does cost this option and seeks to ensure its actions are cost effective. Its second route – merger – is far more cost effective, and it achieves the ultimate strategic objectives of the union of monopoly representation in those enterprises where it operates, plus substantial membership transfer. For these reasons (although the immediate costs of transfers may be at a premium), they can be written off over the longer term as a worthwhile investment.

12 The Electrical, Electronic, Telecommunications and Plumbing Trade Union: accountability and financial control

1 Historical background

The Electrical, Electronic, Telecommunications, and Plumbing Trade Union (EETPU) was formed when the Electrical Trades Union (ETU) amalgamated with the Plumbers' Trade Union in 1968. Both the amalgamating parties have a history going back to the last century. ETU was formed in 1889. Local societies of plumbers existed before 1800 but it was not until 1865 that a national organisation was formed, the United Operative Plumbers' Association of Great Britain and Ireland.

Historically both ETU and PTU were craft unions aiming to control the supply and number of skilled electricians and plumbers through apprenticeship. However, the union now has over 23,000 women members, and a number of white-collar and managerial staff. It is currently facing a challenge to its skilled traditions with the upgrading of maintenance craftsmen to the status of 'technician', and is therefore facing the risk of losing these members to technical and white-collar unions like MSF. It has therefore been attempting to beef up its white-collar section (EESA) through mergers so that its more upwardly mobile skilled members are not tempted to transfer to staff associations or MSF which they may feel the rise in status justifies. The section has been successful in attracting a number of small unions and staff associations.[1] The union's recent expulsion from the TUC has had the effect of increasing the number of white-collar merger partners from outside the TUC.

Skilled members are still the most important group within the union, comprising almost 55% of members. Clerical and technical workers comprise approximately 28%. Membership within the skilled group is not only likely to be lost through individual advancement to technician levels, but also through the growth in self-employment, particularly in the southeast, which threatens established training and pay structures. Thus EETPU is collaborating with the Electrical Contractors' Association and the Joint Industry Board (JIB) to prevent fragmentation of the industry by setting up a registration scheme of qualified self-employed electricians,

185

and is attempting to have some influence over agencies for self-employed electrical contracting workers. It has been criticised by other unions for doing this, because it is seen as sanctioning a breakup of the core of directly employed workers within the sector, similar to that seen in other areas of the construction industry.

Criticism of EETPU's policies has been common among TUC affiliates in recent years. In 1988, the union was expelled from the TUC over the issue of membership competition, particularly concerning the signing of single-union deals.[2] Since it is no longer covered by the Bridlington procedures, it faces potential competition for membership on all fronts but, conversely, provides a focus for non-TUC organisations and an attractive merger partner for small non-affiliates. This has had an important influence on the union's strategy, as we show below.

2   Structure and government

The current political structure of EETPU is difficult to understand without some further discussion of its history, since it is in part a reaction to it. ETU was involved in a number of well-known scandals before its merger with the plumbers in 1968. Between 1894 and 1907 no less than three consecutive General Secretaries were dismissed for defalcation, though such incidents were not unusual at the time (the General Secretary of the plumbers was also dismissed in 1907 for embezzlement and drunkenness). The most serious scandal culminated in a legal battle in the High Court about alleged ballot rigging in 1961. The background to the case began to develop just after the Second World War when the Communist Party won control of ETU. Throughout the 1950s and 1960s the right wingers and communists engaged in a long drawn out struggle for control of the union. In the case of Byrne versus Foulkes, the losing candidate in the election for General Secretary made allegations against 14 defendants of a fraudulent conspiracy to rig the ballot. After a complex 42 day trial, the court found the case proven against five individuals.

Following the case in the High Court, the union underwent major changes under the leadership of Les Cannon and Frank Chapple, to ensure that the union could not become an ideological battle-ground again. ETU was reorganised into a highly centralised structure with a full-time elected Executive Committee (EC), no longer bound by the decisions of Conference delegates. Instead the union computerised its membership for balloting purposes, so that any disagreements over policy could be settled by direct reference to a ballot of all the members.

The EC also took direct control over branch structure and activity by assuming the right to suspend or dissolve branches as necessary, and by putting in full-time officers to supervise branch administration. At the same time the right of appeal by branches against EC decisions was removed. Since 1969 all full-time officers have been appointed by the EC, and members of the Communist Party have been barred from holding any office, including the office of Conference delegate.

In consequence, the supreme governing body of EETPU is not the annual Conference as in most unions, but the Executive Council which is the body responsible for making and carrying out policy. It consists of full-time officers who are elected for five years: the General Secretary, the Plumbing Secretary, and 13 Divisional Members. The President of the union is elected by and from the Divisional Members of the EC each year. The President presides at meetings of the EC and at the union's conferences. The General Secretary is elected by a vote of all the members of the union, while the secretary of the plumbing section is elected by a vote of the members of the three plumbing Divisions of the union. The Divisional Members of the EC are elected by members who are divided into 13 electoral divisions.

EETPU holds conferences biennially 'to consider policy and any other special business affecting the union', but the EC is not bound by Conference decisions. Conference is an advisory body only, though subscription increases must be ratified by Conference if they are to hold. Each branch is entitled to send one delegate, but the Industrial Conferences are also entitled to send delegates. Only delegates can vote at Conference; members of the EC may attend and speak, but they are not entitled to vote. However, the EC is responsible for the agenda, and it determines the number and character of motions and amendments. Every six years the Biennial Conference considers revisions to the rules, but the rules can also be altered by a ballot of all the members, and by a resolution of the EC.

Below the EC, the members are divided into 27 mainly geographically based Areas. The EC determines both Area and branch boundaries, and also the electoral constituencies of the union. Most Areas benefit from an Area office, and there are 29 of these in all. Area officers are responsible to the EC, and carry out its instructions.

Below the Area structure there are 820 branches. The size of the branches varies, the largest ones being based on industries rather than firms (e.g., electrical contracting). However, the branches in EETPU are not held to be as important as the industrial conferences of shop stewards. Each branch receives some direct support from a full-time official, mostly an Area officer.

In addition to the Biennial Delegate Conference, there are also nine National Industrial Conferences, and seven Area Industrial Conferences. Area Industrial Conferences are convened by the full-time Area officials every year. These consist of shop stewards or staff representatives from the above mentioned industries. The Area Industrial Conferences consider motions to submit to National Industrial Conference. They elect delegates to the National Industrial Conference, the Area Industrial Committee, and the Biennial Delegate Conference, and also representatives to the National Industrial Committee. The Area Industrial Committees assist full-time officials to resolve problems in particular industries. They elect delegates to serve on Joint Industrial Councils and Joint TUC Committees, consider reports produced by National Industrial Committees, and submit motions for the National Industrial Conferences. Area Industrial Committees include Area full-time officials, branch full-time officials and the Executive Council Member for that division as well as delegates elected at Area Industrial Conferences.

National Conferences are convened by the EC which determines the method of representation, agenda, and procedure. They elect delegates to the Biennial Delegate Conferences for those industries which do not hold Area Industrial Conferences. They meet twice a year and consist of delegates elected by either the Area Industrial Conferences or the National Industrial Conference, and the National officer for that industry. National officials submit reports of their activities to the National Area Committees. The Committees also consider resolutions from Area Industrial Committees.

The union employs a relatively large number of staff for the size of membership. There are approximately 2,500 members per official. In addition there are 260 head office staff. Each employee is thus supported by approximately 1,000 members.

3   Financial performance

The membership of EETPU peaked in 1979 at just over 440,000 and has since declined by 17% to approximately 367,000 (see Figure 12.1). The membership turnover is about 45,000 p.a. (or 12%). Most of the union's members are relatively young, having been in membership for only about seven years. Recruitment has a high priority within the union, and all officers are expected to recruit. Advancement and approval for officials within the organisation depend on a good recruitment record. Since the union's expulsion from the TUC, new officers have been taken on, some for a trial period of two years. Their individual contracts will only be renewed if their recruitment record has been sound. Membership receives constant attention from the EC, and Divisional Recruitment Officers have to report to the EC regularly, showing where members have been lost and why, and where new members have been won.

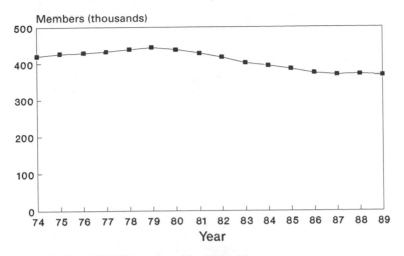

Figure 12.1. EETPU membership, 1974–89

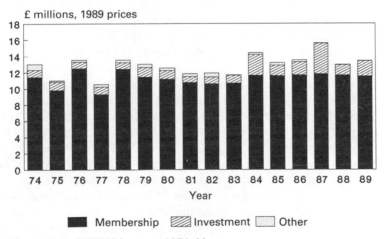

Figure 12.2. EETPU income, 1974–89

The income of the union has not depended solely on membership, in that total real income declined between 1974 and 1978 when membership was rising, but increased after 1984 despite the continuing fall in membership. Figure 12.2 shows the income entering all the unions funds, i.e., the General Fund, the General Purposes Fund, and the Political Fund. The union also has a Computer Reserve Fund, but this is a savings fund, and only contains monies transferred from the General Fund. The level of

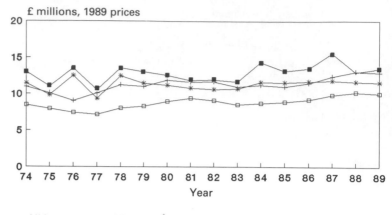

Figure 12.3. EETPU income and expenditure

income from investments has remained fairly stable throughout the period, but in 1987 it increased significantly.[3] The income from other sources includes income from hiring out the union's computer capacity, and income from training activities offered at Esher College and Cudham Hall.

In the aggregate, the union has been able to achieve surpluses between 1974 and 1989. Figure 12.3 shows that the total level of income from all sources has generally exceeded the total level of expenditure. Moreover, total membership income has exceeded administration costs. However, the value of the union's funds and the value of the union's assets fell between 1974 and 1983, suggesting that the surpluses made in the years 1974–83 were too small to maintain the real value of the union's funds and assets. Since 1983 the real value of the union's funds and assets have increased, and they now exceed the level achieved in 1974 (Figure 12.4).

The bulk of the union's expenditure goes on administration, and these costs have not declined despite the fall in membership after 1979 (Figure 12.5). Again the expenditure of all the unions funds is included in the figure. Benefit expenditure accounts for only a small proportion of the total. Most of the new benefits that became available to members in 1986 are self-financing, namely the financial services, including mortgage, insurance and banking discounts, and legal advice. However, the union does provide some of the more traditional benefits, like funeral benefit, strike benefit, disablement grant, fatal accident grant, legal aid, and victimisation benefit. The other expenditure category includes some of the costs of running Esher College and Cudham Hall.

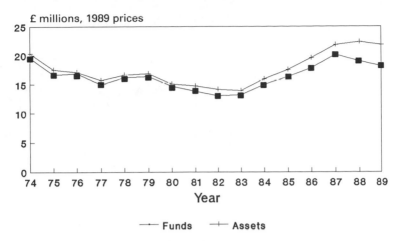

Figure 12.4. EETPU funds and assets

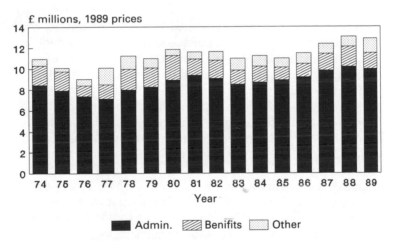

Figure 12.5. EETPU expenditure, 1974–89

The composition of the union's assets have changed over the period 1974–89 (Figure 12.6). The proportion of fixed assets held by the union has increased, while the proportion of quoted securities declined. Until 1987 the union held a lot of its money in equities, and indeed was one of the first trade unions to invest in the stock market. It was also one of the founding unions of Trade Union Unit Trusts. The amount held in cash (other assets) has remained fairly constant over the period. In 1987 the union sold about half its stock market holdings just before the crash in

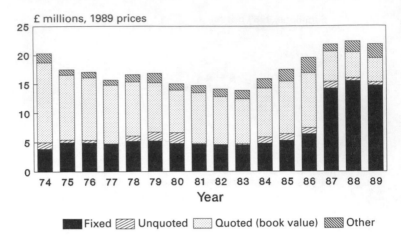

£ millions, 1989 prices

■ Fixed ▨ Unquoted ▢ Quoted (book value) ▧ Other

Figure 12.6. EETPU assets, 1974–89

October of that year to buy Buxted Park in East Sussex, costing about £6 million. Buxted Park was purchased to provide discount leisure facilities to members and to boost the union's training activities at Esher (non-technical training) and Cudham Hall (technical training).

The union's investment strategy is based on three broad principles; getting a good return on the money, avoiding politically sensitive investments, and investing in industries where the union has members. This latter principle conflicts with the investment policies of some other unions which, for example, might avoid nuclear power or defence. All the property and assets of the union are held by West Common Holdings Limited, a company limited by guarantee which acts in place of the lay Trustees whom it replaced in 1970. It does not trade but is registered at Companies House, and has three Directors – the General Secretary, the Finance Officer, and the Head of Administration.

4   Financial management

The EC is formally responsible for the financial management of the union. Under rule 'The general management and control of the Union and the handling of the whole of its affairs shall be vested in the Executive Council.' Also in rule it is stated that 'All money, funds, books and property of every description in the hands of the branch or its officers or members or any other person or persons on its behalf or with its authority are at all times the property of the Union held on behalf of the Executive Council.' On a day-to-day basis, matters are handled by a finance department of 30 people, headed by a qualified accountant. The finance officer reports in detail to the Executive Council monthly.

About 95% of membership income is handled by head office but only about 66% of contribution payments go straight into head office: 9% of contribution income is paid to head office annually in advance and members receive a six week discount if they participate in this scheme, while 57% enters head office through check-off, which costs on average about 2.5% of the subscription bill. Check-off income is not processed through the Area offices. In the past the union has taken the initiative with employers over check-off, and has made every effort to encourage members to participate by offering free bank accounts with £100 on deposit or a loan for as much as four weeks' pay, which is clawed back over 52 weeks. Twenty-five per cent of income comes through to head office from the branches, and another 9% of membership income is received through the Joint Industry Board scheme which is specific to the electrical contracting industry. Since 1988 the union has also run a direct debit scheme, targeted particularly at those who pay through the branches. This has been growing by about 300–400 per week.

Within EETPU, all membership details are recorded on a central computer, the union having invested in computing capacity about 25 years ago. Each member has a computer-generated membership card which includes the name, address, branch number, employer number, date of branch meetings, and name of branch officer, as well as contribution details. The computer records both employment and benefit details, and is also used for balloting purposes. The computerised membership register is normally updated weekly, and it is about 97% accurate.

The computer system is seen as a major source of strength by the union's officers. It can instantly provide details of arrears and automatically produces reminder letters, as well as providing detailed breakdowns of the membership by Area, branch, or industry. The union makes every effort to recover arrears without discouraging members, and offers some incentives to encourage defaulters to pay up, such as reducing the out of benefit period. Currently contribution arrears run at about £1 per member. Arrears problems tend to arise mainly with those paying through the branches, though shop stewards are responsible for checking members' cards and reporting to Area full-time officials. However, subscription yield is not only influenced by those who fall into arrears. Members who are away from work through sickness and losing basic pay, the unemployed, and those on strike, are excused subscription payments. In

1989, there were two contribution rates, 80p per week for skilled, technical, supervisory, and managerial members, and 65p per week for auxiliary, clerical, administrative, and apprentice members. Honorary members pay an annual subscription, but retired members do not pay.

Increases in contribution rates must be ratified by a Biennial Delegate Conference. The EC has the authority in rule to increase contribution rates in between Biennial Delegate Conferences by a maximum of 10p per week, but these increases have to be ratified by the next Conference if they are to hold. If the EC fails to achieve ratification, the contribution increases cease to have effect, but the sums already paid are not refundable to the members.

In adjusting the contribution rate, the Executive Council considers the following factors: the levels members can afford, the income needed by the union, and also what other unions charge. Currently EETPU subscription rate is lower than that of either GMB or AEU, benefits are better and subscription yield is much higher. In principle EETPU likes contribution income to cover expenditure, though this has not always been possible.

On the expenditure side, the union is very careful with its costs. EETPU has always tried to keep its costs low so that it can compete on subscriptions. If costs are in check then EETPU can get away with charging less than other unions. All the new services provided by the union (insurance advice, etc.) are self-financing, and these are considered to be a positive influence on recruitment efforts.

At the beginning of each year the union prepares its budget, under the various major cost centre headings. Income for the ensuing year is calculated on the basis of known membership in October/November. After building in an allowance for a surplus, aggregate estimated expenditure is then divided between a number of cost centres. These include each Area office, and the national overheads like Cudham Hall and Esher College and the activities of head office departments like research, legal aid, and the magazine. Areas are not directly allocated resources. The only allocation they receive is an imprest banking system to deal with day-to-day expenditure.

The expenditure budgets are decided by the General Secretary and the union's auditors, and are constructed from past expenditure, and the rate of inflation. Not all head office expenditure can be easily estimated, particularly benefit payments. The costs of the national overheads, or the central activities undertaken by the head office departments and the colleges are distributed between the Areas by deducting an allowance for these from the expenditure budget for each Area office on a per capita basis. Buxted is run as a purely commercial undertaking and is a separate limited company. However, both Esher College and Cudham Hall are run slightly differently. Here no real attempt is made to break even, but income is measured against expenditure and the commercial rates are set to subsidise as much in-house education as possible.

Monthly management accounts are produced for the EC. If the budgets allocated to the Areas are wildly wrong, the EC can raise income by increasing contribution rates. All staff are paid from head office, but the other costs of the Area offices are funded through the imprest system. Each Area office has to submit an expenditure statement fortnightly. The branches also have to submit financial statements to head office fortnightly, but in practice EETPU branches do not hold much cash as much of the income collected by branches is now paid by cheque. Also branches must submit quarterly to head office the branch contribution ledger, recording all payments made in the period by the members and the money stewards. The honoraria paid to branch officials are paid quarterly in arrears by head office and are taxable: they consist of a small percentage (4–6%) of contributions for the branch secretary and treasurer and flat fees of less than £1 for the branch committee and other officers. These rates are fixed in rule, and can only be changed by a vote at the Biennial Delegate Conference.

In addition, each year the Executive Council allocates 2% of total branch contributions received during the year to the Branch General Purposes Fund. Branches may make claims on this fund from head office, which can be easily monitored, but money from this fund can only be spent on grants 'to members or their dependants, to local organisations or any other worthy cause'. It cannot be used for political purposes, nor for making grants in connection with trade disputes. Various other expenses are payable at the discretion of the EC. For example the rate of strike benefit is fixed in rule, but only the EC has the authority to sanction an official strike. Similarly the EC exercises its discretion over claims for disablement grant, fatal accident grant, victimisation benefit, and legal aid.

The union's investments are managed by the Directors of West Common Holdings Limited in conjunction with the union's stockbrokers. Liquidity is also important in the event of a strike. The union has holdings in government stocks, in equities and unit trusts, and in the overnight money market. The union also has a number of large properties, primarily the head office, the colleges, and the newly purchased leisure/conference centre at Buxted. The property strategy is planned centrally, and there is a central estates department. The strategy is broadly to utilise assets to help the members. The union does not buy property as an asset independent of use. Hayes was bought after the war when the union moved out of bomb-damaged property in Peckham. Esher was also bought some time ago. Cudham was developed into a training college when the union noted that the cost of technical training to employers was prohibitively expensive. The union now runs courses for employers, for employed members, and unemployed members. The union bears most of the costs of training unemployed members.

5   Finance and strategy

EETPU is often regarded as the closest equivalent to American business unionism. Policy could be described as at once authoritarian and populist, dictated from head office. EETPU openly stood apart from other unions by supporting government funding for union ballots, and was in fact prepared to be expelled from the TUC along with AEU over the issue. Most of the other large TUC unions threatened to defy the law because none of them had centralised membership registers, nor effective membership balloting systems unlike both EETPU and AEU. EETPU was actually able to ballot its members on the principle of accepting government money for balloting, and its members approved by a majority of nine to one.

The union has pioneered single-union, no strike agreements. The first agreement was signed in 1981 at Toshiba in Plymouth, but since then approximately 30 more have been signed by the union, many of them in South Wales. Single-union strike-free deals appear to have the support of the members of the union. Eighty-three per cent of the members voted in favour of continuing to negotiate single-status, strike-free agreements and 16% against.

EETPU was expelled amid great acrimony from the TUC. Some of the hostility felt by other unions may be explained by reference to their inability to compete against EETPU in 'beauty contests' staged for employers considering recognition. Other unions have fallen out with the Electricians over their policies and their aggressive recognition efforts. These include NUM's leadership which was, for example, criticised by Hammond of EETPU during the miners' strike, NUR which lost out to EETPU on recognition in the Docklands Light Railway, and the printing unions over EETPU's pact with Eddie Shah, and involvement with News International at Wapping. Moreover, EETPU is considered to be intruding on other unions' territory, particularly in the North Sea among divers, and in satellite television. Its recruitment efforts are often focused on employers rather than individuals.

The effect of the union's expulsion from the TUC however, has been to divest the union of its left wing which has left to form a breakaway union – the Electrical & Plumbing Industries Union, which is now accommodated by MSF. Some of EETPU's members at the Ford Dagenham plant have joined the breakaway, and the left-wing London Press branch has gone to SOGAT. Conversely some smaller, non-TUC unions are attracted by the prospect of merging with EEPTU because it is outside the TUC, such as the Institute of Journalists.

EETPU has also pioneered the services it provides members, and other unions followed its lead. The 'Money-Wise' scheme provides professional financial advice; this includes advice about pensions, discount household insurance, reduced conveyancing fees, personal accident insurance, etc. EETPU has also recently embarked on a joint training scheme with the Electrical Contractors' Association to provide a 'Fast Track' course for the unemployed, who are given the opportunity to qualify as electricians in one year rather than three and a half years. The new range of membership services and training opportunities reflect the union's efforts to hold on to its existing membership.

As well as absorbing smaller unions into its own structure, EETPU has been engaged in lengthy discussion with AEU about a possible merger. The resulting merger would seem to be key to EETPU future strategy. If the union had remained outside the TUC, then merger or federation with other non-TUC unions would have been an appropriate response to TUC competition. Merger with a large, moderate, broadly skilled TUC affiliate such as AEU provides a means of re-entry and a solution to the problems of inter-union competition which attended EETPU's expulsion. However, in the case of AEU, as we have shown, there are massive differences in government and structure to be overcome.

EETPU is a highly competitive union. Its populist policies are based on a philosophy of responding to members' wishes which set it both against certain political stances taken by TUC affiliates and against any regulatory mechanism such as the Bridlington principles. Its benefits are cost effective and are designed to both attract and retain members. Its efficiency in financial management supports both benefit and recruitment expenditure while enabling the union to compete effectively in the membership market. In this sense, financial management, financial strategy, and union objectives are in close alignment.

6   Conclusion

It is appropriate at this point briefly to summarise the findings from the case studies and to assess their implications before proceeding to present the findings of this study as a whole. We have discussed the finances of five unions, two general, two industrial, and one – broadly – craft. In all, financial management has undergone change recently. All have experienced some form of financial problem, even though their financial performance is by no means uniform.

In fact, though these unions are not convergent in structure or policy, the similarities between their experiences are more striking than the differences. All have had to cap benefit expenditure yet move towards a system of benefit provision which is cost effective and appeals to members. The former is perhaps less marked than the latter in NUM, which does not compete for new members, but both trends are marked in the other four. Leaders in all unions have become more concerned with finances across the decade and have centralised financial management: this is perhaps the most striking finding to emerge both here and in the questionnaire analysis. It results in a situation in all unions where control over financial matters is far more centralised than control over policy making through the union's government structure. This government structure is in turn the union's greatest expenditure item and there has emerged in all unions a conflict between centre and periphery in which the centre, with control over finances, has generally prevailed. Ben Roberts' dictum still prevails.

The remarkable aspect of this trend is that it prevails across unions with very different ideological positions. From NUM to EETPU in our case studies, more effective and more centralised financial management has been an objective. This is because, despite the divergent problems these unions faced, financial issues were central to the resolution of the key strategic issue. For BIFU and EETPU this is simply competition for membership. Both seek to succeed through cost effective service provision: in both the fixed costs of a relatively large central overhead need to be spread over a larger membership. In GMB, effective financial management is the key to the 'new' expansionary unionism which must *inter alia* attract low income groups. For AEU and, spectacularly, for NUM, effective, centralised financial management is a necessary ingredient in the resolution of financial crisis. For AEU, it is essentially an income problem which has emerged through poor financial control in the past. For NUM, it is an asset problem exposed by the strike but endemic in the structure of the union. In both, the contest between central control and area or district autonomy is clear.

13 Conclusions: union business and business unionism

1 Introduction

We set ourselves the task of analysing changes in trade unions in the period 1980–9, from a particular perspective. We were concerned to look at financial matters and the internal management systems of unions, rather than, for example, union democracy or bargaining behaviour. We were also concerned to focus on formal union organisation rather than on shop steward networks. Our account is thus by no means a comprehensive picture of change. Nevertheless, we feel that there are some general points about change in trade unions to be made on the basis of our analysis, and they are detailed below. In essence, we shall argue that the changes we have documented are related to more deep seated changes in union organisation and behaviour. Financial variables have responded to broader changes both within the trade union movement and beyond: they have, in turn, influenced union policy responses to change throughout the decade. We shall outline this argument in detail below and assess its implications. However, at the outset it is useful to summarise the empirical work.

2 Summary

Trade unions are not primarily economic organisations and they do not seek in general to maximise financial performance. Nevertheless, they require a certain level of financial resources to survive and to grow. So much was recognised by the Webbs (1907), but many more recent studies have failed to consider financial matters when explaining union behaviour, and no detailed conceptualisation or analysis exists of the financial subsystems of trade unions. This may be because, for many years, unions in the UK have not themselves perceived financial constraints on their behaviour or because the concern of many analysts has been with informal rather than formal unionism. However, if financial matters have been irrelevant in the past, they are unlikely to be so in future.

Data on financial resources, on an aggregated and disaggregated basis, are available throughout the post-war period in the form of statutory returns from all trade unions. However, in order to secure data on the nature and the management of such resources and on the political issues surrounding resource allocation, it was necessary to proceed, via questionnaires and case study analysis, to examination of a smaller set of unions. These data together reveal substantial variability in union financial performance, but the context is one of long-term financial decline.

In the aggregate, UK unions have suffered long-term financial debilitation in the post-war period. Although solvency has been maintained, by a slim margin, the real net worth of trade unions has fallen, particularly during periods of rapid membership growth. The evidence indicates that, at least to 1980, union assets were not inflation proof. The basis of this fall in real assets was an inability to cover expenditure, which has risen consistently in real terms, from subscription income. Union subscriptions in the UK have been low, and indeed falling, through most of the post-war period as a proportion of real earnings.

Ironically, there has been substantial financial improvement during the severe membership losses of the 1980s. Unions have raised real income and reversed the fall in net worth. Fewer members are paying more, and the asset base appears to be both covering the income shortfall and providing a surplus for reinvestment. The interesting question is why should the Thatcher years, so inimical to union organisation, have been reasonably favourable for union financial growth?

A disaggregated analysis was necessary to begin such an answer. Financial performance varied considerably from 1980 onwards. The clearest cases of financial debilitation followed from the experience of national strikes, in steel and coal mining for example. Competing unions also were among the least financially successful. At the other extreme, financial growth was a characteristic of several public-sector white-collar unions which had, comparatively, a weaker financial base at the start of the decade. It was also characteristic of several unions which did not compete for members. However, without analysis of what was actually going on within specific trade unions, it was difficult to understand exactly why some unions were financially successful while others were not. In order to pursue such an analysis, we needed to develop a model of the financial subsystems of trade unions.

In Chapter 4, an approach was developed which saw trade unions as not-for-profit organisations which, to survive, had to achieve success in two related markets; on the one hand, that for employers seeking a bargaining agent and offering recognition and support in the form of facilities and, on the other, that for members to whom a range of services need to be provided in return for subscriptions. Successful operation in both markets ensured financial success, but it was also necessary for the union to achieve bargaining and membership objectives. In this approach, the unions' own resources were seen as important factors in the achievement of overall objectives. A certain level of financial resource was thus essential for union operation.

In fact, it appeared that financial management and the measurement of financial performance were, in the absence both of clear financial objectives and therefore relevant financial measures, essentially political issues. Chapter 5 focused on the policies of such matters, initially discussing the general nature of financial debates within unions and subsequently examining the role of financial managers more specifically.

The questionnaire and case study data indicated the extent of change in financial management within unions. Subscription payments have been automated, leading to an improvement in subscription yield. Subscription levels are increasingly set to an index of earnings, thus avoiding the necessity for debates at conference and helping to protect real subscription income per capita. Expenditure levels are closely monitored and unions have, in several cases, moved towards formal budgeting systems. Increasingly, assets are managed centrally, with few rule book constraints on their disposition.

Several consequences could be identified. Firstly, unions became more centralised in the management of resources and the role of the branch or region was consequently diminished. Secondly, it is likely that, through increased reliance on check-off, unions have become financially more employer-dependent. Thirdly, the management of finances has been to some extent depoliticised, or at least it seems easier for those concerned with the management of union finances to deploy resources according to conventional commercial criteria.

There were differences between unions in all these respects. Naturally enough, poorer case study unions were more concerned about financial matters, making them more central to the governance of the union. There was, however, substantial variance in the level of sophistication of systems of financial management which was unrelated to wealth. It remains the case that several unions lack systems of financial control which generate even the most basic forms of financial data, and they are thus unable to incorporate any detailed financial arguments into the process of policy formulation.

One argument to assess was that there are economies of scale in trade union organisation and that larger unions will *ceteris paribus* be financially more successful. In fact, the largest unions are the richest, though not in per capita terms, and the cheapest, although we have not measured levels of service provision. However, it remained difficult to make generalisations about the effects of size alone. The extent of inter-union competition and the nature of union government – itself related to the level of employer subsidy – are crucial. In addition, the mechanism chosen for growth was also important. Several mechanisms, including growth through merger, do not appear always to have been financially beneficial.

Another argument was that the experience of strike activity was important in explaining variable financial performance: this was examined in detail in Chapter 7. A more varied picture emerged. Unions such as ISTC and NUS, which had experienced large national disputes were indeed financially debilitated by them, but the experience of the civil service dispute indicated that, in certain circumstances, the effect of strike calls on the level of membership income could more than offset expenditure increases, resulting in financial growth. *Ex ante* it appears to be very difficult to assess the likely financial consequences of strike action, even where sequestration of assets is involved.

The final part of the volume sought further to illustrate some of our arguments by discussion of five case study unions in some detail. These cases were picked to demonstrate particular aspects of union management rather than to characterise unions as a whole and we sought in each to demonstrate the relationship between financial considerations and union strategy. The first, NUM, is in structural and policy terms highly idiosyncratic. Its inclusion illustrates perhaps the most complex financial system of any trade union as well as showing clearly the consequences of prosecution of an industrial dispute without reference to financial considerations.

The two largest case study unions, GMB and AEU, show two radically different financial structures and trajectories of change. GMB has halted membership decline through merger and its governance and financial structure have been transformed in consequence. Not all of the mergers could be regarded as financially successful in their own terms, but they have assisted changes in the union promoted by the General Secretary. The AEU financial structure reflects the union's heavy reliance on lay participation and employer support for union government: most of the union's resources are, in fact, 'off balance sheet'. Its history in the 1980s is one of massive membership loss and financial debilitation, followed by partial recovery through the imposition of financial controls.

BIFU displays a very different history. It has experienced steady membership growth but, since it operates in a highly competitive membership market, financial pressures have remained strong. The case illustrates clearly the problems faced by the union in pursuing cost effective growth:

it must operate in both employer and membership markets and the preference therefore is for growth through transfer of engagements, a preference which is reflected in changes to the structure of the union to accommodate incoming groups of members.

In EETPU, one finds a case of the union being run in accordance with strict financial controls and sophisticated control systems. Efficiency in financial management supports recruitment and maintained benefit expenditure while allowing the union to compete in both membership and employer markets. Of all our cases, EETPU has the most highly centralised financial system and one where the union's declared objectives and its systems of financial management were most closely in line. It charged lower subscription levels than many rivals and was, in competition with other unions, highly successful in recognition contests.

Taken together, the cases illustrate an underlying pattern of change in the 1980s. There is greater uniformity in the centralisation of systems for financial control than in the highly variable patterns of union government. The latter indicate more general pressures. All the cases experienced major initiatives to reform financial management based on a keener appreciation of the constraints on policy formation and implementation imposed by financial debilitation in the late 1970s and early 1980s. In all case study unions, financial issues were central to the union's future strategy. We shall return to this point below, but the case study interviews throughout revealed the extent to which union leaders recognised that major financial changes were necessary for union reform.

3   The hypotheses and the model

The first question to emerge from this discussion concerns the usefulness of our model described in Chapter 4. To what extent is it useful to characterise unions in terms of two related product markets, and to focus on institutional or leadership objectives? One way to answer this is to focus on the six hypotheses derived from the model. Several are corroborated, but others perform less well.

The first hypothesis was that formal financial systems would be neither common nor rigorous and that financial issues would only be to the fore in moments of crisis. Some data supported this. Financial centrality was inversely related to wealth and the perception of financial crisis was key to financial reform in NUM, EETPU, and AEU. However, unions such as IRSF and FDA consciously planned for future expenditures and made financial decisions supportive of long-term growth. The extent of formal financial planning and control undoubtedly increased across the decade and not always in response to financial difficulties. Our evidence would point also to the impact of legislation on the computerisation of membership and financial records and, more diffusely, to the tendency for unions to imitate one another in the adoption of such systems.

The second was that unions set subscriptions competitively and avoid raising them unless compelled to do so: they would rather improve subscription yield than subscription levels. Considerable evidence on subscription levels and from case study interviews supports the competitive hypothesis. Subscription levels in competitive sectors converge and finance officers and executives were often required to justify subscription changes in terms of the behaviour of competitor unions. Many unions wish to avoid subscription increases and have moved towards indexation mechanisms in order to prevent having increases debated: they welcome the revenue but not the argument. However, there was contrary evidence from the questionnaire. Many finance officers, particularly in smaller unions where membership competition may be less severe, did not see competitive subscription levels as important. The support for improved yield was almost universal, evidenced in the shift in collection mechanisms.

The third set of hypotheses concerned asset management and were a more accurate description of practice at the beginning of the decade than at the end. We hypothesised that assets would not be managed to secure a competitive rate of return and that rule book provision would constrain asset management. All of the evidence shows that unions now manage investments more commercially, or at least have agents to do so, and that rule book constraints are disappearing: many are, in practice, ignored. These changes fit with the proposition that union leaders have become net revenue maximisers across the decade, but it also should be borne in mind that most of our case study unions experienced a shortfall of subscription income over total expenditure. The role of investment income in such circumstances is less to provide a disposable net revenue to leaders than to cover expenditure on the membership.

The fourth hypothesis concerned income and expenditure. We hypothesised that income would be set to meet expenditure. It too is broadly supported. Few unions planned income levels in order to generate surplus, the prime factor in any income change being a change in expenditure levels. In some unions, the role of the finance officer was to 'deliver' income to cover pre-set expenditure levels, although the more sophisticated ones costed the expenditure implications of conference decisions in advance. In some unions, detailed expenditure data were available based on budgeting systems, but in others they were completely absent. Cost cutting measures were common in the former unions.

The fifth hypothesis was that unions would make financial decisions based on calculations about employer subsidy. It receives little support. Most unions know the importance of but could not put a value on the level of employer subsidy. BIFU, among others, had a policy of seeking facilities improvements from employers, but financial decisions tended to be made in terms of the union's own balance sheet. Certain types of decision, for example to strike, were in practice very likely to depend for their financial consequences on employer reactions, particularly for cash-flow, but the view that such calculations *should* be made was not generally shared: at least unions in general did not see employer dependence as a problem.

The sixth hypothesis, that union leaders would seek control over income and would centralise and depoliticise income and expenditure management did, however, receive substantial support. The installation of automated payment methods, subscription indexation, centralised accounting, and asset management systems, the disappearance of rule book provisions on investment and the emergence of a group of appointed finance officers in the larger unions controlled by the General Secretary or EC all support the proposition that the exercise of managerial discretion supports both the centralisation and depoliticisation of union financial management. The corollary is that the branch, district, or region became financially dependent rather than autonomous and, frequently, its role in union government was diminished. The evidence for this centralisation and depoliticisation emerged consistently from both questionnaire and case study data.

A more general set of considerations concerns the two-product market model itself. It does account for the financial structure of trade unions overall: no union we encountered could, in our judgement, fund day-to-day operations indefinitely from its own resources without massive subscription increases or exhaustion of assets. All are employer-dependent and operate in the employer market in the way we have defined it.

However, this is almost axiomatic, following from the collective bar-gaining focus of unions. The second question is whether union leaders and officers see themselves as two-market organisations and therefore dependent on employers. Some union leaders rejected the idea out of hand. Others indicated that the idea of an employer market was important but could not be articulated within the union where debate had to centre around ideas of independence and service to members' interests. A third set, notably in EETPU and BIFU openly acknowledged the employer market and employer dependence both in debate and in recruitment policy.

In a similar vein, some leaders acknowledged the importance of admin-istrative rationality, particularly during times of membership contraction;

others did not. All referred to the difficulties involved in publicly articulating it, particularly at 'set piece' gatherings such as Executive Committee meetings and Conferences.

In short, then, the approach outlined in Chater 4 performs reasonably well, but its limitations are much as expected. We spell out a model based on assumptions about administrative rationality: i.e., that union leaders would rationally exercise managerial discretion in the interests of institutional objectives on the basis of full information. Where these conditions were approximated, the model performed well. Where leaders lacked discretion or information, it did not: clearly discretion and the ability to secure such information are often related.

The extent to which discretion is a requirement can be seen by contrasting AEU with EETPU. The governance structure of the former, a set of checks and balances, makes centralisation very difficult. That of the latter, a sort of populist autocracy, supports it. The extent to which the perception of competition is important may be seen by contrasting BIFU with ISTC. However, the model fails to account for another, ideological dimension: it does not adequately account, for example, for the history of NUM, where non-economic objectives become paramount.

Three areas of importance to the future of trade unionism emerge as requiring further discussion. We have argued that unions are becoming more employer-dependent but that they do not necessarily perceive this as a problem. Our model suggests that to some extent unions must depend on employer facilities but there clearly is a limit – not least in law in the test of independence – beyond which they would cease to be free agents. The second area is membership competition. Many large unions are seeking new members, often at the expense of competitors but competitive unionism is, as we have shown, financially debilitating. The third area concerns the relationship between union management and union policy. To the extent that unions are managed efficiently and that efficiency becomes an objective, certain policy options may be precluded. Unions which analyse the costs and benefits of courses of action may be contrasted with those pursuing ideological goals. The former may be characterised as more 'realistic', but to what extent does this reaction in fact arise simply from the pursuit of institutional objectives: put another way, if unions are like businesses, will business unionism emerge? We shall discuss each area in turn: in practice, they are, as we shall show, related.

4   Employer-dependence

Collective bargaining in itself implies employer-dependence but the extent of such dependence varies substantially, as do the implications for the union. We may illustrate some of the difficulties here by a simple comparison. AEU is heavily dependent on a combination of lay activism and employer support both for union government and for collective bargaining: most of the union's activity is off the balance sheet. However, we could also take the establishment of such organisation and the concession of facilities as evidence of power over the employer or, as we have put it, success in the employer market. BIFU, particularly during the 1960s and 1970s as NUBE, provides a complete contrast. Dependent on its own resources, particularly full-time officers, without any facilities from employers, it stressed regional and industrial organisation to differentiate itself from the company-based and, in NUBE's view, company-dependent staff associations. However, the union, though not dependent, was arguably marginalised by this independence at the time. It has sought, subsequently, facilities from employers which have made it more dependent but enabled it to provide more services and compete more effectively for membership.

Dependence is thus, to some extent, an indication of negotiating success, given the structure of British unions. Lay involvement, the key to cost control and perhaps to a wider range of union objectives, depends on employer support. But too much employer support may threaten independence and in fact usurp the union's role unless the employer is simultaneously dependent on the union. The issue, then, is one of managing this dependence, of making such dependence mutual.

This raises directly the question of benefits to the employer for the concession of various facilities to the union. Several facilities, notably time-off, balloting facilities, and those for safety representatives, are supported by statute although a number of employers exceed minimum statutory requirements. Supported by this legislation, concession of facilities may be seen by employers as an investment in the 'voice' mechanism: the union serves a function which the employer supports. If the employer goes further, conceding check-off facilities and encouraging new employees to join the union in order to enhance membership and thus the 'representativeness' of the union (Purcell, 1987) the union is in receipt of a revenue stream for very little outlay, and the employer has control, more or less directly, of both the resources to run the union and membership revenue.

Two dangers arise. The first obvious one is that the employer may, in the event of disagreement, withdraw facilities. It is highly likely that this would affect revenue more than resources. Our evidence indicates that the supply of activist support is flexible and, where the dispute is generally supported, the level of lay involvement might substantially increase. The interruption of revenue is more damaging and more immediately effective. Cancellation of check-off would cause immediate revenue interruption, membership loss, and expenditure increases. The conclusion we draw from this is that employer dependence for facilities to encourage lay participation is a *sine qua non* for effective union organisation but that dependence on the employer for revenue and recruitment may be dangerous. Over time, this combination will encourage 'passive' joining decisions and reduced recruitment effort by the union. It makes the current employment situation the channel for communication with members and maintaining the current employment base an objective for the union. Of paramount importance, it makes the union financially dependent upon an employer concession to collect in which, evidence the number of employers charging for check-off, the employer sees little benefit.

If the union deals with a large number of employers, particularly if they do not combine in an employers' association, then overall exposure may be slight. Concerted action across the whole range of recognition agreements is unlikely and cross-subsidisation of affected bodies of membership is possible. However, unions which deal with very few employers but depend on check-off are highly vulnerable: many of these are in the public sector.

Vulnerability is enhanced by the possibility that, for political reasons to do with individual freedom rather than economic ones to do with the value of unions, check-off arrangements may be removed, curtailed, or subject to frequent review. Proposals contained in the 1991 Green Paper requiring written annual consent from the employee for continued subscription deduction *and* to approve subscription changes thus pose a substantial threat to the current income base.[1] It is to be expected that on each renewal occasion there would be membership wastage, prompting both income loss and, in compensatory recruitment, expenditure increases. Since each *levy* would need similar approval, strike levies would also be hit. The Green Paper expressly notes the May 1991 AEU strike levy in support of the 35-hour week dispute, emphasising the fragility of a system which collects funding for disputes from the 'opposition'.

Faced with such uncertainties, retention of reliance on check-off is likely to be associated with the retention of a substantial amount of liquid money as a buffer against interruption. The costs of liquidity, if any, must be set against any benefits from check-off.

The second danger is more insidious, and relates to union policy. Several General Secretaries remarked that such 'cosy' relationships gave unions financial allegiance to existing concentrations of employment. The concern then emerged to preserve this employment base rather than focus on services to members or on expanding employment areas. The protection of jobs then coincided with the protection of the union's revenue base, since disruption of the employment relationship is, under check-off, tantamount to disruption of the membership base. Furthermore, such dependence discouraged development of sizeable financial reserves for future policy implementation since members in such employer-dependent organisations would oppose subscription increases.

These fears may be unfounded, but were fairly widely held by leaders of recruiting unions. Both dangers indicate the desirability of moving away from check-off to a direct debiting system of subscription collection which is both less employer-dependent and less vulnerable to legislative change. This requires that union members have bank accounts, and it is of some interest to note that membership services packages used as incentives in recruitment are frequently inclusive of discounted banking facilities.

5   Competition and membership services

Unions compete for new members, for new recognition agreements, and for merger partners. Despite restrictive agreements such as the Bridlington principles, TUC affiliates are not excluded from such competition, which has a number of clear and mostly negative consequences for unions.

Our evidence is that competition keeps subscription levels down and, where individual recruitment is undertaken, pushes expenditure levels up. Since subscription levels are, historically and internationally speaking, low, this is a matter of some importance. A second consequence of competition between unions is that union resources are transferred from what one might characterise as the 'employer-dependent' sector to those sectors where unions seek recognition. In the former, generally, union revenues exceed costs while in the latter, at least initially, the reverse is true. It may be said, then, that unionised employers are subsidising organisational efforts in the non-union sector, at least indirectly, where they recognise general unions, since their provision of facilities allows the generation of a surplus of funds for transfer.

This transfer creates the political problems we outlined above. It may also cause financial problems if such expansionary recruitment efforts fail. As we have noted, many unions facing this calculus opt for increasing membership through expansion in the existing employer-dependent sector, through merger or consolidatory recruitment. The evidence for this is the increase in membership share of the largest unions while both the number of unions and aggregate membership continues to decline.

Competition – in this case both in the employer and membership market – thus encourages the emergence of a particular form of organisation. Unions seeking to recruit into generally non-union sectors must be able to cross-subsidise from a stable, employer-dependent membership base.

Expansion from such a base may, in principle and from an institutional point of view, seem attractive. If the union has a portfolio of membership revenues in different sectors, occupations, and regions it is better protected from ultimate membership decline than, say, an industry or occupational union.

However, existing, well-organised groups of members must receive something in return for this net outflow of funds. Unless recruitment efforts are focused on other parts of their company or industry it is unlikely *ceteris paribus* that this return will be improved bargaining power. Empirically, it is much more likely to be the granting of some autonomy in a sectoral or trade group structure, allowing the preservation of political autonomy and protecting the group from being 'swamped' by new members.

The 'Undy' argument – that such a sectional structure assists the attraction of merger partners – is thus reinforced by the preferences of existing members. Under such a structure, old and new members are kept seperate and, in the general unions, the leadership manages a membership portfolio which may consist of high market shares in declining sectors and low market shares in expanding ones. Our evidence is that there is much more discussion of merger than practice, that such discussions invariably originate with the leadership, and that financially the consequences are not always immediately beneficial. This is consistent with the proposition that many leaders of large unions are seeking mergers with smaller ones in order to reposition the union in expanding rather than declining job territories. It is also consistent with the proposition that, for attractive merger partners, there are often several suitors.

The final consequence of competition is the development of enhanced packages of membership services. As Chapter 2 showed, union services had tended to collapse in the 1970s around the provision of collective bargaining and representational services. Two problems have followed. The first is the free-rider problem: collective services have tended to generate public goods and diminish the incentive to join. The second is that it is difficult for members to evaluate the benefits of collective bargaining or the relative effectiveness of different unions as bargaining agents. Benefit expenditure remains substantial, in some unions more so than others but, since financial benefits are low in real terms and often dependent on lengthy periods of membership, they do little to attract new recruits.

All of our case study unions had or were developing packages of discounted services such as free banking, cheap legal advice, and sales discounts, in part to attract new members and in part to retain existing ones. This development was seen by some to be 'faddish' or 'consumerist' but it represents a significant development in union services on three counts.

The first is that it offers services to the member as a consumer which are not dependent on a particular workplace, or even on union recognition. The second is that they are membership dependent: the incentive to free-ride may thus be reduced. The third is that they are at worst costless and at best revenue generating. The unions concerned are simply making use of an unused asset in the membership list.

Such developments thus reverse the long-term trend in the decline of industrial benefits, avoiding the cost pressures which had generated such a decline. However, they are also collective benefits in that they do not require transfer of contribution from one member to another, being available to all. In some cases, these developments have been imitative or externally encouraged, for example, in the attempt to reap some benefits from the membership records requirements of the 1984 Trade Union Act. However, in several unions such packages, together with the improvements in subscription yield and the more aggressive approach to investment management, encouraged the view that the union as a whole was being run on more commercial lines. The implications of this are worthy of further discussion.

6   Union business and business unionism

The enhanced level of management information now available in the case study unions make it possible for union leaders to analyse the costs and benefits of recruitment campaigns, strike calls, and policy initiatives. It allows decisions to be made on the cost effectiveness of retaining or discarding particular groups of members or, short of this, reducing service levels or increasing subscription rates for cost-ineffective groups. Similarly, although it does not allow direct evaluation of the extent and distribution of employer subsidy, those parts of the union from which profits on membership servicing are made can be identified. The current level of management information available thus offers union leaders a greater chance to run the union as a business, i.e., to maximise net revenue from members and from return on investments. Although UK unions are not proprietorial there are, as we have noted in Chapter 4, several possible benefits to union leaders from this situation.

However, this information is not exclusive to incumbent union leaders. It is also available to political rivals and, as a consequence in particular of the provisions of the Employment Acts of 1988 and 1990, the unions' financial operations are becoming increasingly transparent to members. The accumulation of large investment portfolios or cash mountains, or even the internal transfer of funds from employer-dependent to marginal areas is becoming increasingly difficult to hide or fudge. In several unions, notably EETPU, members were vociferous concerning the use of union funds for the benefit of *current* members. Money-making ventures not immediately seen to generate such benefits were criticised. The possibility therefore also exists for membership control of union funds, often in the interests of current members rather than of institutional objectives, using recently established statutory rights and perhaps the assistance of the Commissioner for Trade Union Members.[2]

This process may be taken further. Among the proposals contained in the 1991 Green Paper is that for greater investigative powers for the Certification Officer, supported by a statutory duty to use such powers if prompted by a member's complaint. This is associated with a widening of the reporting requirements to include leaders' salaries, and the suggestion that unions be placed under a statutory requirement to disclose certain types of financial information annually to members.[3] If implemented, such proposals might weaken leaders' control over funds.

However, on balance, the tendency we have observed over the last decade is for increasing centralised control of income, expenditure, and assets and this does raise the question of whether financial considerations will come to dominate union policy making to such an extent that only 'profitable' areas are organised or only 'financially viable' policies pursued. Several unions do, as we have seen, cost conference motions and policy initiatives prior to debate: is this mere prudence or a more fundamental shift towards cost–benefit unionism?

It needs to be acknowledged at the outset that one may be naturally drawn to the conclusion that unions are run as businesses by deciding to focus on the financial aspects of union activity which may well not be among the concerns of the median member. This abstract point is, in fact, supported by the evidence: our cases show greater commercial awareness but few indications that financial matters dominate union policy making. Moreover, there appears to be little relationship between the sophistication of financial controls or the level of financial information available on the one hand and the predisposition towards net revenue maximisation by union leaders on the other.

As Chapter 5 indicated, there were considerable differences between what we observed to be the sophistication of financial controls within unions and the centrality of financial matters in union decision making. More specifically, we have considered NUM, particularly since 1984, in terms of a combination of sophisticated accounting controls in internal management combined with policies which remain fundamentally anti-capitalist and unchanged since the early years of the decade. EETPU, described by several respondents as a 'business union', is in fact not a net revenue maximiser but rather characterised by extreme membership accountability. GMB is determined to make its organisation more efficient in order to penetrate low-income membership areas, rather than to avoid them. In summary, although we reach the firm conclusion that unions have become more commercially aware in the management of their own affairs and that this awareness has affected decision making within unions, we found no case of 'cost–benefit' trade unionism as defined above. Unions may be economically more rational in administration, but policy formulation and pursuit, particularly, as we have seen, in areas such as recruitment, is often effected on extra-economic grounds.

What, then, does our analysis indicate about the state of trade unionism in Britain in the late 1980s, and about the prospects for the future? The question is worth asking, since many debates on this issue begin with exogenous factors – the reduction in manufacturing employment, the increase in female and part-time employment, the growth of white-collar and technical work – which change job territories, normally interpreted as being to the detriment of union organisation. Our focus here is less on factors which might alter the demand for the existing set of trade union services and more on the supply side: the ability of unions to recruit and service a changing membership. The difference is, of course, one of emphasis since supply and demand are related, but the supply side has been ignored and is worth consideration: what do the unions do to affect their own fate?

Centralisation, one of the most pervasive trends we observed in financial management, puts greater power in the hands of union leaders and raises questions about the role of local branches and Areas. Many of the changes put the member at arms length to the union and required unions to think about structural changes designed to reestablish contact directly with activists and members. Much depends on the structure of collective bargaining faced by the union, but many of the recent changes to union government and administration encourage membership detachment rather than involvement. The trend away from an activist-based voluntary organisation towards an inertia-selling operation can be something of a caricature of events but many of our case study unions, fearing it, were experimenting with forms of 'delegated autonomy' towards branches and Areas in order to involve members more actively in the life of the union. This was particularly difficult where membership turnover was high.

High levels of lay involvement were pursued as valued ends in themselves, but they do have economic benefits in the control of costs. Often referring to events in the late 1970s and early 1980s, many General Secretaries in our case studies stressed the importance of being 'responsive' to members' wishes. This related both to policy formulation and to service provision. Referring to more recent events, many finance officers stressed the extent to which members demanded services unrelated to their immediate work situations. Those launching packages of discounted financial services often found that the level of financial literacy amongst their share-owning members put strong pressures on the level of service provision. This concern with a new form of lay involvement raises several problems.

The first is simply the extent to which unions can effectively provide collective bargaining representation at the workplace *and* packages of discounts and insurance services away from it. In the post-war period unions developed into pure collective bargaining organisations in which negotiators outnumbered other staff. In the 1980s, developments in service provision have required different forms of expertise. This has in several cases involved cultural changes: the downgrading of the status of negotiator and the attendant changes to the career paths of union officials. For some unions, particularly manual ones with elected officials, this has not been easy.

A second relates to the sources of membership attachment to trade unions. It may well be that the majority of trade union members have always been instrumentally attached to their union, looking for bargaining gains in return for subscriptions. However this might, in the course of events, require active involvement by members in the prosecution of negotiations. By contrast, a collective adherence *only* to the union's services package might imply purely passive behaviour towards the employer combined, perhaps, with an aggressive attitude towards the union as service provider. Several respondents were anxious about the impact of such an orientation on bargaining power and administrative costs. They were also anxious in the present legislative climate, about the focus on services from the union to members rather than on the union's role in exacting concessions from the employer.

The third problem emerges from this combination of calculative attachment with the increased transparency of union financial practice promoted both by the development of systems of financial control and by legislative changes attaching rights to information to individual members. The essence of collective action is that it involves cross-subsidy and many of the principles of cross-subsidisation have simply never been articulated, in rule books or elsewhere. To the extent that they became so, there exists the threat of challenge and of fragmentation if groups of members perceive no common interest across increasingly heterogeneous organisations. Impoverishment does not help: such cross-subsidies involve net gains and losses if they are funded directly from the income stream rather than, as before, from reserves. However, even if there is cross-subsidy from reserves, in non-proprietorial organisations there may be questions about ownership and allocation. It is worth emphasising once more that the expansion of trade unionism into non-union areas and sectors requires such cross-subsidy.

Different types of union organisation face these problems to different degrees and resolve them in correspondingly different ways. Some closed unions, like FDA, pursued policies of restricting membership to highly paid, relatively homogeneous occupational groups who pay high subscriptions and are easily, though relatively lavishly, serviced. FDA differs from the traditional 'closed' craft model primarily in its reliance on full-time appointed officials rather than lay activists. Cross-subsidy takes place, but between individuals rather than diverse occupational groups. Others pursued growth based on cost–benefit analysis. EETPU, formerly a closed craft union but now a more open one based on a sort of populist centralism in government restricts growth to those groups of members which can be recruited and serviced economically. The culture, and the internal accounting systems, make extensive cross-subsidy to loss-making groups difficult. Hence the focus on organising the employer market through single-union deals and on mergers.

However, unions attacking the non-union sector invariably move towards an organisational form based on cross-subsidy within a sectional structure. A portfolio of job territories is managed in which employer-dependent areas cross-subsidise pre-recognition ones. Growth focuses on both, through mergers in the former case and individual recruitment in the latter. Recruitment activity may be subject to cost–benefit analysis but it does not follow that cost-ineffective groups will not be targeted for recruitment or not retained in membership, since membership expansion is pursued as an end in itself. Once recognition is secured, the objectives of the centre *include* shifting the burden of organisation away from the full-time officers of the union and on to employers and members: it goes off the balance sheet. The annual returns of any large successful union thus cover only a fraction of the resources necessary for union operation.

This organisational form, recognised by Undy *et al.* (1981) as appropriate for the attraction of merger partners, is not restricted to general unions. In our case study sample, BIFU also corresponds to it. We would contend that it is the *only* effective expansionary form of trade unionism since, without it, a union head office cannot reallocate resources effectively. It is more effectively adopted by larger rather than smaller unions since, *ceteris paribus* they have more resources to reallocate.

The relevance of financial issues to this argument is, we hope, clear: it leads us to a, perhaps controversial, final conclusion concerning the prospects for trade union expansion. This portfolio form of organisation is a model of a union incorporating managerial discretion, at least over resources. It is not a net revenue-maximising model, but it does require net revenue maximisation in parts of the organisation. Financial centralisation is essential: the funds must be collected to the centre efficiently in order to be reallocated. The financial reforms we have documented are thus the key to the further development of trade unionism in Britain. In short, if unions in Britain are to expand into poorly unionised sectors, a first condition is that union leaders must be able to act independently of current members' interests, and to do so they must have firm hold of the financial reins.

Secondly they must deploy resources from the highly unionised sectors to poorly unionised ones cost effectively. The key to cost effectiveness is the avoidance of competition. With the current structure of the union management in the UK, competition between unions and the expansion of union membership overall are incompatible.

Such expansion will, at least in the interim, generate a large number of members in pre-recognition situations. The development of membership-dependent but not recognition-dependent benefits and services is necessary to retain such members with which negotiating rights can be established. A third condition for expansion is thus the development of membership inducements other than collective-bargaining representation.

However, even with such inducements, the objective of recognition and negotiation with employers remains paramount. The fourth condition for expansion is thus the more effective inducement of recognition from employers. This may occur through pressure or coercion; either the union builds up membership to the point where the employer concedes, or perhaps through the good offices of some future administration a statutory route is provided. Alternatively, unions may become more effective at convincing employers of the benefits of collective bargaining.

Either way, this remains the most critical area. The first three conditions can be fulfilled, in many unions have been fulfilled, by policy development and organisational change within trade unions. Employer support underpins the current pattern of trade union activity; it must underpin its expansion.

APPENDIX 1: Research methods

1 INTRODUCTION

This appendix focuses on the design of the research project. In practice, we are dealing with two distinct phases of research. The first, initially reported in Willman and Morris (1988), was based on the generally available data from the statutory returns, which we briefly describe. The second, from which our case studies emerged, was an attempt to understand financial management *within* trade unions. Data here included those from interviews and documentary material produced by trade unions themselves. It is thus appropriate to include a more detailed discussion of the two projects, before going on to a discussion of our questionnaire design and of the basis of case study selection. Initially, however, we must describe the statutory returns.

2 STATUTORY RETURNS BY TRADE UNIONS

Prior to 1971, all unions registered under the 1871 Trade Union Act were required to submit an annual financial return to the Registrar of Friendly Societies. From 1971 to 1974, under the Industrial Relations Act,[1] a return was required to the Registrar of Trade Unions and Employers' Associations. The current reporting requirements are detailed in the Trade Union and Labour Relations Act 1974 and the Employment Protection Act 1975;[2] the latter Act transferred the functions of the defunct Registrar of Trade Unions and Employers' Associations to the Certification Officer, who also took custody of returns dating back to 1871.

In brief, the requirements are as follows. Each union must, each calendar year, send a return to the Certification Officer detailing a 'true and fair' account of income, expenditure, and assets, an auditor's report, and a copy of the rules. The Act requires that each union keep proper accounts and establish a satisfactory system of control of its accounts in order to provide such data.

The return requires unions to give a breakdown of their income, expenditure, and assets. Unions must outline contributions from members, from investments, and from several other identified sources, for each fund they manage: the form thus requires unions to disclose their fund structure and to indicate where money has been transferred between funds. Various headings are given for classifying expenditure, such as salaries, occupancy costs, and expenses. The union's assets and investments must be detailed. Asset value, depreciation, and book value at the end of the accounting period must be detailed, together with disposals. Investments must be classified into quoted and unquoted securities, and equity holdings must be detailed. A balance sheet must be produced, showing liabilities and year-end funds against assets.

The data are relatively consistent in that the precise reporting requirements and the main headings of income, expenditure, and assets have remained the same throughout the period. There are also few instances of non-compliance, outside of the period 1971–4, when many TUC-affiliated unions refused to register and to complete a return to the Registrar. The series is interrupted across these four years. In addition, it is likely that the returns do generally give a 'true and fair view' as required by the 1974 Act. That Act required returns to be externally audited, although many unions had their returns so audited prior to the requirement.

However, there are certain problems. Latta notes two: first that the coverage of the requirement to report varied during the 1950s and 1960s as several white-collar unions first registered across the period and second that union accounting practice, particularly in the recording of assets and the practice of depreciation, was variable (1972: 394).

The extent of the first problem is clear from a comparison of membership figures in the return with those from the Department of Employment, summarised in Bain and Price (1980). Particularly in the 1950s and 1960s, the membership figures reported by the Certification Officer are substantially less than those yielded by the Department of Employment's estimates. Coverage has tended to increase over time, but the 1974 Act altered the definition of a trade union, thus omitting 31 previously included organisations. Since 1975, the Certification Officer has required all listed trade unions to complete a return, but listing is a voluntary process; it may be that several organisations which fulfil the statutory definition of a trade union are omitted. However, by the 1980s the difference between the two series is much smaller.[3]

The extent of the second problem is more difficult to assess. Accounting practice, particularly in the recording of assets, has probably been variable. Most unions have tended to quote book rather than market value of assets in their returns and to depreciate appreciating assets such as property. However, some do not, and among those who do depreciation practice may vary. Revaluation of assets occur at different intervals in different unions, often with remarkable results for their financial status. However, it is likely that, while some variance between unions in accounting practice remains, the effect of the 1974 Act has been to professionalise accounting practice; there now exists a set of accounting guidelines for trade union accounts. This may have an effect on the content of the returns, increasing the relative accuracy of more recent ones.

The net effect of these two problems is that the returns are likely to be a more accurate picture of the financial status of British trade unions in the 1980s than in the 1950s. In particular, the requirements of the 1984 Trade Union Act are likely to have an effect on the accuracy of membership and subscription records, while the 1988 Act may cause some unions to reconsider accounting practice in light of the prospect of inspection by members.

A final point to be made about the returns is that, although they include the funds held by regions, districts, or branches of trade unions – which may not be available to union leaders in practice – they fail in two respects to give a full picture of the resources available to trade unions. Specifically, they omit two major sources of support for union activity discussed in Chapter 4, namely the time given to union affairs by unpaid lay activists and the support given to union activity by employers who provide facilities.

The value of this support is typically not included in unions' own accounts. The reservations aside, the returns provide an aggregate data set across the post-war period. We use them in Chapters 2, and 3 to discuss financial performance. Moreover, since they provide the only data set consistent between unions, we also use them as the backdrop to the case studies of Chapters 8 to 12. However, as the foregoing discussion has implied, they fail to provide some important data. It was thus necessary to design research instruments to collect additional material. These are discussed in the next three sections.

3 THE TWO PROJECTS

In the first project, our methods involved documentary analysis, supplemented by interviews with officials in the Certification Office and with some trade union officials. To go further, we needed to extend the scope of our documentary analysis, to survey a sample of unions and also to engage in a wider programme of interviewing. We thus required a more elaborate research design and a different sampling method.

Our initial focus was on the 56 unions with over 20,000 members in 1984. We were able to look only briefly at the internal mechanisms for financial management within each union in a set of this size. In addition, the set specifically excluded unions with less than 20,000 members, which constitute the majority. We felt, therefore, that our second project should focus on fewer cases, but on a wider size range.

Initially, we proposed a two-stage research design: first, a postal survey of finance officers in the set of 56 unions following circulation of our initial findings and second a smaller set of case studies. The postal survey was to gather information on the setting of subscriptions, income, expenditure and assets and the availability of financial information. The case studies were to look in more detail at the internal systems of financial management and their relationship to wider union objectives.

However, for a mixture of both practical and methodological reasons, we changed this design. The first reason for change was that we wished to encompass the entire size range of trade unions listed by the Certification Officer (354 in 1988) rather than the set of 56. The second set of reasons had to do with the role of the questionnaire itself. The first purpose was to facilitate access to case studies. However, we came to feel that a questionnaire was not an appropriate vehicle. A second was that, prior to involvement in the cases, we were unsure about what information we needed or could reasonably hope for. We felt that involvement in the cases would sharpen our appreciation of the necessary and appropriate content of the postal survey.

The third set of reasons was purely practical. Several unions were concerned about the kinds of information which might appear in the public domain. Some of those covered by the first project wished to discuss matters informally before proceeding. In addition, the TUC were surveying their affiliated organisations in connection with the work of the Special Review Body. We were keen not to replicate such work and to gain the backing of the TUC for our approaches to affiliates for access. In the event, such support was forthcoming.

These considerations caused us to proceed with the case studies before attempting the questionnaire. However, although the timing was reversed, the general approach to the pursuit of case studies and questionnaire design respectively were maintained.

4 THE CASE STUDIES

It was not immediately clear what the basis of case study selection should be. There is in the UK a highly skewed size distribution of trade unions; about half of UK unions have less than 1,000 members, but only one union still declared more than one million members in 1988. If we stratified our sample by size, we would include a smaller proportion of union members than if we focused on larger unions. On the other hand, smaller unions might be worth inclusion if their financial structures proved distinctive. Our original sample contained both white-collar and manual unions, but many did not fit neatly into either category. The same may be said for the private/public sector distinction. The sample also contained both expanding and contracting unions, but many of the former had grown by mergers or transfers of engagements. More to the point, these various distinctions did not appear necessarily to correspond to variations in financial performance.

We initially considered whether to base our sample on some measure of financial performance, taking subsamples of successful and unsuccessful unions. However, this approach has problems. The most general is that we have no clear definition of financial success. A second is that those unions which have shown particularly poor financial performance may illustrate rather more the outcome of recent litigation than basic financial health or weakness. We felt that those unions with the most traumatic financial histories might, in some respects, prove most interesting, but they might offer only a remote chance of access; moreover they are, almost by definition, untypical. Access was a significant issue, since the chances of access probably related to the financial variables under study. Successful unions and those which were in any event more open about their financial affairs were, we thought, more likely to grant access: those with less openness or with embarrassing returns might be less inclined to do so.

In the event, we decided to stratify our sample by size, focusing on the largest unions but attempting also to cover several omitted from our first *Report* by removing the cut off of 20,000 members. Our intention was to study between eight and ten unions in some detail, and to include among them some of the largest. Table A1 illustrates our initial sample choice. We targeted 18 unions initially, hoping to complete ten case studies.

We looked for a wide distribution according to size and for a rough balance between white-collar and manual unions on the one hand and public and private sector unions on the other, recognizing in both cases the difficulties of so simply classifying the current pattern of union organisations. Table A1 also indicates (in italics) those unions which eventually declined to take part and those unions

Table A1. *The case study sample*

Size Band sampled	Proportion	Targeted	Subsequently included
Over 750K	3/4	GMB, NALGO	AEU
Over 500K	1/2	*MSF*, NUPE*	
Over 250K	2/3	EETPU, *RCN*	USDAW
Over 100K	4/14	NUM, BIFU NAS/ UWT*, NUR	
Over 50K	3/7	IPCS, IRSF, ISTC	
Below 50K	6/324	BETA,* STE, *URTU, LBGSU*, FDA, BFAWU	CMA, EMA

* Incomplete cases

which were selected for inclusion instead. We completed 16 cases, since satisfactory access was generally offered. Four unions declined to take part. Three unions, NUPE, BETA, and NAS/UWT, agreed to cooperate, but we were, for various reasons, unable to complete the cases. The sample badly underrepresents small unions, covering only 4.5% of all unions, but covers approximately 40% of union members as a whole.

For each of these unions, we pursued both documentary and interview data. For each, there were at least two main sources of financial and other information:
(a) the statutory returns to the Certification Officer,
(b) the union's own financial records, including the proceedings of delegate Conferences and committee meetings at which financial matters were debated.
Using these data, we sought to provide:
(i) a more finely disaggregated study of union finances, deriving measures of nominal income and subscription yield, looking at organising and staffing expenditure and looking at the nature of union investments and assets;
(ii) an account of the mechanisms and processes through which subscriptions were raised and expenditure decisions made, primarily from documentary sources.

These data were supplemented by semi-structured interviews with finance officers (or those responsible for financial matters) and General Secretaries (or those responsible for the overall management of the union). Where relevant, Executive Committee members and union trustees were also included. The main functions of these interviews were to:
(a) corroborate conclusions from documentary analysis,
(b) gain factual information on the nature and quality of information systems within the union, and on changes over time,
(c) discover the nature of any planned or imminent changes to financial practice,
(d) ascertain the opinions of finance officers on the financial performance of their own union,
(e) attempt an assessment of the priority accorded to financial issues in union decision making,

Table A2. *Population and sample size distributions, 1988*

Size Bands	Population %	Sample %
Under 100	15.9	11.1
100–499	24.2	5.5
500–999	8.3	5.5
1000–2499	15.0	16.7
2500–4999	8.6	9.7
5000–9999	5.1	12.5
10000–14999	1.3	0
15000–24999	3.5	4.2
25000–49999	7.3	15.3
50000–99999	1.9	2.7
100000–249999	4.1	8.3
More than 250000	3.2	8.3
Membership unknown	100	100

Source: Department of Employment.

(f) explore the accuracy of the collection and reporting of union membership figures over the last decade,

(g) assess the usefulness and relevance of the current system of collection of data on union finances.

We approached those directly responsible for financial matters and those responsible for the union's overall management in slightly different ways. Appendix 3 details the questions used for the semi-structured interviews with financial managers and Appendix 4 the questions used for General Secretaries or their equivalent.

5 THE POSTAL SURVEY

The postal survey was distributed in April 1989. That to TUC affiliates contained a note in the covering letter to the effect that the project was viewed favourably by the TUC. The main issues covered were:

(i)   the setting, raising, and collection of subscriptions,

(ii) expenditure decisions,

(iii) the management of assets,

(iv) the quality and quantity of available financial information,

(v)   if relevant, the financial issues surrounding merger discussions and the financial consequences of merger.

The questionnaire is at Appendix 5. Initially, it was sent to all unions on the Certification Officer's list (354 at the end of 1988). The response rate was initially very slow and some telephone follow-up was required. In the course of this folow-up, it became clear that there were not, in fact, 354 extant unions. Several organisations not completing the questionnaire indicated either that their organisation had ceased to exist or that they no longer considered themselves trade unions and did not complete returns. Several unions on the list are in fact federations with no members of their own. Within the NUM, several branches are listed even though the separately listed areas include their data in returns. Appendix 4 discusses the population size in more detail.

We estimate, on the basis of this experience, that the true population size in 1989 was 319;[4] our response rate (n = 72) is thus approximately 23%. Table A2 above shows the size distribution of our respondents compared to the overall size distribution of trade unions provided by the Department of Employment for 1988. Again, there is a slight oversampling of larger unions, but some smaller union coverage is included. The questionnaire data cover approximately 46% of union membership.[5]

6 THE CASE STUDIES AND THE CERTIFICATION OFFICE RETURNS

In some cases, the data presented in the case study Chapters 8–12 differ from those used in earlier chapters, particularly Chapter 8: the latter are those abstracted by Certification Office (CO) staff from data supplied by the union concerned.

The following factors account for these differences.

AEU

The 'other income' figures for 1974 include the activities of a General Protected Fund which was incorporated into the General Fund in 1975. The activities of the construction, foundry and roll turners are incorporated from 1987, while those of the Political and Superannuation Funds have been included throughout.

BIFU

Our figures differ from those of the Certification Officer in 1989, having been independently calculated from the returns. The CO's figure under other income is £176,000. It should actually be £245,188. Their investment figure is £224,000, while we can only find £177,581 worth of investment income. However, these discrepancies do not affect the aggregate, and we broadly coincide. The CO's total income is £6,446,000, while we arrive at £6,500,099. However, we have included the activities of BIFU's small Strike Fund, and of NORSA, which joined in 1989 bringing in some extra other income.

EETPU

Our figures are £13,410,000 for total income, while the CO's come to £13,421,000. On the expenditure side, we make total expenditure £12,877,000, and the CO's comes to £12,867,192.

Concerning the discrepancies under investment and other income, and administration and other expenditure, we have carefully unpacked the income and expenditure of the Rolls Royce Management Association, United Kingdom Association of Professional Engineers, British Transport Officers Guild, Association of Management & Professional Staffs, and Steel Industry's Management Association. It is not clear that the CO has done this.

GMB

There are two sets of GMB accounts for 1989, one for two months and the other for ten months, reflecting the amalgamation that year. At the end of the day, the excess of income over expenditure is £5,270,000, which increases the year end value of the funds by £5,270,000 – from (nominal) £36,422,726 in 1988 to £41,692,726. Our aggregate excess of income over expenditure (£43,183,283–£37,913,283) conforms exactly to this figure, the CO's does not (£37,605,000–£32,420,000) quite.

It is difficult to tell whether the CO has aggregated both sets of accounts for 1989, and whether they have included the Political Fund, the Central Investment Reserve, the Amalgamation Contingency Fund, the Members Superannuation, and the Branch Commission. We have used both sets of accounts, and aggregated all Funds.

APPENDIX 2: Regression results

Determinants of per capita real net worth

Independent variable	Coefficient	Std. error	t-value	Significance level
Constant	251.901628	38.192346	6.5956	0.0000
Strikes	−0.000808	0.000322	−2.5065	0.0178
Unemployment	4.630796	1.83357	2.5256	0.0171
Shortfall	−124.121587	35.95768	−3.4519	0.0017
Return	−7.917136	1.404729	−5.6361	0.0000

R-SQ. (ADJ.) = 0.8156   SE = 10.600102   Durb Wat = 0.993

APPENDIX 3: Questions for finance officers

Income

(a) SUBSCRIPTIONS

How is subscription income collected?
What proportion is check-off, bankers order, or direct debit by hand ?
How does the union deal with those in arrears?
How quickly can arrears be identified?
How are membership records kept?
How accurate and up to date are they?
How many different contribution scales are there?
What is the distribution of members across contribution scales?
How are adjustments made to subscription rates?
What are the main pressures to raise subscriptions?
What are the main constraints?
Does the union compete with other unions for membership; if so, which unions?
Is the income from different membership groups monitored?
What proportion of due subscriptions are collected?

(b) OTHER INCOME

What are the other main income sources? (other than investment income)

(c) EXPENDITURE

How is money defrayed between (e.g.) head office, branch, regions?
How are HO/branch/regional budgets calculated?
What restrictions are there on the spending of branch officials, regional officers, department heads, etc.?
What is the fund structure of the union?
Are there separate expenditure accounts for (e.g.) strikes, legal, benefits?
How are decisions taken about major expenditure items, e.g., property/computer purchase, strike pay, recruitment drives?
What are the major recurrent expenditure items?
How many officials are there, and what are they paid?
What does the union spend other than on its members?

(d) INVESTMENTS

What are the union's principal investments
  equities
  gilts
  local government securities
What are its major assets?
Who is responsible for investment and asset management?
Are there trustees; if so, who are they and what are their qualifications?
How are decisions about new investments made?
Is there an investment policy?
How frequently are investments reviewed?
Is outside advice sought; if so, from whom?
Does the union make loans to any other union?
Who makes such decisions? What considerations are taken into account and what interest is charged?

(e) DEBT

To whom does the union owe money?
What is the balance between long- and short-term debt?
Who is empowered to undertake debt?

(f) MANAGEMENT ISSUES

Does anyone within the union know monthly what the expenditure position is?
Do the branches/regions submit income and expenditure reports; if so, how often?
Do regions/branches have separate bank accounts?
What proportion of branch/regional income is kept by the branches?
What happens if there is a cash flow problem?
What controls exist to ensure budgets are adhered to?
What are the major costs of recruitment drives?

(g) MERGERS

Are financial factors the basis for the choice of merger partners?
If so, which financial factors?
  income
  expenditure
  assets
Are the costs of potential mergers calculated in advance?

APPENDIX 4: Questions for General Secretaries

(a) FINANCIAL MATTERS, NEC

Assuming the NEC is the responsible authority, who raises financial matters on the NEC?
How often does the NEC discuss finance?
Is monitoring of the financial situation built into the timetable?
What financial issues would worry the NEC? Monthly cash-flow problem?
Is there a financial policy?
Do members of the NEC ever take financial initiatives?
How often do you monitor the accounts?

(b) THE FINANCE OFFICER

How does the finance officer get his advice/views over?
Can he speak to the NEC?
Does he work through the GS?
Does he write financial reports? How often?
Is there a mechanism by which he can address members?

(c) CONFERENCE

As conference decisions tend to involve costs, how does the GS get across to members that there are financial constraints?
Does the Chair of the Finance Committee address Conference?
Are members informed of the costs of strikes, campaigns, etc., and how are they informed? What conference decisions tend to be the most financially challenging?
Fixed levels of strike pay? Campaigning initiatives?

(d) CONTINGENCY PLANS

If the union is in difficulties do you have any contingency plans to cut costs?
What is immediately expendable?

APPENDIX 5: Questionnaire: trade union finances

This questionnaire is designed to gather information about the way financial matters are administered in trade unions. It is divided into several sections and the first deals with general information about you and your union. Subsequent sections cover income, expenditure and investments. There are also some questions about how finance influences important decisions such as undertaking a campaign and the role of the finance officer in the general running of the union.

1 Name of union:
   ....

2 Position of person filling in the questionnaire:
   ....

3 Do you have responsibility for financial administration?
   Please circle appropriate response: Yes No
   If your answer is **yes**, please go to question 6 next.

4 If **no**, is there anyone in the Union with specific responsibility for financial administration?
   Please circle appropriate response: Yes No

5 What is their job title?
   ....

6 If **yes**, are you a qualified/part qualified accountant?
   Please circle appropriate response: Qualified
   Part qualified
   Unqualified

7 How many staff are employed full time by the union?
   Please circle appropriate response:
   less than 10; 11–20; 21–30; 31–40; 41–50; more than 50.

8 How many of these staff are full-time officials?
   Please circle appropriate response:
   less than 10; 11–20; 21–30; 31–40; 41–50; more than 50.

9   Are the records of membership held on computer?
    Please circle appropriate response: Yes   No

10 Are the subscription records of members held on computer?
    Please circle appropriate response: Yes   No

11 What percentage of your members pay by
    check-off   ... %
    direct debit   ... %
    standing order   ... %
    cash/cheque   ... %
    Now we want to ask some questions about the union's *income* and how it is collected.

12 Does a change in subscription levels always require the approval of members?
    Please circle appropriate response: Yes   No

13 When planning to change the subscription level, do you usually make a recommendation to the EC on the new level?
    Please circle appropriate response: Yes   No

14 How far forward are levels of subscription income fixed?
    Please circle appropriate response:
    One year or less; more than one year; more than 2 years; more than 3 years; more than 4 years;

15 What proportion of your due subscription income was collected last year?
    Please circle appropriate response:
    Less than 50%   50–75%   76–90%   More than 90%

16 When planning to raise subscription levels, please **rank** the following factors in order of importance.
    (1 = most important; 6 = least important)

		RANK
(a)	Meeting expected administrative costs	( )
(b)	Subscriptions charged by other unions	( )
(c)	The range or level of benefits provided to members	( )
(d)	The earnings of your members	( )
(e)	Maintaining present levels of union reserve funds	( )
(f)	The level your members will find acceptable	( )

17 Are branches entitled to a proportion of the income of the Union?
    Please circle appropriate response: Yes   No

18 If **yes,** what proportion?   0–20%   21–40%   41–60%
                                        61–80%   +80%
    The next set of questions are about the ways that the union's *investments* are managed.

19 Are there any forms of profitable investment which you would avoid?
    Please circle appropriate response: Yes   No

20 If **yes,** what sort of investments are these?
    ....
    ....

21 Who is *chiefly* responsible for managing the union's current investments?
    Please circle appropriate response:
    (You may circle more than one)

    (a)   Finance officer
    (b)   General/Deputy General Secretary
    (c)   Trustees
    (d)   Executive Committee
    (e)   Specialists employed by the Union, i.e., Stockbrokers
    (f)   Other (please specify)
             ....
             ....

22 By whom would decisions about new investments above, say £10,000 be made?
    Please circle appropriate response(s):

    (a)   Finance Officer
    (b)   General/Deputy General Secretary
    (c)   Trustees
    (d)   Executive Committee
    (e)   Specialists employed by the Union, ie. Stockbrokers
    (f)   Other (please specify)
             ....

23 Is there an investment policy set down for the Union?
    Please circle appropriate response: Yes   No
    If **no,** please go to question 26.

24 If **yes,** where is it set down?
    Please circle appropriate response:

    (a)   Finance officer
    (b)   General Secretary/Deputy General Secretary
    (c)   Trustees
    (d)   Executive Committee

(e)   Annual Delegate Conference/Meeting
(f)   Other (please specify)
....
....

25 In terms of the union's investment policy, please **rank** the following in
    order of importance?
    (1 = most important; 5 = least important)

                                                                RANK

    (a)   Maximise income   ( )
    (b)   Maximise capital growth   ( )
    (c)   Provide income and capital growth   ( )
    (d)   Provide security for members' funds   ( )
    (e)   Generate funds for new projects   ( )

26 If the union has no investment policy, what criteria are used to manage your
    investments?
    ....
    ....

    **In the next section we want to look at the way the union manages its expendit-
    ure. We are interested in the systems of control and use, the responsibilities of
    the finance officer and how certain important items of expenditure, for example,
    recruitment campaigns are managed.**

27 Does the union have a system of budgeting to manage its expenditure?
    Please circle appropriate response   Yes   No
    If **no,** please go to question 30.

28 If **yes,** who is chiefly responsible for setting the budgets?
    Please circle appropriate response:

    (a)   General Secretary/Deputy General Secretary
    (b)   Finance Officer
    (c)   Executive Committee
    (d)   Other (please specify)
    ....
    ....

29 Who is chiefly responsible for monitoring the budgets?
    Please circle appropriate response:

    (a)   General Secretary/Deputy General Secretary
    (b)   Finance officer
    (c)   Executive Committee
    (d)   Other (please specify)

30 If you do **not** have a budgeting system, what is the main method of checking expenditure?
Please circle appropriate response:

(a)   By reference to bank balances
(b)   By reference to internal ledgers
(c)   Some other method (please specify)
. . . .

31 If the expenditure of the union is broken down and monitored in any way (ie by department; by section) please specify how this is done. **Please tick the appropriate boxes:**

by section   ( )   by official   ( )
by branch   ( )   by area/region   ( )
by department   ( )

32 Do branches have their own separate bank accounts?
Please circle appropriate response: Yes   No
If **no,** please go to question 34.

33 If **yes,** can they go overdrawn without permission from headquarters?
Please circle appropriate response: Yes   No

34 Can the finance officer take decisions concerning major items of capital expenditure, such as property or computer purchase?
Please circle appropriate response: Yes   No
If **no,** please go to question 36.

35 If **yes,** is this: **(Please tick appropriate box)**

(a)   alone   ( )
(b)   with the General Secretary/Deputy Gen. Sec. ( )
(c)   with the EC   ( )
(d)   with the Delegate Conference   ( )
(e)   other (please specify)   ( )
. . . .
. . . .

36 In the past 18 months has your union organised a recruitment drive?
Please circle appropriate response: Yes   No
If **no,** please go to question 38.

37 If **yes,** did you monitor the costs and/or benefits of this?
Please circle appropriate response:

(a)   Costs only
(b)   Costs and benefits
(c)   Benefits only
(d)   Neither costs nor benefits

38   Has your union been involved in industrial action in the past five years?
     Please circle appropriate response:
     If **no,** please go to question 40.

39   If **yes,** how important was the financial position of the union in the decision
     to undertake that action?
     Please circle appropriate response:

     (a)   Very important
     (b)   Important
     (c)   Neither important nor unimportant
     (d)   Unimportant
     (e)   Wholly irrelevant

40   How important was the financial position of the union in the decision to take
     up the most recent campaign on behalf of its members (i.e., for better pay,
     to protect jobs?)
     Please circle appropriate response:

     (a)   Very important
     (b)   Important
     (c)   Neither important nor unimportant
     (d)   Unimportant
     (e)   Wholly irrelevant

41   Has your union been involved in merger discussions with another union(s)
     in the past three years?
     Please circle appropriate response: Yes   No
     If **no,** please go to question 45.

42   If **yes,** which other union(s) were involved?
     . . . .
     . . . .

43   How important were the finances of **your** union in the decision to undertake
     merger discussions?
     Please circle appropriate response:

     (a)   Very important
     (b)   Important
     (c)   Neither important nor unimportant
     (d)   Unimportant
     (e)   Wholly irrelevant

44   How important were the finances of **the other** union(s)?
     Please circle the appropriate response:

     (a)   Very important
     (b)   Important
     (c)   Neither important nor unimportant

(d)   Unimportant
(e)   Wholly irrelevant

45   Please **rank** the items below in terms of their importance as reasons for the
     decision to seek a mergers.
     (1 = most important; 7 = least important)

                                                                    RANK

(a)   Decreasing membership of your union   ( )
(b)   Bargaining power of your union   ( )
(c)   Improve membership services   ( )
(d)   Declining reserves of your union   ( )
(e)   Expenditure growing too fast in your union   ( )
(f)   Income not rising fast enough/income   ( )
        declining in your union
(g)   Political position of your union's executive ( )

**The following section is concerned with the *general influence* of financial matters
on the *management* of the union.**

46   Which of the following statements best sums up the job of the finance officer
     in your union?
     Please tick appropriate box
     The job of the finance officer is *mainly* concerned with:

(a)   day-to-day administration   ( )
(b)   longer term planning   ( )
(c)   a mixture of (a) and (b)   ( )
(d)   providing expert advice to the General   ( )
        Secretary and EC

47   How often docs the finance officer formally report to the General Secretary?
     Please circle appropriate response:

(a)   weekly or more often
(b)   every 1 to 4 weeks
(c)   every 1 to 3 months
(d)   every 4 to 6 months
(e)   between 7 months and a year

48   How often does the EC or a finance subcommittee receive a formal report
     from the finance officer?
     Please circle appropriate response:

(a)   weekly   (d)   half-yearly
(b)   monthly   (e)   annually
(c)   quarterly

49 In your view, how important are financial factors in the general pattern of decision making in your union?
    Please circle appropriate response:

    (a)   Very important
    (b)   Important
    (c)   Neither important nor unimportant
    (d)   Unimportant
    (e)   Wholly irrelevant

50 To what extent do you agree that the job of the finance officer **should** be **primarily** concerned with long-term financial planning/management?
    Please circle appropriate response:

    (a)   Completely agree
    (b)   Broadly agree
    (c)   Neither agree nor disagree
    (d)   Disagree somewhat
    (e)   Entirely disagree

51 To what extent is the finance officer involved with the executive in decisions which have financial consequences?
    Please circle appropriate response:

    (a)   Completely   (d)   Rarely
    (b)   A great deal   (e)   Never
    (c)   Sometimes

52 To what extent do you think that the job of the finance officer should be primarily concerned with giving advice to the executive of the union?
    Please circle appropriate response:

    (a)   Completely agree
    (b)   Broadly agree
    (c)   Neither agree nor disagree
    (d)   Disagree somewhat
    (e)   Entirely disagree

53 To what extent do you agree that the finance officer should be actively involved with the executive in all decisions which have financial consequences for the Union?
    Please circle appropriate response:

    (a)   Completely agree
    (b)   Broadly agree
    (c)   Neither agree nor disagree
    (d)   Disagree somewhat
    (e)   Entirely disagree

Thank you very much for your co-operation. Please place the completed questionnaire in the attached, self-addressed pre-paid envelope.

APPENDIX 6: The number of trade unions

The Certification Officer's report for 1988 lists (pp. 26–39) 354 trade unions. Of these:

(a) Nineteen are areas of NUM which no longer exist or branches of NUM which have listed in order to present a distinct financial return but whose financial and membership data are contained within extant areas or the returns of the national union.

(b) Three, including APEX and AIT, have disappeared through merger.

(c) Eight are associations consisting of other unions which submit a separate return.

(d) Three are staff associations which no longer exist.

(e) Two are organizations of self-employed or owner operators.

If one deducts these from the given total, the resultant population figure is 319.

Notes

2 THE FINANCIAL STATUS OF BRITISH TRADE UNIONS, 1950-89

1 An earlier version of this chapter has appeared as Willman (1990).
2 Roberts (1956) p. 389, f.n. It is of interest to compare his speculations with the current role of Unity Trust and with TUC initiatives on the provision of Services to members. See TUC (1988).
3 There are, in fact, several possible explanations for the observed correlation. They are explored in Chapter 6.
4 The difference is spelt out in the Certification Officer's Report, most recently 1990: p. 45.
5 The category 'other income' is the finest classification available across the whole period. It is composed primarily of income from assets, including rental income from property.
6 The series on administrative expenditure is effectively interrupted in 1987, with a change to a more inclusive definition which includes thereafter all non-benefit expenditure.
7 The earnings measure used here is the weekly gross earnings of full-time manual males, over 21 (subsequently on adult rates), whose pay was unaffected by absence. This is a proxy for average earnings, a full series of which from 1950 was unavailable.
8 $r = -0.9251$, significant beyond $a = 0.001$
9 The coefficients are (income from members) $r = 0.8344$ and (administrative expenditure) $r = 0.8061$.
10 These are crude measures, but on average the rate of return exceeded inflation by 0.2% per annum between 1950 and 1968, fell short by 3.8% per annum between 1968 and 1980 and exceeded once more by 10% per annum between 1981 and 1989.
11 See Chapter 5, below.
12 See Chapter 5, below.
13 This 'profit' was £5.60 per capita per annum in 1986. However, if one includes benefit expenditure the annual 'profit' per member is only £0.82.

3 FINANCIAL DIFFERENCES BETWEEN UNIONS

1 The correlations are as follows for 1989. Subscription dependency and net worth per capita, $r = -0.6307$; subscription dependency and solvency, $r =$

−0.6298; net worth per capita and solvency, r = 0.5534. All are significant beyond 0.001. The correlation is particularly strong given that, purely for accounting reasons, RCN declares subscription dependency and solvency of 1 and net worth of £0.

2 ISTC earned £1.91 million from investments in 1989.

3 The correlations are: subscriptions and administrative cost per capita, r = 0.9065 (0.001); subscriptions per capita and membership, r = −0.2805 (0.04); subscriptions per capita and net worth per capita, r = 0.2282 (0.04).

4 By this expression, we refer to the excess of subscription income over administrative expenditure, i.e., the revenue from members minus the costs of servicing them.

5 See endnote 6, Chapter 2.

6 RCN, AMMA, EQUITY, and NAHT all gained over 50%.

7 The correlation is; r = 0.8483, significant beyond 0.001.

8 The position of NUM, where membership falls more rapidly than wealth, giving above average increases in real net worth per capita is discussed in Chapter 8.

9 MSF has real subscriptions per capita less than the average of TASS and ASTMS in 1980; see Table 3.3.

4 THE ROLE OF FINANCIAL MATTERS IN UNION ORGANISATION

1 The paradox may be more apparent than real. Burton (1984) has indicated that the Ross model, implicitly a model of the union as a non-profit organisation, can be specified in formal economic terms.

2 It is of some interest that recent TUC proposals suggest a 'staged' process of recognition, in which rights accrue to unions based on membership percentage. At 10% it is proposed that some facilities be granted, at 20% consultative rights, and at 40% full bargaining rights. At any level of membership, individual rights are proposed, but: 'an individual's right should be against the employer and not against the union, so that the union would not be under a formal statutory duty to act for its members. Given the resource constraints on unions, it would be unreasonable to impose any absolute duty on unions to represent their members' (TUC, 1991: 37).

3 For a fuller discussion of the implications of this, see Martin 1980.

4 There is in practice, a fifth, for individual trade unions, i.e., subsidies from other trade unions, but this appears to be of lesser importance.

5 See Chapter 8.

6 For a review of the relevant literature, see Hirsch and Addison 1986: 75–112. One needs to discriminate here between the impact of strikes on members and on union funds. Although members may generally experience a net financial loss from strike activity, there is some evidence to suggest that union funds may grow. See Willman and Morris, 1988: 53–71, and Chapter 7 below.

7 The analysis here relies on Willman (1989).

8 The definition of an independent trade union is at TULRA, 1974, Section 30. The criteria used in the test are outlined in the Certification Officer's First Report, 1976: 7–17.

9 There is, of course, debate about the benefits of trade union recognition for employers. For the UK, see Metcalf (1989, 1990) and Nolan and Marginson (1990).

10 The analogy here is with the economics of the newspaper industry, where the two related product markets are readership and advertising; see Reddaway (1963).

5 THE POLITICS OF UNION FINANCES

1 There was, of course, a size difference between affiliates and non-affiliates. Seventy-five per cent of non-TUC respondents were below 5,000 in membership, compared with 15% of affiliates. Thirty per cent of TUC affiliates had more than 100,000 members; only 6% of non-affiliates were in this size band.

2 The questionnaire is reproduced at Appendix 5.

3 Several respondents did not understand the term, and inserted 'deductions from salary'; these were included in the check-off figure. The relevant figure is derived by multiplying percentage responses to q11 by actual union membership in 1988 (year end).

4 $r = 0.1888$, significant beyond 0.001.

5 $r = -0.2020$, significant beyond 0.001.

6 $r = 0.3792$, significant beyond 0.001.

7 $r = -0.3229$ on benefits and $r = -0.1800$ on reserves; both significant beyond 0.001.

8 Chi square $= 18.4$, d.f. $= 10$, sig 0.04.

9 Larger unions were more likely to identify cost centres at branch, section, or Area level. For many respondents, however, there were no such internal divisions.

10 The correlation between membership level and the total number of employees was $r = 0.5921$; that between membership level and the number of full-time officials was $r = 0.7850$. Both are significant beyond 0.001.

11 This is a far higher proportion than that observed in the sample of unions with over 100,000 members covered in the first project. See Willman and Morris, 1988: 53–85.

12 $r = 0.2409$, significant beyond 0.001.

13 $r = 0.3622$, significant beyond 0.001.

14 The relevant questions are 10, 27 and 51.

15 All questions were closed-ended involving selection of response from a five-point scale. The maximum possible score (i.e., lowest centrality) was 25, the minimum (highest) was 5.

16 All questions were closed-ended and dichotomous. The minimum score (maximum sophistication) is thus 4 and the maximum 8.

17 In other unions, such as EETPU, the executive has the power to raise subscriptions by a fixed amount (10p in EETPU) but must seek endorsement of this from the next annual conference.

18 Quotes are from ISTC *Banner*, Conference Specials 1981 and 1982.

19 NUM Finance and General Purposes Committee *Report*, Item xii, in *NUM Conference Report*, 1987.

20 Annual Report, ADM, 1980: 17.

21 BFAWU Treasurer's Report to Conference, 1976: 1.
22 BIFU, Financial Satement to Members, 1988.
23 Quotes from Annual Reports to the ADM, 1979: 7, 1978: 7, and 1981: 17.
24 One exception may be noted in EETPU. In October 1987, the union moved some assets out of equities just before the crash in order to purchase a property which would be developed as a commercial conference centre. They avoided the substantial losses many others experienced at the time, but the General Secretary was criticised at the 1989 Conference because the fees of the centre were alleged to be too high for members to afford.

6 UNION SIZE, GROWTH, AND FINANCIAL PERFORMANCE

1 The total 'profit' of TGWU, GMB, AEU, and NALGO was £12.1 million in 1988 but they showed a deficit of £1.6 million on membership servicing in 1989.
2 The relationship appears strong. Chi square for membership and recruitment (19.6, d.f. = 10) is significant at 0.032. That for TUC affiliation and recruitment (2.35, d.f. = 1) is significant at 0.013.
3 These are: remuneration and expenses of staff, including separate items on salaries, auditors' fees, occupancy fees, stationery, postage and telephone costs, executive committee expenses, conference expenses, other expenses.
4 That is, the last year for which data on administrative costs are available under the more restrictive definition.
5 The relationship is weak, negative, and not significant where both actual and percentages changes on costs and membership are used.
6 In 1985, for example, r = −0.1990, significant beyond 0.005.
7 The significance level for the union type effect was 0.1014 and for the inter-active effect of type and size 0.2109.
8 F ratio for 'shelteredness' = 6.068 (significant beyond 0.005); for membership F = 1.21 (not significant). There is no interactive effect between membership and shelteredness.
9 Chi-square = 4.789, d.f. = 1. Significant at 0.03.
10 It will be recalled that the definition of administrative cost used from 1987 onwards is more inclusive.
11 In McCarthy and Undy's 1989 survey of 34 merging unions, 76% of cases involved competitive bidding (R. Undy, personal communication).

7 STRIKE ACTIVITY AND UNION FINANCES

1 ADM Report, 1979: 10.
2 Taxes, 1978: 343.
3 Taxes, 1986: 112.
4 ISTC *Phoenix*, November 1986: 2.

8 THE NATIONAL UNION OF MINEWORKERS: STRIKE AND FINANCIAL DISASTER

1 The figures used in the case study Chapters 8–12 differ in some respects from those presented in the Certification Officers' Reports. For an account of these differences, see Appendix 1.
2 The National Coal Board was subsequently renamed British Coal; the text reflects this, using the latter name where appropriate.
3 Monopolies and Mergers Commission, (1983).
4 There has been considerable debate about the measures of efficiency and profitability of pits or areas of British Coal. See Cooper *et al.* (1990).
5 The votes were cast 125,233 against action, 81,592 for.
6 See Aston, Morris, and Willman (1990) for more details of the litigation during the dispute.
7 See Aston, Morris, and Willman (1990). These figures refer to the official accounts of NUM and Areas. Other monies are discussed below.
8 The accounts of NUM are the most complicated submitted to the Certification Office, and over 40 separate sets of accounts are now involved. One set of accounts obtain to the national union, and the rest belong to each of the 'constituent associations' named above. The number of accounts processed by the Certification Office has increased over the years from 29 in 1975 to over 40 in 1988.
9 The Mineworkers' Trust was established immediately prior to the strike to insulate approximately £1 million of property assets from the sequestrators. See Lightman, 1990: 21–2.
10 NEC Report to Conference, para. 16.7.
11 Conference Report, 1984: 435.

9 THE GMB: MERGER AND FINANCIAL REFORM

1 'GMB' is currently the registered name of the union, rather than an acronym. Previously the union was named GMBATU (The General, Municipal, Boilermakers' and Allied Trades Union), but it was felt that, given the diversity of membership and the union's ambitions, such a name was inappropriate.
2 There may have been some substance to this belief. When the union *did* expand in the later 1970s, the net growth in funds from membership contributions was very small. Conference Report, 1980: 782.
3 Rules, 1987: 5, 55.
4 All figures from *Financial Review and Report on the Survey of Contributions and Benefits*; *Special Report to the Sixth Congress*, 1988: 4–6.
5 Source as note 4.
6 Conference Report, 1981: 790.
7 This is handled for the union by Unity Trust. It is estimated to be worth £80,000 per year.
8 *Decision* 84 para. 34, where the growth in funds attributed to members' contributions from 1973 to 1982 is £0.

9 Conference Report, 1977: 563.
10 Conference Report, 1989: 880–1.
11 Conference Report, 1979: 663.
12 Conference Report, 1989: 870, 872.
13 *Branch Financial Administration for the 80s*, Conference Report 1980: 830–3
14 General Secretary's Report to Conference, 1989: 37.
15 Conference Report, 1986: 637.

10 THE AMALGAMATED ENGINEERING UNION: BACK FROM THE BRINK

1 The skilled sections are Sections 1 and 2.
2 Subscription yield in 1985 was £18.46 per capita, and the declared membership 914,683; the *paying* membership was thus equivalent to approximately 464,000 full-paying Section 1 members.
3 A small Roll-Turning Section numbered 428.
4 Rule 13, paras. 10 and 11. Byelaws exist for the foundry and construction sections. For the purposes of this rule, the EC is considered to be a branch and may propose rule changes.
5 Rule 14, para. 18,2.
6 Rule 12, para. 11.
7 See Undy 1979 and Undy *et al.*, 1981: 101–16 for a detailed account.
8 See Certification Officer's Report, 1990: 60.
9 See General Secretary's Statement, 1988: 4.
10 See General Secretary's Reports , various years. Figures in the Certification Officer's Reports vary slightly, showing a rise in benefit expenditure from 18% to 20% between 1985 and 1989.
11 General Secretary's Report, 1985: 9.
12 General Secretary's Report, 1985: 7.
13 Rule 1, para. 20.
14 Rule 22, para. 1:2
15 In practice, since large employers such as GEC are themselves decentralised, there are more than 3,000 payment points.
16 The vehicle for this was the recalled 1985 rules revision meeting.
17 The Finance Manager estimated that, prior to 1986, branch account records were up to nine months in arrears. Since then, there have been monthly statements of income, expenditure and balances and branch accounts are subject to a quarterly audit undertaken by the general office.
18 Rule 12, para. 1.
19 General Secretary's Report, 1988. These proportions were substantially the same in 1985.
20 Rule 26, para. 3.
21 Rule 36, para. 3: 2.
22 The trustes are not financially qualified and in practice the union takes the advice of Midland Montague on investment and pension fund management.
23 Survey evidence indicated in 1989 that this package was not particularly popular with members in the East Midlands; 1989 *Survey of AEU Membership in the East Midlands*, Trent Surveys, for the AEU, March 1989: A2.
24 AEU, Annual Report and Accounts, 1991.

11 THE BANKING, INSURANCE AND FINANCE UNION: COMPETITIVE UNIONISM AND FINANCIAL SURVIVAL

1 Bank Officers' Guild *Journal* 1920, November. The union was initially called the Bank Officers' Guild. It became the National Union of Bank Employees in 1946 and the Banking, Insurance and Finance Union in 1980.
2 The union has recently experienced dissaffection which led to the attempted departure of a recently amalgamated staff association at Eagle Star Insurance Company.
3 The dispute with MSF over recruiting rights in the Midland Bank was resolved by a TUC intermediary, Bill Keys of SOGAT, who proposed sole recognition rights for BIFU and transfer of the engagements of MSF members.
4 For example, BIFU in 1989 absorbed Northern Rock and North of England Building Society staff associations.
5 Rule G (v).
6 Financial Statement to Members, 1988.

12 THE ELECTRICAL, ELECTRONIC, TELECOMMUNICATIONS AND PLUMBING TRADE UNION: ACCOUNTABILITY AND FINANCIAL CONTROL

1 Recent transfers of engagements have included several small staff associations and the Institute of Journalists.
2 See *The EETPU: General Council's Report to Congress*, TUC 1988.
3 This followed the sale of certain investments in order to purchase property; we discuss this further below.

13 CONCLUSIONS: UNION BUSINESS AND BUSINESS UNIONISM

1 See *Industrial Relations in the 1900s*, Cm 1602, London, HMSO, 1991, p. 26.
2 The first and second reports of the Commissioner list several complaints made on financial grounds.
3 See *Industrial Relations in the 1990s*, p. 31.

APPENDIX 1: RESEARCH METHODS

1 The relevant sections are Ss 87 to 91.
2 Specifically, Ss 10 to 12 and Schedule 2 of the 1974 Act and Ss 7 to 9 of the 1975 Act.
3 For illustration, the membership reported to the Certification Officer as a percentage of that reported by the DE is as follows in selected years.

1950	85.6%	1955	87.4%	1960	86.8%
1965	84.1%	1970	N/A	1975	96.8%
1980	97.6%	1985	99.0%		

4 This fits with the fact that, in 1987, only 304 of the listed 354 unions submitted returns. See Certification Officer's *Report*, 1988 p. 4, 9.

5 Based on Certification Office membership data. This series is used throughout, for compatibility with the financial data. It may, of course, slightly overstate the real level of trade union membership, see Bailey and Kelly, 1990.

References

Adeney, M. and Lloyd, J., 1985, *The Miners Strike 1984–1985; Loss Without Limit*, London, Routledge.

Ashenfelter, O. and Johnson, G., 1969, 'Bargaining Theory, Trade Unions and Industrial Strike Activity', *American Economic Review*, 59: 35–49.

Aston, B., 1987, 'Trade Union Mergers in Britain, 1950–1982', London University PhD Thesis, unpublished.

Aston, B., Morris, T.J., and Willman, P., 1990, 'Still Balancing the Books; the 1984–5 Miners' Strike and the NUM', *Industrial Relations Journal*, 21 (4).

Atherton, W., 1973, *The Theory of Union Bargaining Goals*, Princeton University Press.

Bailey, R. and Kelly, J., 1990, 'An Index Measure of Trade Union Density', *British Journal of Industrial Relations*, 28 (2).

Bain, G. S., 1970, *The Growth of White Collar Unionism*, Oxford University Press.

1986, 'Introduction' to 'Symposium on the Role and Influence of Trades Unions in a Recession', *British Journal of Industrial Relations*, 24 (2).

Bain, G.S. and Elsheikh, F., 1976, *Union Growth and the Business Cycle*, Oxford, Blackwell.

Bain, G.S. and Price, R., 1980, *Profiles of Union Growth*, Oxford, Blackwell.

Berkowitz, M., 1954, 'The Economics of Trade Union Organization and Administration', *Industrial and Labour Relations Review*, 7: 512–23.

Booth, A., 1983, 'A Reconsideration of Trade Union Growth in the United Kingdom', *British Journal of Industrial Relations*, 21 (2).

Buchanan, R., 1981, 'Union Concentration and the Largest Unions', *British Journal of Industrial Relations*, 19 (2): 232–7.

Burton, J., 1984, 'The Economic Analysis of the Trade Union as a Political Institution', in Rosa, J.J. (ed.), *The Economics of Trade Unions; New Directions*, Boston, Kluwer Nijhoff, pp. 123–54.

Campbell, A. and Warner, M., 1985, 'Changes in the Balance of Power in the British Mineworkers' Union; an Analysis of National Top-Office Elections 1974–1984', *British Journal of Industrial Relations*, 23 (1).

Carruth, A. and Disney, R., 1988, 'Where Have Two Million Union Members Gone?', *Economica*, 55: 1–19.

Certification Officers' Reports, London, HMSO, various years.

Chaison, G., 1986, *When Unions Merge*, Kentucky, Lexington Books.

Child, J., Loveridge, R., and Warner, M., 1973, 'Towards an Organizational Study of Trade Unions', *Sociology*, 71 (1): 71–91.

Commission on Industrial Relations, 1973, Report No. 35, *William and Glyns Bank*, London, HMSO.

Commissioner for the Rights of Trade Union Members, 1990, *Annual Report, 1989–1990*, Warrington, COI.

Cooper, D. and Hopper, T., 1988, *Debating Coal Closures: Economic Calculation in the Coal Dispute 1984–5*, Cambridge Studies in Management, 10. Cambridge University Press.

Crouch, C., 1982, *Trade Unions: The Logic of Collective Action*, London, Fontana.

Daniel, W.W. and Millward, N., 1983, *Workplace Industrial Relations in Britain; The DE/PSI/SSRC survey*, London, Heinemann.

Durcan, J., Mc Carthy, W.E.J., and Redman, G.P., 1983, *Strikes in Post-War Britain*, London, Allen and Unwin.

Eaton, J. and Gill, C., 1983, *The Trade Union Directory; A Guide to all TUC Unions*, Pluto Press, Workers Handbook.

Edwards, P.K. and Bain, G.S., 1988, 'Why are Unions Becoming More Popular? Trade Unions and Public Opinion in Britain', *British Journal of Industrial Relations*, 26 (2): 311–26.

Freeman, R. and Medoff, J., 1984, *What Do Unions Do?* New York, Basic Books.

Gennard, J., 1982, 'The Financial Costs and Returns of Strikes', *British Journal of Industrial Relations*, 20 (2): 247–57.

1990, *A History of the National Graphical Association*, London, Unwin Hyman.

Gerth, H. and Mills, C.W., 1954, *Character and Social Structure*, London, Routledge and Kegan Paul.

Heery, E., 1987, 'The Pay and Employment Conditions of Full-time Officials', mimeo, London School of Economics.

Hirsch, B.T. and Addison, J.T., 1986, *The Economic Analysis of Trade Unions; New Approaches and Evidence*, London, Allen and Unwin.

Hirschmann, A., 1970, *Exit, Voice and Loyalty*, Cambridge MA, Harvard University Press.

Hyman, R., 1971, *Marxism and the Sociology of Trade Unionism*, London, Pluto Press.

Kelly, J. and Heery, E., 1989, 'Full-time Officers and Trade Union Recruitment', *British Journal of Industrial Relations*, 27 (2).

Latta, G., 1972, 'Trade Union Finances', *British Journal of Industrial Relations*, 10 (2).

Lightman, G., 1990, *The Lightman Report on the NUM*, Harmondsworth, Penguin Books.

Martin, D.L., 1980, *An Ownership Theory of the Trade Union*, Berkeley, University of California Press.

Martin, R., 1989, *Trade Unionism; Purposes and Forms*, Oxford, Clarendon Press.

Metcalf, D., 1989, 'Water Notes Dry Up', *British Journal of Industrial Relations*, 27 (1).

1990, 'Union Presence and Labour Productivity in British Manufacturing Industry', *British Journal of Industrial Relations*, 28 (2).

Michels, R., 1915, *Political Parties: A Sociological Study of the Oligarchical Tendencies of Modern Democracy*, Glencoe, Free Press.

Mills, C.W., 1963, 'Situated Actions and Vocabularies of Motive', in Horowitz (ed.), *Power, Politics and People*, Oxford, Oxford University Press, pp. 439–52.

Millward, N. and Stevens, M., 1986, *British Workplace Industrial Relations, 1980–1984*, Aldershot, Gower.

Monopolies and Mergers Commission, 1983, *The National Coal Board; A Report on Efficiency and Costs in the Development, Production and Supply of Coal by the NCB*, London, HMSO, Cmnd 8920 (2 vols).

Morris, T.J., 1986, *Innovations in Banking; Business Strategies and Employee Relations*, Croom Helm.

Nolan, P. and Marginson P., 1990, 'Skating on Thin Ice: David Metcalf on Trade Unions and Productivity', *British Journal of Industrial Relations*, 28 (2): 227–49.

Offe, C. and Wiesenthal, H., 1980, 'Two Logics of Collective Action; Notes on Social Class and Organizational Form', *Political Power and Social Theory*, 1: 67–115.

Olson, M., 1965, *The Logic of Collective Action: Public Goods and the Theory of Groups*, Cambridge MA, Harvard University Press.

Oram, S., 1987, 'Printing Trade Unions; A Financial Study of Multi-Millionaires', *Employee Relations*, 9 (4): 17–23.

Pencavel, J., 1971, 'The Demand for Union Services; An Exercise', *Industrial and Labor Relations Review*, 24 (2): 180–90.

Purcell, J., 1987, 'Management Control through Collective Bargaining; A Future Strategy', in Thurley, K. and Wood, S. (eds.), *Industrial Relations and Management Strategy*, Cambridge University Press, pp. 53–62.

Reddaway, W.B., 1963, 'The Economics of Newspapers', *Economic Journal*, 73: 201–18.

Richardson, R. and Wood, S., 1989, 'Productivity Change in the Coal Industry and the New Industrial Relations', *British Journal of Industrial Relations*, 28 (1): 33–57.

Roberts, B.C., 1956, *Trade Union Government and Administration*, London, Bell and Sons.

Ross, A., 1948, *Trade Union Wage Policy*, Berkeley, University of California Press.

Swabe, A. and Price, P., 1984, 'Building a Permanent Association', *British Journal of Industrial Relations*, 22 (2).

Swint, M. J. and Nelson, W. B., 1978, 'The Influence of Negotiators' Self-Interest on the Duration of Strikes', *Industrial and Labor Relations Review*, 32 (1): 56–66.

1980, 'Self-Motivated Bargaining and Rational Strikes; A Multi-Party Model and its Implications for Strike Activity', *Southern Economic Journal*, 47 (2): 317–31.

Trades Union Congress, 1988, *The EETPU; General Council's Report to Congress*, TUC, August.

TUC, 1991, 'Trade Union Recognition', A TUC Consultative Document.

Turner, H.A., 1962, *Trade Union Growth, Structure and Policy*, London, Allen and Unwin.

Undy, R., 1979, 'The Electoral Influence of the Opposition Party in the AUEW Engineering Section, 1965–1975', *British Journal of Industrial Relations*, 17 (1).

Undy, R., Ellis, V., McCarthy, W.E.J. and Halmos, A.M., 1981, *Change in Trade Unions; The Development of U.K. Unions since 1960*, London, Hutchinson.

Voos, P., 1984, 'Union Organizing; Costs and Benefits', *Industrial and Labor Relations Review*, 36 (4): 576–91.

1986, 'Trends in Union Organizing Expenditures', *Industrial and Labor Relations Review*, 38 (1): 52–63.

Webb, S. and Webb, B., 1907, *The History of Trade Unionism*, London, Longman, Green and Co.

Willman, P., 1989, 'The Logic of Market-Share Trade Unionism; Is Membership Decline Inevitable?', *Industrial Relations Journal*, 20 (4).

1990, 'The Financial Performance of British Trade Unions', *British Journal of Industrial Relations*, 28 (3).

Willman, P. and Morris, T.J., 1986, 'Union Growth and Membership Diversification', Working Paper G5-17-86, London Business School.

1988, *The Finances of British Trade Unions, 1975–1985*, Research Paper No. 62, Department of Employment.

Willman, P., Morris, T.J. and Aston, B., 1989, 'The Management of Financial Resources in British Trade Unions', Report for the Department of Employment, London Business School.

Subject Index

Index of trade unions

ACTT, 23, 24, 25, 29
AEU, 2, 5, 21, 24, 25, 26, 27, 29, 31, 32,
  68, 71, 72, 81, 82, 85, 86, 88, 100,
  154–69, 194, 196–7, 202, 203, 221,
  223, 241, 243
AMMA, 24, 25, 93, 239
ASLEF, 25, 27
ASTMS, 40, 91, 96–8, 239

BACM, 121
BFAWU, 24, 68, 71–2, 81, 221, 241
BGSU, 21, 25, 26, 28, 93
BIFU, 5, 24, 26, 27, 33, 40, 68, 71–2, 81,
  85, 88, 93, 170–84, 198, 202, 205, 221,
  223, 241, 244

CATU, 24, 25
CMA, 71–2, 221
COCSU, 106–12
COHSE, 27, 29, 91, 93
CPSA, 31, 93, 104, 106, 107, 108, 112
CSU, 26, 107, 108, 112

EETPU
  expulsion of, 1, 2, 5, 29, 71–2, 81, 91,
    96, 100, 185–98, 203, 205, 221, 223,
    240–1, 244
  merger with AEU, 168–9
EIS, 28
EMA, 29, 68, 71–2, 221
EQUITY, 24, 28, 239

FBU, 25, 82
FDA, 70–2, 81, 102, 106, 108, 109, 203,
  221
FTAT, 29

GMB, as NUGMW, 3, 98–9, 5, 21, 24, 25,
  28, 29, 71–3, 81, 82, 87, 93, 96, 100,
  133, 140–53, 159, 168, 194, 198, 202,
  221, 223, 241, 242

IPMS, 68, 71–2, 81, 87, 93, 102, 106, 107,
  108, 109, 221
IRSF, 25, 68, 71–3, 102, 106, 107, 108,
  109, 110, 112, 203, 221
ISTC, 21, 24, 25, 26, 68, 71–3, 81, 102,
  105, 106, 112–15, 202, 221, 241

LBGSU, 24, 25, 28, 93, 221

MSF, 2, 21, 25, 28, 31, 33, 82, 87, 91, 96–
  8, 169, 173, 182, 185, 197, 221, 239,
  244
MU, 21, 24, 25

NAHT, 24, 26, 93
NACODS, 121
NALGO, 21, 22, 24, 25, 26, 27, 28, 29, 31,
  32, 33, 68, 71–2, 82, 87, 93, 159, 221,
  241
NAS/UWT, 87, 93, 221
NATFHE, 21, 24
NCU, 23, 25, 26, 104
NGA, 21, 24, 28, 31, 32, 33, 40, 82, 96,
  102, 117, 118, 119
NUCPS, 26, 93
NUFLAT, 25
NUJ, 23, 24
NUM, 2, 5, 12, 25, 26, 27, 31, 32, 48, 68,
  71–3, 87, 105, 106, 117, 120, 121–39,
  196, 198, 202, 203, 221, 237, 239, 240,
  242
NUPE, 2, 21, 24, 27, 29, 31, 91, 93, 221
NUR, 3, 20, 24, 28, 68, 71–2, 105, 116,
  196, 221
NUS, 3, 21, 23, 24, 25, 26, 27, 105, 115–
  17, 120, 202
NUSMW, 96–7
NUSMWCH & DE, 96
NUT, 21, 24, 25, 26, 28, 93, 105
NUTGW, 23, 24, 29
NWGSU, 26, 93

Author Index